How We Learn Where We Live

How We Learn Where We Live

Thomas Bernhard, Architecture, and Bildung

✦

Fatima Naqvi

NORTHWESTERN UNIVERSITY PRESS
EVANSTON, ILLINOIS

Northwestern University Press
www.nupress.northwestern.edu

Printed in the United States of America

10 9 8 7 6 5 4 3 2 1

Library of Congress Cataloging-in-Publication Data

Names: Naqvi, Fatima, author.
Title: How we learn where we live : Thomas Bernhard, architecture, and bildung / Fatima Naqvi.
Description: Evanston, Illinois : Northwestern University Press, 2015. | Includes bibliographical references and index.
Identifiers: LCCN 2015040896| ISBN 9780810132016 (paperback) | ISBN 9780810131996 (cloth)
Subjects: LCSH: Bernhard, Thomas—Criticism and interpretation. | Architecture and literature. | Education in literature. | BISAC: LITERARY CRITICISM / European / German.
Classification: LCC PT2662.E7 Z7873 2015 | DDC 838/.91409—dc23 LC record available at http://lccn.loc.gov/2015040896

For Abba,

Mohsin Naqvi

(*Sandila, ca. 1940–New York City, December 20, 2013*)

Thought [. . .] is always represented as a building inhabitable for shorter or longer periods. It is generally pictured as an intellectual edifice in which everybody, the philosophers and their followers, can go in and out with more or less excitement.

Das Denken wird immer als ein kürzer oder länger bewohnbares Gebäude dargestellt, jedermann spricht vom *Denkgebäude*, in welchem alles, die Philosophen und ihre Gläubiger, mehr oder weniger aufgeregt aus und ein geht.

—Thomas Bernhard, *Gargoyles* (*Verstörung*)

CONTENTS

ILLUSTRATIONS

ACKNOWLEDGMENTS

A closeness to Bernhard is not like other affinities. His prose, with its repetitive, loquacious, condemnatory, maddening pace, often leads readers to first embrace him passionately—and then to flee, fatigued or perturbed, and sometimes a combination of both. I am greatly indebted to Wendelin Schmidt-Dengler (Zagreb, May 20, 1942–Vienna, September 7, 2008). His dedication to his students and passion for Thomas Bernhard rekindled mine at a point when I feared it had flagged. Without Schmidt-Dengler's enthusiastic suggestion—"Why don't you look at the relationship between Novalis's *Notes to a Romantic Encyclopaedia* (*Das Allgemeine Brouillon*) and Bernhard's *Amras*? Could be fruitful! I'll give you the typescript!"—spoken in his typical rapid-fire speed and Austrian cadence between office and university corridor, I might never have pursued this project. I miss his ebullience and knowledge and greatly wish that he could have seen the completion of this book. His contributions to scholarship on Bernhard are inestimable, with his essay collection *Der Übertreibungskünstler* (*The Exaggeration Artist*, 1986, with a 2nd expanded edition, 1989) and the twenty-two-volume *Werke* begun under his direction. His many afterwords to the collected works, written together with Martin Huber, Manfred Mittermayer, and other Bernhard specialists, are extremely valuable to both the scholar and general reader.

At Northwestern University Press thanks go to Henry Carrigan for his fondness for Austrian writers and to Nathan MacBrien for shepherding the book through to completion. I am also very grateful to my colleagues at Rutgers. They put up with all sorts of semester stress while I was on sabbatical in Austria, where the executor of Bernhard's estate, Dr. Peter Fabjan, guided me through his half-brother's homes in Upper Austria. A sincere thank-you goes to Dr. Fabjan as well, for his support of this project. A much appreciated grant from the Rutgers University Research Council helped fund my research and the acquisition of reproduction rights. A very generous subsidy from the Botstiber Foundation for Austrian-American Studies further supported this book's publication with its many images. Christina Mandt, my research assistant, was wonderful in helping with copyright issues. I would also like to express my appreciation to the many interlocutors along the way—to Bernhard Judex at the Bernhard Archive in Gmunden and Manfred Mittermayer at the University of Salzburg; associates from the Werfel Stipendium in Vienna; colleagues and students at Rutgers, Harvard, Brown, Princeton, Columbia, the Universities of Vienna, St. Gallen, and Szeged (thanks, Attila!), who commented on various Bernhard talks; my friends Karin Schiefer (who supported me both intellectually and familially, taking care of my children on some of the many Austrian school holidays) and Andrea Grill (who spurred my first visits to Upper Austria and encouraged me during the ups-and-downs of writing). Michael G. Levine offered helpful suggestions that allowed me to do what Bernhard's protagonists do: revise. Henry Sussman's advice is also greatly appreciated. Christoph Holzhey's acuity in the final stages was tremendously valuable; thank you, Christoph, you are still the most thorough reader I know!

Earlier versions of the chapter on *Amras* appeared in Attila Bombitz and Martin Huber's compendium of Bernhard essays entitled *"Ist es eine Komödie? Ist es eine Tragödie?": Ein Symposium zum Werk von Thomas Bernhard*; an article on Bernhard's *Old Masters* in *Monatshefte* 96, no. 2 (2004): 252–72 was the predecessor for Chapter 3.

I am endlessly indebted to Chris for reading the manuscript in his minimal spare time, my mother Brita for reading and rereading everything, and my daughter Malena for inspecting snippets on screen and offering encouragement. She once commented endearingly: "This is actually pretty interesting!" Gratitude is due to my sweet Amelie, who often asked why I left her in kindergarten for so long, but got used to it and will hopefully forgive me. As for Beatriz, who is still too young to realize what I am doing when I am sitting at the computer: I promise you some future work.

This book is for my father, Mohsin Naqvi, whose untimely death came in the midst of the manuscript's completion. I feel his absence acutely and will be forever sorry that his last months were spent in architecturally heinous New York hospitals, without any views or connection to the outside world. They were anathema to his agile, peripatetic thought and extroverted nature.

PREFACE

Propædeutics, n.

The body of principles or rules introductory to any art, science, or subject of special study; preliminary learning; an instance of this.

1842 W. T. Brande *Dict. Sci., Lit. & Art* 91/1 *Propædeutics*, a term used by German writers to signify the preliminary learning connected with any art or science: that in which it is necessary to be instructed, in order to study with advantage the art or science itself.

Edification, n.

under 2**b**. Mental or moral improvement, intellectual profit; instruction. (Now often *ironical*.)

1875 B. Jowett tr. Plato *Dialogues* (ed. 2) III. 206 Kindly answer, for the edification of the company and myself.

—*Oxford English Dictionary* (1989)

"How will this book be relevant outside the Thomas Bernhard community?" This was the rather inane question an interviewer, a comparatist by training, once asked me. We were seated in a tight, windowless seminar room, partitioned off from the neighboring offices and hallways through a thin skin of sheetrock. An oval, pinkish-tinged laminate table took up most of the space. The whiteboard along the ten-foot wall hardly reflected the incandescent light above us. That's a good question, I answered slightly duplicitously, distracted by the claustrophobic setting.

The reason we get up in the morning, I was tempted to respond, and go to the library day in, day out, and spend many hours in climate-controlled, slightly stale-smelling archives, finally imparting our thoughts to students in windowless rooms such as this one, is: we firmly believe that the authors, filmmakers, and visual artists we write and talk about are important enough to transcend the borders of any "community." In their dense particularity, we sense that they have something to say about the way we live, think, and feel that no one else has said previously in such a pertinent formulation; with their unique contributions, they structure the way we conceive of ourselves. They are not universal truths, certainly, but do apply to and encompass a larger multitude. Granted, we often stake out claims based on their works that are too broadly formulated. But we may be forgiven for being hyperbolic, as the stock that society places in the labor we do has steadily declined.

His question was indicative. He had so internalized society's disdain for the *Geisteswissenschaften*—the German word for the humanities, but more literally and poetically the "sciences of the spirit"—that he felt we scholars needed to "account" for our projects before this wider audience, beyond just stating our specific case and assuming others recognize its value and validity. A case no longer speaks for itself. Maybe I have internalized this contempt to some degree, too, which is why the vocabulary of capitalism (stock, account, value) invades this description. I cannot yet cogently make the argument for the liberal arts' "value" outside of that paradigm. But perhaps, in the allusions to grounds and grounding, staking, and borders, there is a more persuasive argument to be made, albeit not entirely free from real estate speculations.

Later I thought about this question more than I care to admit. I thought about it while I made my daily pilgrimage across Vienna's infamous Heldenplatz into the Austrian National Library, housed in the former Imperial Palace. I mulled it over while the newly installed humidifiers in the renovated reading room went on and sprayed readers and books with a fine mist. I contemplated it when I came out into the early twilight and recrossed the vast, empty square toward the subway, with the roof of the Burgtheater, the former Imperial Court Theater, part of my magnificent view. I pondered it still, while casting a short look over at the Kunsthistorisches Museum, the Art History Museum, on the further side of the arch that closes off the Heroes Square from the Ringstrasse, before ducking my chin down into my scarf (it was a very cold winter). Occasionally, I would wander across the five-lane boulevard into the Kunsthistorisches Museum, hoping to peruse Tintoretto's painting *White-Bearded Man* in search of a convincing answer.

These sites will be immediately recognizable to any reader of the Austrian author Thomas Bernhard (1931–1989). In his early novel *Amras* from 1964, the Habsburgs' art collection is brought into play—the *Kunst-* and *Wunderkammer* in Innsbruck's Castle Ambras is the implicit setting, a cabinet of art and curiosities eventually absorbed into the Art History Museum's holdings. In his late novel, *Old Masters* (*Alte Meister*), published more than twenty years later in 1985, the museum, with its constant temperature of eighteen degrees centigrade and the Tintoretto portrait of the white-bearded dignitary, is the focus of attention. The prestigious Hotel Ambassador, located on the Ringstrasse I crossed so often during that winter, as well as the Burgtheater are secondary and tertiary places of interest in this book. Finally, Bernhard's last play, written fifty years after the Anschluss to work through that event—when the First Austrian Republic was annexed to Nazi Germany—takes as its title the Heldenplatz or Heroes Square, located immediately in front of the Imperial Palace's new wing. Here, an estimated 200,000 people cheered Hitler's announcement from the balcony that Austria had come "home" to the Reich. By a strange coincidence, my research had me moving about in this Bernhardian triangle day after day, plotting my paths within the trajectories of his fictive characters. In unintended ways, it emplaced me within their convoluted and often opaque textual anxieties.

The act of walking into and out of these imposing buildings and across these squares and streets, simultaneously symbols of barbarism and culture, had, needless to say, a profound effect on this project. Sitting in the Art History Museum and National Library for long periods of time, I reflected on the question the interviewer had put to me, as well as on the challenges the humanities face and the declining persuasiveness of the study of art and literature. These spatial experiences combined to let me think of the object of my research in a different way: I began to see the enfant terrible of the German cultural establishment and Austrian society as someone who not only thought about what we learn, but about *how* we learn in certain spaces. Our learning is intimately connected to the quality of the places in which we live and through which we move. We get a very clear sense when reading Bernhard that the materiality and historicity of these places matter, that their walls, stairs, and windows shape people. Whether we are located in shoddy buildings or carefully constructed edifices is not a matter of indifference, and the layered histories that are congealed in these structures influence our perception of the present and our receptivity to the insights cultural artifacts offer. In Bernhard's novel *Old Masters*, for instance, the elderly critic's method of teaching in the Art History Museum works on the assumption that the open space and carefully controlled atmosphere of the Bordone Room stands in a close relation to his students' aesthetic receptiveness and ethical judgment. His *Bildungs*-project in the Kunsthistorisches Museum, circling around the works of the late Renaissance within a late nineteenth-century building, is an implicit condemnation of the cinder block walls and otherwise gutted structures in which we more often than not discuss artworks with our students.

Other sites played an equally important role in shaping my thoughts about the necessity of propaedeutics, a *Vor-Wissen* or pre-knowledge that makes *Wissen* or knowledge through art possible: Bernhard's houses in the province known as Oberösterreich or "Upper Austria." Bernhard was a notorious collector of real estate or, to use the old-fashioned Austrian word he preferred, "Realitäten" ("realities"). He transmuted the experience of acquiring and meticulously restoring these "realities" into his fiction, becoming a "Realitätenvermittler" (a "real estate agent," but literally a "mediator of realities") in a different sense than his former friend, the realtor Karl Ignaz Hennetmair. While he continuously polemicized against mediation in art as well as against any nineteenth-century conception of verisimilitude in artistic representation, Bernhard should be seen as both "negotiating" and "mediating" various realities through the prism of a particular place or space. By the middle of his life, he owned three farmhouses near the provincial city of Gmunden, as well as an apartment in Gmunden proper. In each home, his attention to historic architectural detail is evident in his careful restorations. He sought to return many features to their original condition, modulating his adaptations with his predilection for asceticism. The farmhouses were sparingly furnished with Biedermeier and late nineteenth-century furniture bought at various antique dealers; his apartment contained rectilinear tables, shelves, coffee tables, and plain lamps of his own design.[1] With their simplicity and conservativism (in the sense that they remain beholden to an Austrian heritage of interior design), the homes emulate the aristocratic and haute bourgeois culture Bernhard witnessed in his patrons' homes as a young man. The executor of Bernhard's literary estate and Bernhard's half-brother, Dr. Peter Fabjan, led me through the main Vierkanthof in Ohlsdorf, an old farm built on a square floor plan around an inner courtyard, as well as his brother's house in Ottnang, a simple brick structure that once housed a miner's family.[2] Bernhard is said to have written *Heldenplatz* and been inspired to further write about the Castle Wolfsegg (see *Extinction/Auslöschung*, 1986), across the valley on top of a hill, while staying in his rustic home in Ottnang.[3]

In these houses, Bernhard's whole discourse of ups and downs, highs and lows in relation to his educational model take on new significance.[4] Bernhard's homes proved to be a kind of counterpoint to the sensation of vertiginous verticality I experience when I read his up-and-down passages, with their paratactic sentence structure, comparative and superlative adjectives denoting directionality, and disorienting emplacement of the reader. While his characters are often literally forced to move to higher ground in their efforts to educate themselves and reach a better, "higher" station in life (only to then suffer downward setbacks), he walked through rooms that were arranged horizontally, especially along a vast stretch on the second floor of his main house, the farm in Obernathal. Even the small library that functioned as a study is open to both sides, a pass-through inviting movement across. Perhaps knowledge in Bernhard's model of education, picking up on the modernist aesthetic of flowing space with its democratic ethic, should be envisioned as a kind of passageway or extended threshold.[5] We gladly saunter through, without stagnating or remaining fixed in place, and are aware of what came before with a view to what might come later.

In his prose works, Bernhard reflects on our positioning in relation to the higher education we purportedly value: are we up or down, in or out with what we learn? Does education actually give us access to the higher social status we think we desire? Does learning in an ideal scenario locate us in an in-between or threshold space? How do we create a solid foundation or protective walls? Or should we learn to live without them? Can the constraints of closed, hermetic spaces actually become creative, that is, the condition for the possibility of a new kind of education?

Bernhard's locations in his works are iconic, as I indicated: these are spaces of representation and self-representation, meant for the display of power, wealth, and status.[6] The places themselves are often a kind of cultural "capital" in the doubled sense of the phrase, embodiments of accrued cultural significance and anchoring sites of national and regional identity in capital cities such as Vienna and Innsbruck. However, each of these places in Bernhard's books refers beyond the actual site or building itself—the city district Amras of Innsbruck, the Habsburg Art History Museum, the Castle Wolfsegg, the Heldenplatz, and so on—to imply a certain intellectual atmosphere, political history, and accreted emotion. The genius loci is the Roman spirit of a specific site,[7] and Bernhard is not far from invoking these spirits, their generative capacities and their innate being (which is one reason why there is a whole problematic discourse in Bernhard where culture is persistently naturalized). In such representative, iconic, architecturally unusual places, the figures sense an intangible "spirit," adapting themselves to its contours and demands. Here they may, under the right circumstances, allow learning in an emphatic sense to take place. Summoning up the sociocultural and historical character, the genius loci makes itself felt in ways rational and irrational. It serves as the figures' guiding force in the present, when it imposes demands and imparts obligations. As such, the stories of decline and possibility Bernhard tells in his oeuvre and against which he sets his propaedeutics are embedded in a larger geographical and architectural context. Perhaps there is something nostalgic about Bernhard's undertaking, as some theoreticians of both space and place have argued about the vengeance with which they have returned to the center of our concerns in the last decades.[8] His interest lies in situating man within material and tectonic coordinates that have a binding importance. He reasserts their structuring function over and against the dematerialization or disappearance of our physical world.[9]

Buildings come into being in specific landscapes with specific histories. They inflect the architectonics of our thinking, which Bernhard calls our "Denkgebäude," or "thought structures"—and we neglect their larger histories at our own peril. I was reminded of this during my sabbatical in Vienna in 2012. The first years of the new millennium have been a boom time for developers, especially after the economic turmoil of 2008. The lack of confidence in immaterial goods and services has led many investors to seek out the solid "realities" Bernhard also preferred (but for different reasons and different in kind). Throughout the city, buildings from the nineteenth century are being knocked down at an astonishing rate, making way for larger apartment blocks and shopping complexes. A few prominent architectural cases call to mind the vehement debate about the near-demolition of the Wittgenstein House in the early 1970s. These buildings and interiors (e.g., the Sophiensäle, the Roman Bath on the Praterstern) have garnered media attention, but unfortunately to relatively little avail. The rampant demolition of smaller buildings, without fanfare or objection, evinces city planners' willingness to extinguish this formative architectural period, which shaped philosophers and architects such as Ludwig Wittgenstein, Adolf Loos, and Wittgenstein's collaborator Paul Engelmann—even if only in opposition. The obliteration of vast swaths of the city proceeds in the name of a global modernity and urban modernization supposedly befitting a future-oriented populace.

The destruction is as sad as the new cynical watchword of "lifelong learning," whereby we are supposed to become the ephemeral, flexible humans in command of the skills that the neoliberal economy needs at any given moment, only to be discarded the next, when these skills have lost their relevance. At a juncture when our traditional model of the B.A. (as it has been put in place in the United States in the twentieth century) is increasingly eviscerated of its breadth and broad cultural competence seems like a mere marketing slogan for a global bank rather than a goal of higher education, Bernhard's propaedeutic project is more timely than ever. His *home*ly reflections raise the question: What can a proper preparatory training in particular spaces achieve? What are the ideal spaces for fostering innovative ideas? In the buildings in which learning happens, we now perhaps focus on *Ausbildung* to the detriment of *Bildung*, on pre-professionalization rather than creative-critical thinking.

The latter requires schooling in sensibility and sensitivity, in receptivity and rebelliousness. Bernhard's writings insist: learning has always been a lifelong process. In the particular landscapes and buildings that circumscribe our lives we do not learn because of outside imperatives, but for the sheer pleasure of constructing thoughts without end or resolution, occasionally building hubristic towers of Babel.[10] We cannot divorce the places in which we live from what we learn and how well and creatively we think. The famous, infamous, and little known sites that we have formed also form us over time, as well as those who come after us.[11] This does not mean, however, that we are infinitely permeable, amorphous beings that can be randomly shaped for present needs, especially not by buildings designed to have such an effect with translucent walls, clusters of workstations with low partitions, or open floor plans. There is a correlation between our openness and the openings in our buildings, but it is indirect, hard to grasp, and difficult to explain—the openings leading from inner to outer world and vice versa, the passageways directing us from one space to another, the antechambers preparing us for certain transitions and requiring a differentiated geometry. In our thoughts, we balance this openness while maintaining the foundations and retaining walls that support our "Denkgebäude."

ABBREVIATIONS AND TRANSLATIONS

The quotations from Bernhard's oeuvre are taken from the 22-volume standard edition, *Werke* (Frankfurt am Main: Suhrkamp, 2003–2013), unless otherwise noted. Because of the difficulty of Bernhard's prose, I have generally chosen to use both the published English translation and the German original; I mention where there are critical divergences between the two. With few exceptions that have been marked, emphases are in the original. The following abbreviations are used throughout:

A	*Amras* (English)
Am	*Amras* (German)
AM	*Alte Meister*
Aus	*Auslöschung*
B	*Beton*
C	*Correction*
Cn	*Concrete*
E	*Ereignisse*
Ext	*Extinction*
G	*Gargoyles*
I	*In der Höhe*
Ind	*Indication of the Cause*
K	*Korrektur*
M	*On the Mountain*
MP	*My Prizes*
MPr	*Meine Preise*
OM	*Old Masters*
P	*Prose*
Pr	*Prosa*
U	*Die Ursache*
V	*Verstörung*

In the case of many architectural texts, I often cite Johannes Porsch's invaluable compendium, *The Austrian Phenomenon: Architektur Avantgarde Österreich 1956–1973*. The longer essays from the German volume have been partially collected in a separate English book by the same title; these translations are at times too literal, so I offer my own. For other writings that were originally published in French or German, I give the original in the main body of the text where I thought it might add clarity.

How We Learn
Where We Live

Introduction

✦

The Floor Plan

This book is about a number of things:

elementary architectures and the thought structures they engender;
two-dimensional squares and 3D-cones;
up, down, and middle positions;
the concentration and dispersion of attention;
visionary architects (Raimund Abraham, Hans Hollein, Walter Pichler, Richard Neutra, Mies van der Rohe) and philosophers (Ernst Bloch, Ludwig Wittgenstein);
humic and *human*ist constructions;
panoptic and synoptic views telescoping or otherwise distending time and space;
students' *pre-positioning* and teachers' propaedeutics;
cabinets of curiosities and modern museums; and
performances and concepts (*Vorstellungen*).

But it is mainly about *Bildung*, understood as an encompassing education, and *Gebilde*, meaning structures of various sorts, as this relationship manifests itself in the work of the late, great Austrian novelist, playwright, and poet Thomas Bernhard (1931–1989).

In order to shed some introductory light on these many issues, it is helpful to begin with a floor plan, what in German is called a *Grundriss*. This literally is a two-dimensional line drawing of the ground.[1] We might think of its most basic element as a square with a black outline. The black square encases the proposed spatial area. The lines and proportions connote simplicity. The length—let's say 120 mm by 120 mm—indicates that the building is drawn to scale, shrunken and hence reduced to a manageable scope. The *Grundriss* provides a survey, an overview: emplaced directly above, we look down upon the ground. From here, we have a sure sense of the occupied surface. The *Grundriss* often functions to document an existing structure, but it may also be used when planning further construction or alteration to a site. The square may mark the location for a foundation, where the groundwork is to be laid for a future structure. It may also show the perimeter of the walls, without windows or doors. Then it marks the outer, load-bearing walls that have already been erected, freeing and emptying the inside for any possible number of spatial combinations: divisions based on movable partitions, different materials, varying light sources, and so on, which come later.

Let us change our viewing angle, so that the square becomes an *Aufriss*, a view from the side. We are no longer looking at the ground from an aerial position, but are now on the same plane as the object, seeing it head-on. This front elevation would show us a flat representation of a plain façade. We could, however, also be looking at the cross-section of a box: a two-dimensional representation of a three-dimensional receptacle. The black line would suggest the containment of whatever is put within the box, as the *Grundriss* did. In both cases, the square could be seen as a limit—or, put more positively, as a creative constraint, carving out an area for a particular purpose.

For a proponent of experimental poetry such as Friedrich Achleitner, this black outline conjures up a number of literal and metaphorical possibilities. For the trained architect and architectural critic, it might be the basic element of an architect's handicraft;[2] a tool for visualizing a design; a schematic drawing of a wall, door or window; a measurement unit that carries with it the potential and drawbacks of standardization; an architectural example of modernist minimalism. For Achleitner as an avatar of avant-garde poetry, the square could suggest the material ground for textual production, namely, the blank page; a metaphorical foundation for concrete poetry, which uses language in its typographic and imagistic dimension; the importance of the visual ground for such writing. It might signify a confining structure—the social, linguistic, historical, and economic restrictions an experimental writer faces. The square may be a container for bringing order to the imagination's myriad ideas or a limiting constraint that the blocked writer needs to propel him forward. Perhaps it suggests a "magical square" with affinities to Dürer's mathematical square in his engraving *Melencolia I* (1514), signifying a deep harmony between geometry and arithmetic. In this case, it perhaps conjures up a special affinity between architecture and writing as well as the reconciliation between an applied art (architecture) and the fine arts (poetry and drawing/printmaking).[3]

A *Grundriss* in German also is used figuratively in the sense of a short treatise, primer, or tract meant to give an overview or provide guidance. For Achleitner, this may be, ultimately, the most interesting connotation: the square as the groundwork for a redefined genre with a new orientation—a reconfigured novel of education or *Bildung*. The square that I have been using as an example is Achleitner's geometric springboard in his playful 1973 book entitled *quadratroman*, or *square novel*. The programmatic lowercase letters, straining against orthographic convention (which would capitalize all German nouns), are neatly printed with right justification in the bounds of a 120 mm by 120 mm large square. The subtitle Achleitner gives his 176-page-long work is telling. He calls it "1 new bildungsroman 1 new novel of development etc.etc.etc." ("1 neuer bildungsroman 1 neuer entwicklungsroman etc.etc.etc."), explicitly locating his work in a celebrated literary historical lineage that reaches back to Johann Wolfgang von Goethe.[4] The lowercase letters indicate that we can no longer expect a Bildungsroman such as Goethe's *Wilhelm Meister's Apprenticeship* (*Wilhelm Meisters Lehrjahre*, 1795–96); the "etc.etc.etc." pokes fun at what has been considered a serious genre. The narrative unfolding of a young man's evolution until he fits into bourgeois society is clearly not the point of Achleitner's *quadratroman*, which lacks protagonist, plot, or development. There are no heroic gestures in 1973, just a small, stumbling, humorous listing of the many possibilities inherent in the elementary architecture of a square. Achleitner does not make the image (*Abbild*) fit the picture (*Bild*) we have of education (*Bildung*);[5] rather, he shows how *Bildung* and structures (*Gebilde*) are interrelated.[6] The *Bildung* of the Bildungsroman is here understood in its widest sense, as enlightenment, clarification, elucidation, and especially critical, analytical thought. The content of the squares can problematize, foil, or potentiate one another. The words in them take on a life of their own, recounting mini-narratives in space and time. One square's constraint is another's creative impetus: in order for the box to become the condition for the possibility of enlightenment and growth, it must be reimagined, turned inside out, written over (and under), pulled through the inky muck, and made to speak beyond itself.

Let us turn, for illustration, to the square on p. 43 of the *square novel* (figure 1). In a manner typical for a number of squares in the book, simple typewritten text fills the box. The words "oben" ("up") and "unten" ("down") are repeated in row after row; their slight shift from line to line creates visual diagonals across the page. Of course, something is wrong: "oben" or "up" is not at the top of the page. Instead, the word "unten" or "down" has pride of place in the first line. The facing page, p. 42, shows the word "unten" arranged in seven straight columns. "Unten" fills the square, except for the last row. At the bottom, the word "oben" is reproduced eight times, breaking up the rigid typographic pillars formed above. The page ends with a single "o," since the "-ben" no longer fits within the square's outline. Is it an exclamation that the downs and ups have gotten jumbled, the German interjection "O!" that is equivalent to our English "Oh!"? Or is the "o" a graphic mark to indicate that an aberrant row of words has destroyed the established symmetry? Picking up on both possibilities, the square on p. 43 refuses to restore any semblance of order or meaning disrupted on the preceding page. A single line of the word "unten," repeated seven times, replicates the mixing of hierarchies we already confronted on p. 42 and wreaks havoc with deictic markers of space (there is no up or down there!). To further confuse things, the word "oben" forms a border on two sides of the square, that is, "oben" runs vertically down the perimeter walls, while "unten" is a kind of

```
unten unten unten unten unten unten unten
oben oben oben oben oben oben oben oben o
ben oben oben oben oben oben oben oben ob
en oben oben oben oben oben oben oben obe
n oben oben oben oben oben oben oben oben
oben oben oben oben oben oben oben oben o
ben oben oben oben oben oben oben oben ob
en oben oben oben oben oben oben oben obe
n oben oben oben oben oben oben oben oben
oben oben oben oben oben oben oben oben o
ben oben oben oben oben oben oben oben ob
en oben oben oben oben oben oben oben obe
n oben oben oben oben oben oben oben oben
oben oben oben oben oben oben oben oben o
ben oben oben oben oben oben oben oben ob
en oben oben oben oben oben oben oben obe
n oben oben oben oben oben oben oben oben
oben oben oben oben oben oben oben oben o
ben oben oben oben oben oben oben oben ob
en oben oben oben oben oben oben oben obe
n oben oben oben oben oben oben oben oben
oben oben oben oben oben oben oben oben o
ben oben oben oben oben oben oben oben ob
en oben oben oben oben oben oben oben obe
n oben oben oben oben oben oben oben oben
oben oben oben oben oben oben oben oben o
ben oben oben oben oben oben oben oben ob
```

Figure 1. Friedrich Achleitner, *quadratroman* (1973), p. 43. © Zsolnay Verlag.

porous top and "oben" is a leaky bottom—the spacing between words suggests permeability.

On these pages, the unspoken assumptions underpinning education and academic rankings are systematically subverted: gone are symmetry, proportion, harmony. Undermined are the rankings with which we decide what is valuable and located "above" or "on top" versus what is negligible and "down" or "below." The unsystematic presentation of the adverbs of place profoundly destabilizes; better said, the adverbs pretend to be systematically arranged but flout standard usage by cropping up in the wrong places. The second square with the same words, but with a slightly different arrangement, even outdoes the preceding page. The destabilization becomes palpable through the glimmering afterimage that remains on the retina. The words seem to flicker because of the optical illusion the white striations create. The use of a single row of "oben" and "unten" on both pages reinvigorates the German idiom "aus der Reihe tanzen": when an individual tries to "march to a different tune" in German, he "dances out of the row"—just like the words "oben" and "unten."

We are prepared for this *détournement* earlier in the book, which draws much of its rhetorical power from the play with spatial markers. On p. 20 (figure 2), another idiom "drunter und drüber," or "helter-skelter," creates a

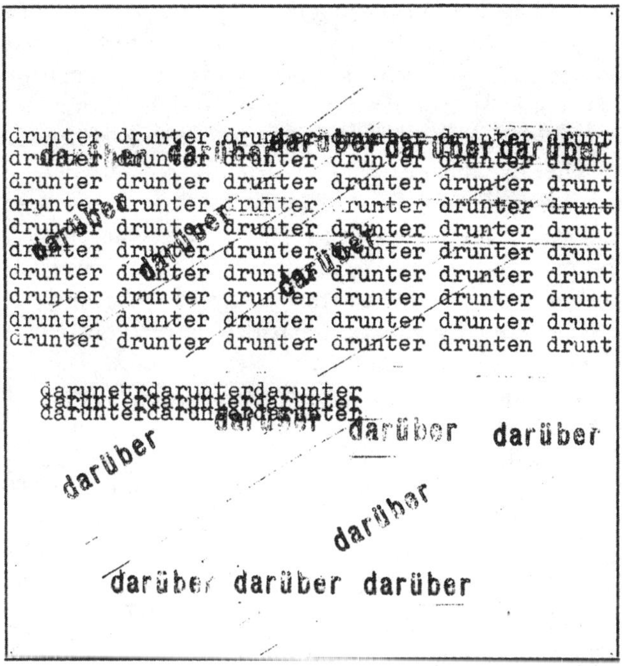

Figure 2. Friedrich Achleitner, *quadratroman*, p. 20. © Zsolnay Verlag.

similar muddle within the square's confines. Things go "higgledy-piggledy" when the adverbs of place are typed every which way; the "drunter" or "below" is indeed overwritten with the word "darüber" or "over." Nonetheless, the "drunter" fills the top of the page as well as the middle, reaching into the lower half and giving pause—the word "below" is actually on top. The "darüber" is engaged in an agonistic contest with it for the upper hand; it is "above" and "across." The idiom is also distorted ever so slightly: instead of the colloquial "drunter and drüber," the letter "a" is inserted into "drunter" and "drüber," turning both abbreviated everyday words into their High German variants. What becomes of a colloquialism that aspires to proper standard German? Is it seeking to repress the topsy-turvy nature it expresses? Does the "darüber," in other words, have the advantage?

Only to a degree: the suppressed "drunter" is ultimately irrepressible. The "darunter" that stands below the alternatively spelled "drunter" is agitated, with mixed up letters and incorrect line spacing, leading to a kind of visual oscillation and melding. Energy emanates from these run-on "darunters," at odds with the efforts of the "darüber" and the black borders to confine them to the square space (the -er of the "darunter" is cut off in the last column). The "darüber" is forced to give way and move to the bottom of the page—where its meaning is obliterated.

Achleitner's reflections on the bounds and thresholds of the square as an elementary architectural form arise from his effort to take seriously the implications of architecture for perception and thought—and hence education. Two of his 173 squares cite the philosopher Ernst Cassirer's *Philosophy of Symbolic Forms* (*Philosophie der symbolischen Formen*) from 1925.[7] The excerpts Achleitner chooses from the second volume on *Mythical Thought* (*Das mythische Denken*) stress the difference between abstract mathematical space and the perceived space of haptic and optic experience. Implicitly, his manipulation of squares demonstrates the divergence between the homogenous space of abstract reflection and the heterogeneous space of lived experience, which Cassirer thematizes in these sections of his multivolume work. The "here" and "there" always possess a definite tonality ("Tönung"); they are never "merely" present.[8] Cassirer argues in the subsequent, unquoted passages from *Mythical Thought* that in order to break through to the "Gedankenraum"—the "thought space"—of pure mathematics, one would have to reverse one's perspective and suspend everything that appeared immediate to perception.[9] Mythical space occupies a middle ground ("Mittelstellung") between the spaces of sensory perception and mathematical abstraction, but in the end is closer to immediately perceived space than the thought space of mathematics.

These architectonics implicit in thought are the basis for the *square novel*. In the passage from Cassirer that Achleitner quotes, the German philosopher uses significant building terms to describe the proximity of perceptive and mythical space and thought. Both spaces are "concrete structures" of consciousness ("konkrete Bewußtseinsgebilde").[10] Space and place are not opposite one another as imaginative/abstract and real/concrete terms respectively; both work together in consciousness. A novel of development, even one as tongue-in-cheek as Achleitner's, comes down in favor of this site-specific, emplaced, haptic-optic, instant experience. The visual arrangement of words on a page has a substantial reality for readers. It elicits a very particular space for thought that is comprehended immediately via sensory perception. There is no such thing as a reader's indifferent positioning. The closing sentence from Cassirer to which Achleitner refers reads: "Each element [every position in space] has a special distinguishing character which cannot be described in general concepts but which is immediately experienced as such."[11] Here and there, right and left, up and down can only be experienced as special and individual; their "distinctive character," "mode," and "value" in turn give rise to a particular thought-space (which, for Cassirer, is not yet that of abstract thought).[12] When right and left, as well as up and down are repurposed, as in Achleitner's case, they overturn previous sensory experience, thereby giving rise to new thought spaces—including abstract ones. In the *square novel*, emplacement allows insights into sociocultural existence beyond the lighthearted typography and play with idioms. Being on the right or the left politically and up or down socially no longer come across as natural; they are removed from the realm of habit and custom, becoming tangible and available to experience, reflection, and, finally, change.

Taking my cue from a lexicon entry cited in one of Achleitner's last squares, I would argue that the *square novel*, relating the fundamental *Grundriss* of *Gebilde* to the metaphorical building blocks of *Bildung*, also raises his reflections to a higher power. To square something, in German as in English, means to take it to the power of two ("zweite Potenz"). If the word *Quadrat* is combined with another noun into a composite word denoting measurement, a unit of length is transformed into an area. Squaring increases the unit's "Potenz," its power, potency, and potentiality:

> Square . . . (Lat.) Modifier of composite
> words with the meaning
> "to the second power"; as prefix
> before units of length (that there-
> by become units of area) Abbr. q,
> in Germany.
>
> Quadrat . . . (lat.) Bestimmungswort von Zusammen
> setzungen mit der Bedeutung
> "zweite Potenz"; als Vorsatz
> von Längeneinheiten (die da-
> durch zu Flächeneinheiten wer-
> den) Abk.q, in Dtschld.[13]

With humor and impudence, Achleitner overturns the belief in the edifying properties of *Bildung* and its foundational aspect for personal growth and sociocultural development. He also insists on national specificity, stressing the distinctions between Austria and Germany. This is clear in his allusion to Ernst Jandl's famous 1962 poem "vienna: heroes square" ("wien: heldenplatz") on one page of the *quadratroman*, where the letters of the word "Platz," or "square," stretch to mimic an empty square within a black square. Achleitner's empty "Platz" serves as a counterpoint to the crowded Heldenplatz, which Jandl's poem describes as a "sea of little men" ("männchenmeere") on the day Hitler announced Austria's annexation to the Third Reich in March 1938.[14] The vacant square within the black square suggests an alternative history—if only it had been so in reality, then the novel of development might possibly lead toward some kind of resolution.

A post-World War II, post-1968 Bildungsroman topples our ideas of what constitutes up and down (upward or downward social mobility), in and out (insider or outsider status), high and low (culture), all the while suggesting its own lack of progress and irresolvable nature. The final page of Achleitner's book attempts to take back whatever has been achieved developmentally—most notably the upending of our conservative habits of thought or automatic reactions—and dismantles the very literary tradition it has used as a foil. The "dear reader" is asked, in the last square, to forgive and forget all he or she has read. A "terrible mistake" has been discovered, namely that the square is not a square: it is a rectangle measuring 120 mm by 119 mm.[15]

My own efforts have been to "square" Bernhard's overlapping geometries, directional mobility, up-and-down hierarchies, and emphatic emplacement with his pedagogical intervention. I position Bernhard's novels within the discourse around architecture and the interventions in higher education that began in the 1960s in the German-speaking world. In his highly stylized, multivolume autobiography, drawn together in English as *Gathering Evidence* (comprised of *An Indication of the Cause / Die Ursache. Eine Andeutung* [1975], *The Cellar: An Escape / Der Keller. Eine Entziehung* [1976], *Breath: A Decision / Der Atem. Eine Entscheidung* [1978], *In the Cold / Die Kälte. Eine Isolation* [1981], *A Child / Ein Kind* [1982]), he charts his own dismal experiences in Austrian corporatist, National Socialist, and post-1945 schools. Their lip service to the nineteenth-century ideal of *Bildung*, with its belief in the organic, all-encompassing development of the autonomous, reason-centered subject, and their hypocritical appeal to edification, meant to vouchsafe the moral structuring of the individual, are unmasked as shams in Bernhard's indictment. *Bildung*, unchanged after the National Socialist catastrophe, is a travesty, continuing the authoritarian pedagogical methods with the same content. In his works, he does not equate *Bildung* with a person's cultivation of particular intellectual faculties; instead, he stresses the schooling of what he calls a "creative-critical," irreverent voice with a physical, emotional, and artistic investment in life.

The early 1960s, when Bernhard begins to publish in earnest, are a seminal moment in postwar German culture. Bernhard's fascination with education should be seen against the backdrop of the first stirrings of confrontation with the conservative status quo. In Austria, an environment of cultural fermentation makes itself felt, which eventually leads to visceral artistic interventions in the public sphere such as those of the Viennese *Aktionisten*—while admittedly never giving rise to the widespread open rebellions that shake the Federal Republic of Germany.[16] Bernhard participates in the burgeoning interest in the relationship between education (*Bildung*), upbringing (*Erziehung*), and authoritarianism that characterizes this defiant cultural moment. He engages with the works of Ernst Bloch, Heinz-Joachim Heydorn, and Alexander Mitscherlich, reading their writings on utopian thought and architecture, the aporias of inherited *Bildung*, and the problems with current urban and rural planning respectively.[17] Indeed, the titles from Bernhard's own prestigious publishing house Suhrkamp that can be found in his Obernathal library suggest an ongoing interest in pedagogy, which has not yet been examined: from Theodor W. Adorno's *Education for Maturity and Responsibility* (*Erziehung zur Mündigkeit*, 1969), Ernst Bloch's *Pädagogica* (1971), Paul Feyerabend's *Knowledge for Free Beings* (*Erkenntnis für freie Menschen*, 1979), to a series of scholarly works such as Dietlind Eckensberger's *Socialization Conditions of Public Education* (*Sozialisationsbedingungen der öffentlichen Erziehung*, 1971), Joachim Hirsch and Stephan Leibfried's *Materials for Science and Education Policy* (*Materialien zur Wissenschafts- und Bildungspolitik*, 1971), Walter Schäfer's *The Problems of School in Times of Social Change* (*Probleme der Schule im gesellschaftlichen Wandel*, 1971), and Brigitte Eckstein's *University Didactics and Conflicts in Society as a Whole* (*Hochschuldidaktik und gesamtgesellschaftliche Konflikte*, 1972).[18]

In his prose works in particular, Bernhard disparages the state of humanist education because its deterioration has gone hand-in-hand with the decline of the public sphere and the increasing dominance of science.[19] The open space of discussion that guarantees a democratic society is closed with the turn away from what Bernhard construes to be teaching in its true form—a discursive education that takes place in *other* spaces.[20] In 1965, when he receives the city of Bremen's prestigious Literature Prize for his first novel *Frost* (1963), he openly lambastes the "Wissenschaftswelt," meaning the scholarly world of research with its belief in the universal applicability of the scientific method. In a rebellious gesture decapitating all paternal authority associated with youth's education, Bernhard claims that the scientistic, quantitative drive has led to the pervasive disenchantment of the twentieth century; "the fairytales are past," he maintains.[21] Disenchantment has taken place behind the backs of the "blind fathers" ("blinde [. . .] Väter") and "stupid teachers" ("blöde [. . .] Lehrer"), who are unaware of their actions. The young are left without guidance during the "most audacious chapter in the book of world history" ("kühnste Kapitel des Weltgeschichtsbuchs"). Within this period marked by youths' upheaval against an increasingly administered life,[22] a new propaedeutic becomes necessary within new kinds of spaces, and Bernhard's oeuvre sketches out the possibilities for such a preparatory course of study. The goal of rethinking buildings and their relation to *Bildung* is not to impart a specific knowledge, but to prepare the young to be receptive to new insights within the parameters the "Wissenschaftswelt" sets.[23]

One book in his library is particularly pertinent in this regard: Heinz-Joachim Heydorn's untranslated *Toward a Reformulation of the Concept of Bildung* (*Zu einer Neufassung des Bildungsbegriffs*).[24] The professor of pedagogy polemicizes against the idea of *Bildung* as it has been passed down from the German Enlightenment to his contemporaries in 1972. Orienting his critique along those of the Frankfurt School, he impugns late capitalist West German society for having given up on *Bildung*'s most fundamental tenet: the goal of emancipation for an entire class. Instead of "reflection, sensitivity, productive development and unfolding" through *Bildung*, he finds a "system of total quantifiability" and "useless life." Rather than providing a *Grundriss* or blueprint, education now furthers "Risslosigkeit," the lack of gaps or "Risse." It results in human deformation, uninterrupted profit-seeking, and total administration without the fissures enabling creative thought and freedom:

> Behind the unbroken chain of concepts of balance sheets in late positivism, no expectation is concealed, only a deformed human being. Reflection, sensitivity, productive development turn into signs of worthless life in a system of total quantification. [. . .] In that manner, the process of alienation finally has reached *Bildung*, it is subject to the same norms of production as everything else.
>
> Hinter dem rißlosen Begriffsalphabet der Bilanzbuchhaltung des Spätpositivismus verbirgt sich keine Erwartung, sondern ein deformierter Mensch. Reflexion, Empfindsamkeit, produktive Entfaltung werden im System der totalen Quantifizierung zu Merkmalen wertlosen Lebens. [. . .] Damit hat der Entfremdungsprozess die Bildung endgültig erreicht, sie unterliegt den gleichen Normen wie alle Produktion. (Heydorn, *Zu einer Neufassung*, 119)

In the "gapless state of profitability" ("lückenlosen Rentabilitätsverfassung"), humans can only become empowered to act ("Handlungsbefähigung") if their education has not given up on humanity as a collective concern and on class emancipation. The divergence between the individual and the middle class is palpable in the development of the institutions of *Bildung*. With the turn away from the collective in education toward the intensive focus on individual edification and development, *Bildung* has lost its emancipatory, progressive moment.

In returning to the etymological distinctions inherent in words related to learning, Heydorn resuscitates a Kantian belief in autonomous reason. The contradictions within the system of education become legible in the words' roots, which imply a down or up direction:

> The antagonistic relationship that weighs on institutionalized *Bildung* is very well expressed in the terminology when one explores its origins. Upbringing is discipline, necessary submission that we have to traverse, acquisition that we cannot avoid; *Bildung* is man's control over himself, liberation. [. . .] Upbringing is supposed to become obsolete, *Bildung* should become reality.
>
> Das antagonistische Verhältnis, das sich über die institutionalisierte Bildung niederschlägt, wird über die Terminologie selber vorzüglich ausgedrückt, wenn man ihren Ursprüngen nachgeht. Erziehung ist Zucht, notwendige Unterwerfung, die wir durchlaufen müssen,

> Aneignung, um die wir nicht herumkommen; Bildung ist Verfügung des Menschen über sich selber, Befreitsein. [. . .] Erziehung soll obsolet, Bildung Wirklichkeit werden. (Heydorn, *Zu einer Neufassung*, 120)

Heydorn distinguishes between *Erziehung* and its downward pull (stressing the "Unterwerfung" or *sub*mission rather than the upward pull inherent in the German term *Erziehung*) and *Bildung* and its upward thrust. He comes down firmly on the side of upward development via education conceived as *Bildung*. The Latin word "educatio," he continues, already signals the movement via *up*bringing to true education. Education is also movement forward, which leads out of the imposed strictures perpetuating dependency. Heydorn conceptualizes his model, taking his cue from an entire Enlightenment tradition, as one of *Aufstieg*, of ascendant movement and stepping up. All the practical suggestions that Heydorn proffers toward the end of his treatise are couched in the language of upward advancement, be it universal higher education, general admission to all institutions of higher learning, the reconciliation of practical and theoretical training, or the removal of functional imperatives from university life.

Rather than limiting the individual, Heydorn argues that *Bildung* should be without borders, as in Kant's "Idea for a Universal History with a Cosmopolitan Purpose" ("Idee zu einer allgemeinen Geschichte in weltbürgerlicher Absicht," 1784): "Reason knows no borders."[25] From the sublation of alienation, the "Aufhebung" (literally the "lifting up"), to raising consciousness to the heights of the technological revolution, Heydorn conceives his radical project as one that explodes institutions from within and eradicates borders through upward striving (*Zu einer Neufassung*, 122–24). There is no confining square in his *Grundriss* for a new kind of education.

In Heydorn's plea for a return to *Bildung* as an instrument in class struggle,[26] the teacher has a special function that can only be described as architectonic. The pedagogue is to work for the present in the service of the future, laying foundations and giving form. Heydorn's view of the teacher has a utopian component: "He is confronted with the human being at a certain age, but he does not teach him for that age, but for a coming world" ("Er hat den Menschen in einem bestimmten Alter vor sich, aber er bildet ihn nicht für dieses Alter, sondern für eine kommende Welt"). In his person, the teacher externalizes and actualizes the promise of this future moment, *becoming* structure: "He himself is concrete future in the midst of the present, a qualitative reference for his pupils" ("Er ist selber konkrete Zukunft inmitten von Gegenwart, qualitativer Hinweis für seine Schüler"). Concretizing and hence shaping the future as his own *Gebilde*, the teacher comes to both create/educate (*bilden*) and represent (*darstellen*): "He must himself already represent the future for which he instructs, in the breaking open of human liberation ("Die Zukunft, für die er bildet, muß er bereits selber darstellen, in der Aufbrechung menschlicher Befreiung," 125–26). The tension-riddled imperatives inadvertently come to the fore in this passage: the teacher must shape and also break open the mold. On the one hand, the teacher is form and can thus give form to impressionable youngsters; on the other, he must initiate the process of forcing open past confinement and destroying structure so that liberation can be achieved. Moreover, he has to witness and propel the development of minors who are not capable of taking their own learning in hand; at the same time, he is supposed to increasingly disappear into the background of their development.

For Heydorn, the contemporary school has mutated into a "supersized holding institution" ("überdimensionale [. . .] Bewahranstalt," 100). Bernhard echoes this conception of education in its institutionalized form as a kind of retainer or holding pen for intellectually hungry youths from *Amras* to *Old Masters*, as we see in Chapters 2 and 3, even where he elides the social frame for his young men. Indeed, his Cone in *Correction*, modeled on the Wittgenstein House's extreme precision, is at first meant as a counter-building to the familial estate of Altensam, a confining structure (see the Conclusion). It becomes yet another way of conceptualizing the imbrications of the "composite of masonry and men," the "Gebilde von Mauern und Menschen," present in *Bildung*.[27]

While Bernhard studiously avoids any affiliation with the Left, he takes on yet more of Heydorn's assumptions. Making no distinction between *Erziehung* and *Bildung*, Bernhard utilizes the same upward trajectory in all his writings in order to gesture toward the autonomy and emancipation from inherited structures. A common figure is the pedagogue or guide, who uses form to articulate thought patterns and shed light on societal grievances. However, Bernhard's educational project is entirely private: from the outset, the reform of institutions from within—the long "march through the institutions," to use a catchphrase of the 1960s student movement—is not even contemplated. The perfect education can only be realized in the dialogue between an older man and his disciple *outside* the constraints of state-sanctioned schools. The voluble teacher who guides but must also efface himself is largely realized only in Bernhard's late work, in *Old Masters* (1985) and *Extinction* (*Auslöschung*, publ. 1986, but written prior to *Old Masters*).[28] Bernhard's prose records the ongoing search for this kind of person, for someone who can tolerate the strain of standing in opposition to the society he orbits.[29]

Heydorn ends with a utopian appeal of nearly expressionistic, revolutionary character. *Bildung* has an emancipatory character for the pupil and the social class to which he or she belongs. The process, however, influences educators as well as students, drawing together different temporal moments:

> The process to which *Bildung* gives birth understands itself as a process concerning the social base. All *Bildung* is aimed at the human being as one's interlocutor; he is its real object, as a living, tangible person. *Bildung* is the path from below. In the way in which it

> manages to represent conscious life, the educator himself is educated. With its success, *Bildung* is self-help; man is supposed to gain himself through others. [. . .] It is self-doing as mutual aid, in this manner the constant initiation of liberation. It is an experiment on oneself. This is its anticipatory character, with which it sets man above and beyond his imposed border. It is the future within the contemporaneous. With *Bildung*, man takes possession of himself. It begins now.
>
> Der Prozeß, den die Bildung entbindet, begreift sich als Prozeß an der gesellschaftlichen Basis. Alle Bildung ist auf den Menschen als Gegenüber gerichtet; er ist ihr wirklicher Gegenstand, als lebender, erfahrbarer Mensch. Sie ist Weg von unten. In der Weise, mit der sie bewußtes Leben zur Darstellung bringt, wird der Erzieher selbst erzogen. Mit ihrem Ausgang ist Bildung Selbsthilfe, der Mensch soll sich am Menschen gewinnen. [. . .] Sie ist Selbsttun als gegenseitige Hilfe, damit ständige Initiierung von Befreiung. Sie ist Selbstversuch. Dies ist ihr antizipatorischer Charakter, mit dem sie den Menschen über seine verhängte Grenze setzt. Sie ist Zukunft im Gegenwärtigen. Mit ihr ergreift der Mensch von sich Besitz. Sie beginnt jetzt.[30]

Heydorn's conceptualization of *Bildung* as an anticipatory process and, more importantly, as a pathway ("Weg") going from the lower social orders upward, from down to up ("von unten"), leads to the self-tutelage and self-development with which Bernhard grapples. For Bernhard, any education furthering independent thought can only have the effect of supplanting or superseding the model of teacher-student, since the teacher is also changed in the course of educating. As a permanent process of initiation—we will look at initiation rites in *Amras*—*Bildung* needs to move beyond the sorely lacking present. Bernhard fuses the utopianism of Heydorn with the principles of hope in architecture he finds in Ernst Bloch's work, which I discuss below. *Bildung*, according to Bernhard, must take seriously the buildings in which it takes place. It does so by moving beyond any instrumental conception of edifices. It has a duty to care for these spaces and their accreted histories. In a best-case scenario, these sites literally and metaphorically open up to experiences from the outside.

"I am not really a writer, I told Gambetti, only a literary broker dealing in literature, a kind of literary realtor, as it were, a dealer in literary real estate," states the German-speaking teacher of Bernhard's second-to-last novel when conversing with his Italian student Gambetti in *Extinction* ("Ich bin nicht eigentlich Schriftsteller, habe ich zu Gambetti gesagt, nur ein Vermittler von Literatur. . . . Eine Art literarischer Realitätenvermittler . . . , ich vermittle literarische Liegenschaften sozusagen").[31] In appropriating the old-fashioned term "Realitätenvermittler" for himself and taking it literally, the teacher makes the explicit connection between real estate ("Realitäten") and its mediating function ("Vermittlung") in education. The teacher has to mediate between literature's realities and its thought structures on the one hand and the student on the other. He continues the German romantic project—where philosophical thought ends, poetry begins to carry it onward.

Bernhard's own penchant for acquiring homes brings us back to the importance of the square floor plan for his pedagogical designs and to the peculiar mediating function he has in mind for his teachers. His *Vierkanthof* is a traditional farm that is laid out on a square foundation with an interior courtyard only accessible through one central gate. Bernhard uses the farm building as a model to describe the relationship between architectonic environment and learning. In writing about the importance of space and place in its relation to mental development and artistic production, Bernhard participates in the ongoing parallelism that thinkers have postulated between actual architecture and psychology and/or philosophies of the self. As the architectural theorist and historian Mark Jarzombek has shown, this combination can be traced back to Hegel's linking of interiority with cultural and civilizational progress. Jarzombek argues against the "philosophical insistence on interiority (as a trope of romantic philosophy)" and its automatic association with "interiority as a topic in the context of architectural history." He considers the coupling a throwback, occluding the myriad meanings inherent in certain architectural features and their importance for modern life. He writes: "The seemingly persistent philosophical yearning for thresholds, windows, and views is [. . .] an atavism lurking within the modern philosophical project."[32] Nonetheless, I think it is important to stress that Bernhard's pedagogical project—like Ernst Bloch's—is grounded in this "atavistic" yearning. In their case, the modern project has become highly questionable after the excesses of the twentieth century; it stands to reason that their undertakings engage with this intellectual legacy of interiority, cultural development, and civilizational superiority in spatial terms. Bernhard's early works look at closed-off structures facilitating interiority and development from the perspective of the young person seeking enlightenment. Examining the potential solitude that hermetic constructs offer, he participates in the totalizing architectonic conceptions some young Austrian architects such as Hans Hollein and Walter Pichler develop during the 1960s and 1970s (Chapter 1).

In an autobiographical essay for the daily newspaper *Die Presse* from 1965 entitled "My Own Solitude" ("Meine eigene Einsamkeit"), Bernhard delves into the salutary aspects of his square *Grundriss* in Obernathal. He eschews any organic societal or topographic roots, which might be expected given that the farm has the traditional design for the province of Upper Austria. Instead, the *Vierkanthof* is conceived as an inorganic structural anchor and bastion. His renovated farmhouse is the precondition for the desired discipline; it enables the self's education and rearing. The square's starkness promises an ordering of thoughts.[33] Bernhard writes of his farm: "I believe

[it] will not kill me, but discipline me for the future, make me concentrate on my goal, and confuse me as little as possible."[34] The precondition for analyzing, dissecting, and segmenting ("zergliedern") is his incarceration there. In permitting concentration to take place, it becomes both instigator and receptacle for new thoughts. Bernhard creates the neologism "Vierkantarbeitskerker" or "square labor dungeon" to refer to his *Vierkanthof*. The home is a sealed enclosure that becomes the condition for productivity. As a tight vessel, it can be filled with radically new ideas conceived in an idealized dialogue with libraries and books, real and imagined, in untold number. The private aspect of Bernhard's pedagogical model emerges in this description; the social component is only present in the imagination, not in any left-leaning conception of social change. Bernhard ironically uses a Marxist term to describe his self-willed isolation: "my comrades are the real and imagined libraries of thousands and hundreds of thousands and millions of imagined and real, written and unwritten books."[35]

Within the square, Bernhard emphasizes his transformational movement between the actual walls, with its barns, and the world of thought, exemplified by the books in his library.[36] His own concentration is linked to the austerity of the traditionalist interior: "The walls are white, the doors green, the floors from larch wood boards. Alone with the white walls, the green doors and the larch wood boards, I now succeed in concentrating in the best manner."[37] The physical restriction or concentration in an ascetic space is linked to psychical concentration. Paradoxically, confinement leads to mental expansiveness and intellectual mobility, to the passage from the material to the immaterial. The square explodes its own borders. As such, Bernhard's metaphorical incarceration leads him to alternate between the literal and literary world:

> I alternately walk back and forth between the world of pigs and cows and the world of philosophies and cacophonies. I hear what I have not yet heard, I see what I have not yet seen, I think what I have not yet thought, I feel what I have not yet felt. To dissect the world as it is and *appears*, those are the things with which I fill my solitude, *one, my own* solitude out of the billions of solitudes, with it I fill my farmhouse, my dungeon, my square labor dungeon.

> Abwechselnd gehe ich in der Welt der Schweine und Kühe und in der Welt der Philosophien und Kakaphonien hin und her. Ich höre, was ich noch nicht gehört habe, ich sehe, was ich noch nicht gesehen habe, ich denke, was ich noch nie gedacht habe, ich fühle, was ich noch nie gefühlt habe. Die Welt wie sie ist und *erscheint*, zu zergliedern, damit fülle ich meine Einsamkeit aus, *eine, meine eigene* von den Milliarden Einsamkeiten, damit fülle ich meinen Hof aus, meinen Kerker, meinen Vierkantarbeitskerker.[38]

There is something supremely reassuring about this idea of holing oneself up, reading and writing in absolute solitude but in communication with the spirit of countless texts—all the while grounded in the material realm of immediate sensation. Within the tightly controlled confines of the farm, the writer can make the necessary movement to and fro between Cassirer's perceptive space with its "here" and "now," and mathematical, abstract space with its exchangeable positions of the "anyplace" lacking emotional valences. Bernhard moves from the realm of the squealing pigs to the noisy world of philosophers' thought structures and back.

The essay "My Own Solitude" reveals something important about Bernhard's utilization of location: the spaces he develops in his works engage meaningfully with the history of specific places. In the way in which the farm in Obernathal possesses a precise historical reality, with its barns, courtyard, and floor plan harkening back to a whole tradition of rural building, the sites of his books are more than mere instigators of abstract thought experiments. By conjuring up the accumulated historical vicissitudes of places,[39] he can do away with the dichotomy established in critical literature between abstracted, imaginative space and existent places. No location is ever just one exclusive place, either. By allowing the oscillation between the locales of experience and the abstracted realm of thought, he explodes the sites' hermeticism and perforates any seeming enclosures. A box becomes a space of psychical concentration and a place of physical confinement; a square becomes a space of mental entrapment and corporeal expansiveness. In this book, I show how Bernhard draws on the Castle of Ambras in Innsbruck (Chapter 2) and the Art History Museum in Vienna (Chapter 3), as well as the Wittgenstein House in Vienna (Conclusion). He demonstrates how desirable porousness is with respect to a person's emplacement and ability to learn in, through, and about a site: we learn where we are in more ways than one.

In Bernhard's reflections on architecture, he participates enthusiastically in the reception of Ernst Bloch's popular *Outlines of a Better World* (*Grundrisse einer besseren Welt*), written from 1938 to 1947 in the United States and published in West Germany in 1959.[40] In the *Grundrisse*, the second volume of *The Principle of Hope* (*Das Prinzip Hoffnung*), Bloch outlines architecture's role in articulating and keeping alive a sense of utopian possibility in human life—architecture is placed alongside medicine, social systems, technology, geography, and perspective in art. Carrying over the subtitle of his book into his reflections on architecture, Bloch begins his disquisitions by lauding the architectural floor plan and its beauty. As a delicate being from another realm, such a floor plan conjures up a vision of the future that cannot be realized in any built structure, regardless of how great the effort at materialization. The *Grundriss* possesses its own enchantment: "A special appeal of plans and elevations has always been noted. Most of it goes into the finished house, and yet the creation on paper, so delicately traced, was different" ("Immer schon wurde ein eigener Reiz der Pläne und Aufrisse bemerkt. Das meiste davon geht ins fertige Haus ein, und doch war das Geschöpf auf dem Papier, das zart ausgezogene, ein anderes"). He foregrounds the erotic dimension of the plan in the metaphor of the delicate creature, whose lines are literally traced, but which is figuratively denuded ("ausgezogen . . .").[41] The discrepancy between imagined beauty—which can also be staged in shop windows showing a domestic interior—and lived architecture is an outgrowth of this erotic dimension and the harmony it conjures up.[42] In the vitrine "the appealing plan lives on, though one which has become corporeal; a striking freshness of design still lives on in the unentered room" ("Auch hier [in der Auslage] also lebt der reizvolle Plan fort, wenngleich als körperlich gewordener; eine täuschende Frische des Entwurfs lebt im unbetretenen Raum noch fort").

Architecture, in Bloch's view, has always utilized this artistic, erotic aspect of sheer beauty to transcend the limiting constraints of human life in the present. Every *Grundriss* seeks to activate this fantastical dimension, giving it form that might be embodied in rooms like the one in the shop window. New outlooks emerge, views that are an integral part of the free play of the imagination. In an effort to grasp the utopian, forward-looking element inherent in architecture, Bloch goes back in time from the quintessential Weimar shop window to the mosaics in Pompeii, which employ playfulness and fantasy. In the look "through" the mosaics' window an enchanting vista opens up, Bloch asserts: "A perspective view, vedutas run riot, fragilely beautiful, impossible building shapes are conjured on to the wall" (*Principle*, 700; "Perspektivischer Blick, Veduten toben sich aus, zerbrechlich schöne, unmögliche Baugebilde werden an die Wand gezaubert," *Prinzip*, 820). The irreality of these magical structures is unimportant; their desire to transcend the status quo is significant. The fragility they convey is part and parcel of their charm.

Bloch relates the desire for fanciful, expansive views to later instances of mise-en-scène and theatricality in European baroque and rococo festivals. The same drive to potentiate, to raise to a higher power, is just as much at work in the wild ornamental fantasies of the sixteenth century as it was in the designs of the ancient Italian builders of Pompeii: baroque festivals utilize old and new perspectives in the service of representing life in intensified form, in "further superelevated reflection" ("nochmals überhöhter Spiegelung"). The desire for the wondrous ("Wunder") animates the theatricalization of experience and exponentializes the mirroring effects and the play with illusion, where wall and ceiling appear as one, real columns continue in painted form, and ceilings pretend to open to the outside through the paintings that adorn them.[43] Enchantment derives from a complex interplay of mirroring and potentiating ("potenziert"), interweaving heaven and hell and evoking counterspaces, ones that can be realized via those that are imagined.[44] "This kind of thing embodies," Bloch writes with evident pleasure in the fantastical architectures he describes, "in a masterly unsound manner, nothing less than the wishful image again to live in a different space from the existing one, in fact in a deliberately impossible space. It is a daredevil architectural hurly-burly of perspective, it is simultaneously a work of art composed of exaggerating illusion, of architectural travelling." Like Achleitner's *square novel*, which potentiates the possibilities inherent in the most basic floor plan to stimulate the imagination, Bloch envisions a segue from drawing to *Dichtung* or poetry. "Fictitious building" or "erdichteter Bau" is the enchantment emanating from the drawn or described structure that lives on in the construct, but only as fragment.[45] This appeal radiates outward through the epochs, infusing the yet-to-be into the here-and-now.

The entire section devoted to architecture stands under the sign of the romantic dream: in architectural symbols such as the Egyptian pyramid—which Bloch correlates to a "crystal of death" ("Todeskristall") or excessive rigidity—and the Gothic cathedral—Bloch's "tree of life" ("Lebensbaum") or superabundance and upward movement—one senses the aesthetically dormant alternatives to the status quo, "answering counterimages" ("antwortende Gegenbilder") to the deficient present.[46] Counterspaces can arise from these counterimages; the utopian alternatives need to be excavated from existent plastic-architectonic forms, and the successors of the death crystal or life tree must be traced through the stylistic eras to speak anew to the present. In Bloch's view, the social mediation of religious ideologies underpins the architectonic styles of the distant past. For him, the latent symbols in the structures themselves allow an understanding of the society in which they arose. The Gothic cathedral, to take one example, can then be read as a preparatory space, a "Vor-Raum," pointing upwards from the earth to the coming heaven.

The present needs to retrieve some of this latent yearning for a better world, moving away from late capitalism's nihilistic architecture ("völlig nihilisierte [. . .] Architektur," *Prinzip*, 858). Its empty modernist spaces are akin to sterile sickrooms or ships signifying the flight from the status quo. In the increasingly anarchic economic and cultural conditions, their powerful geometry exerts an inexorable attraction, albeit a sentimental one. The ambivalences animating Bernhard's spatial conceptions appear in Bloch's description of the contradictory pulls of contemporary architecture toward the in- and outside. While modern architecture of the twentieth century seeks to perforate closed walls, letting in light and opening the interior to the exterior, the desire for closure and safety has grown under the capitalist-fascist threat of the 1930s and 1940s. As Bloch argues:

> The essential feature with which the new architecture began was openness: it broke the dark stone caves, it opened up fields of vision through light glass walls, but this will towards an adjustment with the outside world was undoubtedly premature. The de-internalization turned into hollowness, the southern pleasure in the outside world did not, at the present sight of the capitalist outside world, turn into happiness. For nothing good happens here in the street, in the sun; the open door, the tremendously opened windows are threatening in

> the age of growing fascism, the house prefers to become a fortress again, if not a catacomb. (*Principle*, 734)

> Der begonnene Grundzug der neuen Baukunst war Offenheit: sie brach die dunklen Steinhöhlen, sie öffnete Blickfelder durch leichte Glaswände, doch dieser Ausgleichswille mit der äußeren Welt war zweifelsohne verfrüht. Die Entinnerlichung wurde Hohlheit, die südliche Lust zur Außenwelt wurde, beim gegenwärtigen Anblick der kapitalistischen Außenwelt, kein Glück. Denn nichts Gutes geschieht hier auf der Straße, an der Sonne; die offene Tür, die riesig geöffneten Fenster sind im Zeitalter der Faschisierung bedrohlich, das Haus mag wieder zur Festung werden, wo nicht zur Katakombe. (*Prinzip*, 859)

The development of plans for underground cities after World War I, the design of "earthscrapers" rather than skyscrapers, Frank Lloyd Wright's anti-urban Broadacre City and Le Corbusier's pseudo-Greek La Ville Radieuse—these designs participate in the socio-political flight from a reality that only promises annihilation. In functionalist design the human being remains an abstract, undifferentiated entity, standardized, inorganic, and, above all, entirely private.[47]

For many German and Austrian thinkers of the late 1950s and 1960s, Bloch articulates a general anxiety about modernism, which the Nazis denigrated and whose rehabilitation is an uneasy one. When the Austrian neo-avant-garde architects of the 1960s develop underground cities that resemble fortresses below the earth or "hard body" skyscrapers armed to the teeth, they participate in the widespread fear of a militarized, thoroughly capitalist society that threatens to devour itself (see Chapter 1). Bloch sees an architectural openness and utopian transcending in Marxism. In contradistinction, the "visionary architects" and Bernhard attempt to glean positive meaning from the triumph of atemporal, elementary forms divorced from an explicitly historical model. Their cubes, cones, or cylinders share in the anticipatory thrust animating Bloch's proposed reconciliation between crystallized Egyptian geometry and the Gothic upward striving of organic life in a new order based on human freedom. Despite their misgivings about a directly political platform, for them, too, it is a small step from the house as "Höhle," or protective "den," to the house as "Hölle," or "hell," as well as from the "Höhle" to the "Hohlraum," or "hollow space," of a thoroughly commodified subjective interiority. The "visionary architects" carefully situate their designs at the cusp, in the hope of achieving another, very different *Heimat* (which Bloch terms a "homeland" arising from the midst of hard-edged geometric forms).[48] While Hans Hollein, Walter Pichler, and Raimund Abraham are less hesitant than Thomas Bernhard in their embrace of new spatial configurations, all of their designs also hint at the latent dangers and delimitations of these innovative forms.

Bernhard links Bloch's reflections to *Bildung* via buildings. In his 1967 novel *Gargoyles* (*Verstörung*), one of the first stops on the young narrator's journey of education brings him into contact with a paternal figure actually named Bloch in the text. This older man is in possession of Nietzsche's *About the Future of Our Educational Institutions* (*Über die Zukunft unserer Bildungsanstalten*), a posthumously published lecture series that Nietzsche gave in Basel in 1872. While the lectures are not explicitly discussed in the novel, they are present in the architectonic metaphors and topographic emplacement of the figures, which rehearse some of the up-down, in-out figurations I have been discussing.[49] Nietzsche's five lectures seek to resuscitate the ideal of an intimate dialogue between a paternal teacher and his filial student, of careful guidance of the young mind. They emphatically disparage the state's instrumental relationship to education, which has turned its back on the teaching of classical Greek culture and eviscerated the tight relationship between tutor and tutee. The discussions take place outdoors, away from the physical instantiations of state-sponsored education.

This model of teacher/father and student/son is clearly emulated in *Gargoyles*, where the fundamental relationship underpinning education is that between an older and younger man. In Bernhard's novel, the father and son move from station to station along a circuitous path toward a higher vantage point, with the father instructing the son in all manner of life issues. The son accompanies his parent on what amounts to a literalization of the *Bildungsweg*, or path of instruction. The student narrating *Gargoyles* fears the "hollow space" or "Hohlraum" that exists between students like himself and the wider world. When he leaves behind his parents' tutelage for that of outsiders, this hollow space threatens with its indistinction—it is neither here nor there, neither up nor down. The pertinent passage in *Gargoyles* reads:

> Students were always prey to a kind of restlessness, I said, because as long as they are at school they live in a no-man's land [Hohlraum] between the parents they have left behind and the world they cannot yet attain, and their instincts still draw them back to their parents rather than toward the world. There are often tragedies inside that no-man's land, which happen when they realize that they can neither return to their parents nor step out into the world.
>
> Unter den Studierenden sei immer eine Unruhe, sagte ich, weil sie sich, solange sie studieren, in dem Hohlraum zwischen ihren von ihnen verlassenen Eltern und der von ihnen noch nicht erreichten Welt befänden und immer noch mehr zu ihren Eltern zurück als zu der Welt hin tendierten. In diesem Hohlraum komme es oft plötzlich zur Katastrophe, dann, wenn sie einzusehen glaubten, daß sie weder zu ihren Eltern zurück, noch in die Welt hineinkönnten.[50]

In the manner in which Bernhard's first-person narrator disparages the "Hohlraum," Nietzsche's philosopher in the lectures denigrates the hollow space as well. *Bildung*, as the German idealists conceived of it a hundred years earlier, has thrust the late nineteenth-century student into this very "Hohlraum." The elderly philosopher heaps scorn on the paradoxical desire behind *Bildung* as practiced: it calls for a student to be taught to become independent through tutelage, something he in reality can only undertake on his own. The student, once he reaches university, is left to his own devices in the hope that he will somehow become someone special with unusual talents, although then the required guidance is lacking.[51] In other words, the process of maturation presupposes maturity. Furthermore, the student is supposed to be unafraid of the hollow space between himself and the world, a space that education is meant to fill or at least bridge. Rather than pre-positioning him, however, the hollow space leaves him in a vacuum. The model fails on its internal paradoxes and conflicting imperatives.

While the imagistic mélange drawn from architectural, biological, and military terminology in Nietzsche's lectures does not offer itself up to a single reading, a number of building metaphors are worth noting. For the student pursuing a university degree, he finds himself on "sandy ground" ("thönernem Grunde"), on which he can only construct an inferior structure with a "crumbling foundation" ("auf zerbröckelndem Fundamente"). The building "slants to one side, trembling before the whirlwind's blast" ("steht ihr Gebäude schiefgerichtet und unsicher bei dem Anhauche der Wirbelwinde"). The student searches for something to grab and save himself from the straits of pre-professionalism ("the limits of a narrow profession" or "enge [. . .] kleinliche [. . .] Fachmäßigkeit")—and inevitably is disappointed. He sinks down, as "these supports give way, and he finds he has clutched at broken reeds."[52] The student's resulting melancholy, which he seeks to dissipate in unnecessary activity, leads to a fall from the "heights" of learning into a kind of hollow space. For Nietzsche's rudderless student, his inner emptiness is described as an internal hollowness: "He looks into his own breast, analyses his faculties, and finds he is only peering into hollow and chaotic vacuity" ("Er zergliedert seine Fähigkeiten und glaubt in hohle oder chaotisch ausgefüllte Räume zu sehen").[53] While a student is supposed to be self-reliant, externalizing his formation in an architectonic self-construction, independence threatens his well-being and maturation. He is thrust either into empty space or the chaotic realm of university life, which repeatedly intrudes in the form of drunken, reveling students in Nietzsche's lectures.

Bernhard's *Gargoyles* can be read as an elaboration on Nietzsche's pedagogical suggestions, combined with Ernst Bloch's reflections on architecture. Self-sponsorship, that is, the ability to emancipate oneself by teaching oneself, returns in Bernhard, but divested of negative qualities. Bernhard, dissociating his pedagogical method slightly from that espoused in Nietzsche's fifth lecture, charts a process of emancipation via tutelage and not from tutelage per se. The narrating son is primarily taught the need for distance from inherited structures—without this teaching occurring in any overt way—and the beneficial aspects of seclusion. In *Gargoyles*, there is a tension between the heights the student tries to reach with his university (*Hoch*-schule) studies and through high culture and the downward movement toward independence from inherited structures and patterns. The burrowing dominates the first half, where the son moves into dimly lit interiors replete with the trappings of bourgeois learning or into ravines and valleys where the lessons of nature are imparted.[54] In the second half, life lessons are conveyed from the superior vantage point of a castle on a hill.

The character named Bloch is one of the first mediators the young man meets during his pedagogical journey. Bloch, like the first-person narrator of *Extinction*, negotiates complex realities: he is the Jewish owner of a real estate office in a small Styrian town ("Realitätenbürobesitzer," *V* 23), whose father was murdered by the Nazis. Bloch resides in the most beautiful old house in the main square, and its freshly whitewashed interior brings to mind the description of Bernhard's farm in "My Own Solitude." The relationship between the young man's father and Bloch is characterized as highly "philosophical," intellectually adventurous, and interdisciplinary—in contradistinction to the father's association with the remaining townspeople, who are described as dull and closed-minded. The young man recounts his father's positive evaluation of his affiliation with the realtor. Bloch and the father fuse disciplinary fields that are usually separated, utilizing a medical, dissecting approach to historical, political, scientific, and literary problems:

> I might find it hard to believe, my father said, considering the general tenor of things in Stiwoll, but the two of them conducted "autopsies on the body of nature" as well as "on the body of the world and its history." They discussed "comparative political science, applied natural history, literary criticism," and dealt "unsparingly with society and the state."
>
> [H]ier würden, was man in Anbetracht der Zustände, die in Stiwoll zweifellos herrschen, nicht für möglich halte, "Autopsien an dem Körper der Natur" sowie "an dem Körper der Welt und ihrer Geschichte" vorgenommen, hier betreibe man "vergleichende politische Wissenschaften, angewandte Naturgeschichte, Literaturgeschichte" und da sei man "rücksichtslos gegen die Gesellschaft und genauso rücksichtslos gegen den Staat."

Bloch's library is located above the *Vorhaus*—literally the "pre-house," a vestibule that positions and prepares the malleable youth for his encounter with erudition. The library is extremely large, without the contemplative bibliophile character the narrator disparages as bourgeois pretentiousness; only books that are in constant use are worth owning, the narrator remarks. The library functions as a foundation for Bloch. It grounds man as a political animal and establishes a view of the world devoid of ideological illusions. Note the proliferation of words related to substance, foundations, and openings in the German original:

> But in general the main theme in Bloch's house was politics, and they tended to talk about people more in regard to their political than their private beings. Meeting in a first-floor study, they conducted an analysis of the world on the most stringent intellectual principles, and left no margin for any illusions whatsoever. Most of the time the arts were rather scanted, my father said, but occasionally they would turn to them out of courtesy to Bloch's wife. (*G* 20–21)

> Im allgemeinen aber herrsche im Blochschen Haus das Politische, und von den Menschen sei auch mehr im Hinblick auf ihre politische Substanz als auf ihre private die Rede. Man leiste sich in einer über dem Vorhaus gelegenen Bibliothek ein auf der äußersten Geistesanstrengung fundiertes Durchschauen der Welt und gebe sich keinerlei Illusionen hin. Die Künste kämen die meiste Zeit zu kurz, aber Blochs Frau zuliebe öffne man sich auch ihnen zeitweilig. (*V* 24)

In the end, the house reconciles and transcends old and new style, nature and history, art and science, masculine and feminine. The interior glass walls in the *Vorhaus* provide a modernist touch and the literal "view through" ("Durchschauen"), which are the vistas that Ernst Bloch's architectural *Grundriss* extolled. The young man can witness Bloch's aroused, excited, fully embodied ("erregt") approach to his work. "Durchschauen" is the word most associated with the fictive Bloch during the encounter in *Gargoyles*; it is a central aspect of his pedagogical endeavors within his own family.[55] The house, with its library, old walls, and modern glass, allows private individuals to engage in political discussions with a philosophical bent, relying on books such as Marx's *Dissertation*, Kant's *Prolegomena*, Pascal's *Pensées*, and Diderot's *Mystification*. The older and younger generations come together here in an effort to penetrate life's "mechanism" in a manner bridging technology and art, science and nature, philosophy and poetry.

We have become so accustomed to relating to Bernhard's protagonists as eccentric, if not pathological, that it may be difficult to take seriously the author's pedagogical intervention.[56] In the main characters' methods, it is not the madness often ascribed to Bernhard's figures that lurks—nor solely the destabilization of satire, as the German writer and Bernhard admirer W. G. Sebald has contended.[57] Indeed, although the relationship between student and teacher is one of the most persistent and least ridiculous features of Bernhard's oeuvre, beginning with his first novel *Frost* in 1963 through his final novel *Extinction* and including the five-part autobiography *Gathering Evidence*, the theme of an unorthodox teaching style and content and the continual commentary on the *Bildungs*-project have not received sustained attention.[58] The novels are, admittedly, less educational dialogues than meticulous records of teachings or discussions. Some texts—such as the second part of *Correction* or large stretches of *Old Masters*—read like recorded instructional sessions or verbatim transcriptions, posthumously published. The ripostes of the students are largely effaced; like rejoinders in Socratic dialogues, the sparse interjections only further the continuation of the teacher's argument. Even when the informal disquisitions are laughable in their melding of high cultural references and allusions to bodily functions or in their hyperbolic disqualification of the assumptions about art most of us hold dear, they retain their faith in rhetorical persuasion, or, better said, verbal inundation.[59]

Few of Bernhard's prose works are situated in a locus classicus of pedagogy; only sections of the autobiography and parts of *Amras* take place in the halls of academia. Traditional schools and universities are sites to be avoided, broken open, or even replaced through the radical intervention of oppositional and subversive teachers. Bernhard's books repeatedly stage the intimate scene of pedagogy—the dialogue between an elder and younger man—in museums, inns, castles, private homes, and in nature (such as the Pincio Hill near Rome).

I can imagine some immediate objections from readers familiar with Bernhard: what is it, precisely, that we learn in his texts? The figures admire Novalis, Montaigne, Schopenhauer, Goethe, and other literary and philosophical greats, all of whom they cite without specifying details. Even in the moments before their planned suicide, the brothers in *Amras* have books lying on the table in front of them: Stifter, Jean Paul, Lermontov.[60] But here, as elsewhere, we do not find out what makes these writers or philosophers compelling. While his characters seem to cling tenaciously to high culture, they have done away with its content. Bernhard anticipated the ephemeral nature of bookishness, the unspoken but ever-present ideal of the academic tribe. In articulating his own variant of traditional *Bildung* (with its dual goal of knowledge acquistion and self-willed independence), he takes aim at any encyclopedic illusions. In the characters' insistence on the importance of these names divorced from any particular content, they already envision a moment in bourgeois Western culture that no longer prizes intimate familiarity with these writers' texts, or any texts for that matter. In the era of Wikipedia, word searches on e-books, and the general surfeit of the Internet, we, too, have watched encompassing learnedness become largely irrelevant. Even if I can recall something promptly, the computer with the search engines at its disposal can always do it faster. However, familiarity with the name still possesses a certain cachet. It suffices to "drop" the name to activate its aura.

Thus learning has to be about something other than broad-based content and needs to be more than simply disposing of cultural capital (implicit in the idea of "name-dropping") in the service of self-aggrandizement, national status, or regional identity, which is what the museum or theater, prominently displaying a cultural heritage, would seem to do. In Bernhard's works, teachers seek the proper environmental conditions to make their students receptive to another kind of thinking; they reevaluate sites of national cultural significance in order to find these ideal conditions. Occasionally, the students who are encouraged to construct intellectual edifices put their blinkered views, haphazard guesses, and prejudices on display in the self-eliding and self-subverting thought systems that they develop, much as their teachers do. The point is not that they get "it" wrong—the point is that they engage at all. And engage they do, with a monumental zeal at times bordering on fanaticism.

For Bernhard, a steady stream of "monstrous" pedagogues accompanies his characters' efforts at edification. They are as essential to the continuation of the Enlightenment project of *Bildung* as is the cabinet of curiosities to the development of the modern museum.[61] It is as if Bernhard, too, required a cabinet of curiosities to articulate his propaedeutics. Bernhard looks to unlikely sources: he begins with the radical articulations of the Austrian visionary architects of the 1960s (Chapter 1), continues on through Musil's utopian "Other Condition" in *The Man without Qualities* (*Der Mann ohne Eigenschaften*, 1930; 1932; 1943; 1952; 1978) and Novalis's anti- and interdisciplinary musings in the fragmentary *Notes for a Romantic Encyclopaedia* (*Das Allgemeine Brouillon*, Chapter 2), and moves to Wittgenstein's architecture ("Conclusion").

This is not intended to be an exhaustive study of all texts in which Bernhard thematizes architecture; if it had been, *The Lime Works* (*Kalkwerk*, 1976), *Yes* (*Ja*, 1978), and *Extinction* (*Auslöschung*, 1986) would have had to be included prominently, as well as *Concrete* (*Beton*, 1982) and *The Loser* (*Der Untergeher*, 1983). Indeed, once we become aware of the importance of architect Hans Hollein's programmatic 1967 statement "everything is architecture" for Bernhard ("Alles ist Architektur" is Hollein's title for an issue of the influential journal *Bau*),[62] it is difficult not to see every one of Bernhard's works as engaging with a widely defined concept of architecture and the architectonics of thinking. For Hollein—and Bernhard—architecture becomes a way of enlarging the human domain and a means to influence the immediate environment beyond the actual buildings themselves. "The expansion of the human domain and the means of determining the surrounding world go beyond any built instantiation," Hollein writes in his eponymous piece ("Die Erweiterung des menschlichen Bereiches und der Mittel der Bestimmung der Um-'Welt' geht weit über eine bauliche Feststellung hinaus"). With new technologies and media at its disposal, architecture becomes, in Hollein's view, a way to explore the "psychic possibilities of an artificial environment" ("psychische Möglichkeiten einer künstlichen Umwelt"). Hollein singles out the school building as a site of potential change. He imagines a moment when the new means of communication might lead to the disappearance of "doctrinal systems and buildings for learning (schools)" ("Lehr- und Lerngebäudes [Schule]").[63] While Bernhard is not interested in new media per se, he, too, seeks to revamp the philosophical schemes ("Lehrgebäude") and the spaces in which they are communicated ("Lerngebäude"). Architecture and architectonics become the encompassing figurations that make legible his oeuvre in light of its *Bildungs*-project.

While I have tried to construct something of an arch between Bernhard's early work and his late texts, it has, I acknowledge, a somewhat insufficient arc. As such the following chapters are not clear-cut studies of single works. "Foundational" texts bleed into various chapters, with references to *Amras* and *Gargoyles* in particular throughout my argument. Such is, I think, the nature of Bernhard's novels, with their patterns and recurrences, their backtrackings and feints.

A final word is in order about the edifices within certain geographical coordinates required for a Bernhardian moral and intellectual edification. A person's emplacement has to be beneficial for the shaping of unusual thoughts and the exploration of presuppositions and prejudices. While the etymological history of "edification" speaks to the implicit relation between learning and construction, the word nowadays sounds ironic. As the *Oxford English Dictionary* definition of "edification" at the beginning of this book suggests, the faint allusion to the act of building moral character in addition to intellectual formation seems somehow retrograde, and we may be tempted to dismiss the term out of hand. However, as Susan Bernstein has argued in *Housing Problems: Writing and Architecture in Goethe, Walpole, Freud, and Heidegger* (2008), Western philosophical thought is indeed deeply indebted to the word's architectural underpinnings: both philosophy and architecture establish, structure, construct, systematize, and institutionalize. She argues that "edification," from the Latin *aedes* meaning "temple" or "house" and *facere* meaning "to make," reveals the relation between self-formation and construction. Indeed, the "laying of foundations" in theoretical thinking and the "defining of the border between inside and outside" turn the act of building into an attractive analogue for "epistemological structure" and the creation of thought itself.[64] How we know, as I have claimed, is linked to *where* we learn something; this *where* helps ground and demarcate the *what* that is the substance of learning and the *wherefore*, the sociopolitical grounds for any specific knowledge. More importantly, the where becomes the condition of possibility for receptiveness to any particular content, modality of thinking, or somatic investment.

For Bernstein, the process of *Bildung* articulates itself via the individual's relationship to his home; the construction of the self is refracted in the house proper. She writes: "*Bildung* installs a certain architectonic of selfhood according to which a narrative unfolds, progressing through various stages of conflict and resolution that allow an interior to be distinguished from an exterior." A house becomes an "inscriptional space"; it allows "subjectivity to inscribe itself and externalize itself in its residence." In the process of delineating an outer from an inner self, an individual is also inscribed upon within a multilayered space that is local, regional, national, and supranational in character. He or she is shaped into a particular exemplar expressing certain (presumably) shared values. But, much like the subject that is supposed to be molded and integrated into a larger social whole, the house is always more than an empty receptacle, hollow repository, or clear expression of the subject's education. As in the case of Bernhard's structures, the edifice subverts or problematizes the "mirroring relation of inside and outside."[65]

For Bernhard, as we will see, the development and construction of an individual is a process that must also fail if it is to be at all successful. The structures in which this formation takes place must continually open themselves toward the outside if any development is to occur. A building's openings reveal its permeability to the outer environment, in the way in which a subject's formation must constantly be undermined or breached by his or her involvement with the world. This does not mean, however, that the foundations or load-bearing walls are irrelevant. Quite the contrary: special spaces—the material rooms and immaterial atmospheres[66]—embedded within special places (towns, cities, landscapes) are the prerequisite for a person's engagement with the in- and outside. They become the precondition for thinking outside the box.

Way Station 1

✦

From Box to Cone

At the time when Bernhard begins his first forays into writing in the late 1950s and early 1960s, questions about the genius loci are in the air. An entire discourse around space comes into being, one that continues for the next half century—space seen as a topophilia (Bachelard), a contested arena for public and private desires (Arendt), a simultaneously perceived, conceived, and lived entity (Lefebvre), an area "tacticians" of quotidian life traverse (DeCerteau), to name but a few approaches.[1] In a 1967 talk entitled "Of Other Spaces" ("Des espaces autres"), Michel Foucault pays homage to the monumental work of Gaston Bachelard, especially *The Poetics of Space* (*La Poétique de l'éspace*, 1958). Charting an epistemic sea change, Foucault detects a movement away from the preponderance of time in Western efforts to emplace the human being. Instead, man is situated in spatial relations of interconnected networks. In what has become a key text for the spatial turn in the liberal arts, Foucault describes sites such as cemeteries, prisons, museums, libraries, bordellos, and psychiatric clinics as *heterotopias*—they call into question a society's norms, power relations, and dominant assumptions. They are, he states, "something like counter-sites, a kind of effectively enacted utopia in which the real sites, all the other real sites that can be found within the culture, are simultaneously represented, contested, and inverted. Places of this kind are outside of all places, even though it may be possible to indicate their location in reality" ("des sortes de contre-emplacements, sortes d'utopies effectivement réalisées dans lesquelles les emplacements réels, tous les autres emplacements réels que l'on peut trouver à l'intérieur de la culture sont à la fois représentés, contestés et inversés, des sortes de lieux qui sont hors de tous les lieux, bien que pourtant ils soient effectivement localisables").[2] Simultaneously excluded from society and thus included all the more—since we need that which we shut out to help define us—these are recalcitrant, unruly locations.

In Foucault's view, then, heterotopias contest the regulative structures of a given society; in spaces such as prisons and insane asylums, a society attempts to cordon off members considered deviant. Such spaces cut through the diachronic unfolding of time to reveal multiple overlapping temporalities or "slices of time" ("des découpages du temps"), which Foucault terms "heterochronologies" in analogy to "heterotopias." The modern museum and library, collecting all things from all epochs, represent such discordant, overlapping sites. Attempting to place themselves in an atemporal space outside of time, they amass things from every age beneath their roofs and become indicators of modern man's conflicted relationship to what preceded him. Time, in Foucault's description, turns into a spatial element, as it is heaped up higher and higher, gathered together in a pile. As Foucault writes:

> Museums and libraries have become heterotopias in which time never stops building up and topping its own summit, whereas in the seventeenth century, even at the end of the century, museums and libraries were the expression of an individual choice. By contrast, the idea of accumulating everything, of establishing a sort of general archive, the will to enclose in one place all times, all epochs, all forms, all tastes, the idea of constituting a place of all times that is itself outside of time and inaccessible to its ravages, the project of organizing in this way a sort of perpetual and indefinite accumulation of time in an immobile place, this whole idea belongs to our modernity.
>
> Musées et bibliothèques sont des hétérotopies dans lesquelles le temps ne cesse de s'amonceler et de se jucher au sommet de lui-même, alors qu'au XVIIe, jusqu'à la fin du XVIIe siècle encore, les musées et les bibliothèques étaient l'expression d'un choix individuel. En revanche, l'idée de tout accumuler, l'idée de constituer une sorte d'archive générale, la volonté d'enfermer dans un lieu tous les temps, toutes les époques, toutes les formes, tous les goûts, l'idée de constituer un lieu de tous les temps qui soit lui-même hors du temps, et inaccessible à sa morsure, le projet d'organiser ainsi une sorte d'accumulation perpétuelle et indéfinie du temps dans un lieu qui ne bougerait pas, eh bien, tout cela appartient à notre modernité.[3]

Simultaneously the pinnacle of human achievement (the mountain's "summit," or "sommet"), receptacle for the accumulation of time, and enclosure for the entirety of material artifacts, the museum or library should not, however, be conceived of as either a cone or a box in Foucault's view. Euclidean geometry cannot do justice to the complexity of heterotopias (only topological spaces could). Society's tensions crisscross such paradoxical sites lying both inside and outside; incommensurable temporal orders are placed in spatial proximity to one another within their walls. Bernhard's own use of the museum is a nod toward this emergent view of it as a problematic space. The gallery does not stand in any clear relationship to the culture from which it emerges, but molds society's self-understanding in powerful ways.

The heterotopia that Foucault tellingly leaves out is the university, which particularly at the time of his speech functions as both an institution replicating societal norms and as a space in which dissent to the norm is articulated. In the German-speaking world as in the French system during the 1960s, turmoil convulses higher education. The question arises: what is the role of the university within the evolving social dynamic and how does it situate itself and the students within its confines in relation to the whole? Historically stylized as an ivory tower, especially in the nineteenth century, the university claims to be outside of temporality yet provides an overview of history; it pursues *Bildung* as an atemporal end while being indebted to the society and special interests underwriting it; it espouses the rhetoric of democratic equality while being accessible to relatively few. Bernhard uses the cone as an ideal structure to symbolize academia or, more accurately, higher education and its spatiotemporal aspirations leading upward and out of time, while at the same time being a social anchor (an "immobile place").

In Austria, the upheaval at the universities is not as pronounced as in other European countries, but its reverberations are nonetheless felt. Traces are evident in the statements of the other Austrian literary star of the period, Peter Handke, who links his anti-establishment reflections to a criticism of schools and teachers. He espouses formal innovation and literary experimentation as a means of self-perception and self-cognition, away from the constraints of any formalized *Erziehung* or *Bildung*. Handke explicitly connects his literary formalism with living in an academic "ivory tower" ("Elfenbeinturm"); he picks up on the concepts of intellectual self-sufficiency and independence inherent in the ideology regarding the modern university of German provenance. In the author's widely circulated and reprinted 1967 essay "I Am an Inhabitant of the Ivory Tower" ("Ich bin ein Bewohner des Elfenbeinturms"), he continues the polemic he began at Princeton University against the *littérature engagée* of the successful German literary Gruppe 47 (Group 47)—the powerful group of writers that had formed in 1947 to call for socio-democratic change after the experience of National Socialism. During their conference in 1966, Handke excoriated the German writers' "descriptive impotence" ("Beschreibungsimpotenz") and took issue with their view of language as a transparent means of political understanding and aesthetic representation.[4]

Handke emphatically allies himself with the "formalists"—the decried denizens of the ivory tower[5]—in the essay and so provides a link to Bernhard's rethinking of the actual ivory tower as a space for enlightenment, (self-)tutelage, and sensory awakening.[6] While the young Handke is interested in delineating his conception of literature and literary experience from a naive and reductive understanding of literary language, his brief text raises the issue of youths' formation. In "I Am an Inhabitant of the Ivory Tower," literature is located above the vagaries of everyday life, where it becomes an anti-educational counterspace: "Thus I was actually never *brought up* by official pedagogues; instead, I always allowed literature to change me" ("So bin ich eigentlich nie von den offiziellen Erziehern *erzogen* worden, sondern habe mich immer von der Literatur verändern lassen").[7] Via literature, young people like Handke can transcend the strictures in which traditional methods of disciplining (*Erziehung/Zucht*) would place them. Against and outside the confines that "official pedagogues" determine for education, the personal experience of literature becomes a means to cognition, or "Erkenntnis." For Handke, literature is a preparatory training for political and social intervention in the name of the single and singular individual. Admittedly, Handke's goal in the essay is to dispense with a simplistic literary realism that has declined to the level of cliché. He wants to install formal and linguistic innovation as the *non plus ultra* in creating literature that actually has something to say about the way people live in the present (he recognizes that this writing style will become outmoded eventually, once it has been widely adopted and devolved into a mannerism).

Like Handke, Bernhard has every reason to search for new linguistic and literary methods to overcome the harm of "official pedagogues" and established culture. While Handke only uses the term "ivory tower" in the metaphorical sense, Bernhard literalizes—concretizes—his and our understanding of it, returning readers to a conical structure to think about the potentials inherent in the ivory tower. In the short parable entitled "Two Young People" ("Zwei junge Leute"), Bernhard tests out an early variant of the cone dynamics that will run as a leitmotif through his prose. The text, first published in 1964, but later included in the collection entitled *Events* or *Ereignisse* in 1969, rewards careful attention. I reproduce it in its entirety:

> TWO YOUNG PEOPLE flee into a tower that served the defense of the city, and they mount it without speaking a word. They don't want to obliterate their silence through a betrayal and execute their plan with thoughtless haste. At the mid-point of the tower they behold an incalculable section of the landscape in which the tower stands. The coldness of the walls lets them stagger upward as in a lump of ice: with open mouths and arms stretched out in front of them, in the idea that they might, through these half-true gestures, artificially decrease the distance, which they want to traverse. Now it is revealed that the girl can create greater speed through her imagination than the mentally limited young man, and it is important to note that the girl, although she ascends eight to ten stairs behind the young man, her lover, is in truth eight or ten stair lengths ahead of him. The completely windowless tower is an early stage of the darkness and clearly recognizable as such. When they finally reach the top, they undress and fall into each other's arms, naked.

> ZWEI JUNGE LEUTE flüchten in einen Turm, der zur Verteidigung der Stadt diente, und besteigen ihn, ohne ein Wort zu sprechen. Sie wollen ihr Schweigen nicht durch einen Verrat auslöschen und gehen mit gedankenloser Schnelligkeit an ihr Vorhaben. In halber Höhe des

> Turms erblicken sie einen nicht errechenbaren Ausschnitt der Landschaft, in welcher der Turm steht. Die Kälte der Mauern läßt sie wie in einem Eisklumpen zur Höhe taumeln: mit offenen Mündern und nach vorn ausgestreckten Armen, in der Idee, daß sie durch diese halbwahren Gebärden die Entfernung, die sie zurücklegen wollen, künstlich verringern könnten. Nun zeigt sich, daß das Mädchen durch ihre Phantasie größere Schnelligkeit betreiben kann als der geistig beschränkte junge Mann, und es ist wichtig, festzustellen, daß das Mädchen, obwohl es acht oder zehn Treppen hinter dem jungen Mann, ihrem Liebhaber, emporsteigt, in Wahrheit ihm um fünfzehn oder zwanzig Treppenlängen voraus ist. Der völlig fensterlose Turm ist eine Vorstufe der Finsternis und als solche ganz deutlich erkennbar. Als sie endlich oben angekommen sind, ziehen sie sich aus und fallen sich nackt in die Arme.[8]

What do we have here? This text, at the beginning of thirty-one brief passages collected in *Events*, offers a quasi-biblical narrative about carnal knowledge, cognition, and recognition. Admittedly, it is a potpourri of parables, a rewriting of Adam and Eve as well as of the Gospel according to John ("The word was made flesh"). Man and woman are joined as one; but in the beginning there is silence and not the word or God ("In the beginning was the Word, and the Word was with God, and the Word was God"). A notation in Bernhard's typescript emphasizes the story's importance as the incipit for the thirty texts that follow. Bernhard scrawls and underlines the words "To the beginning" ("An den Anfang") in the lower right-hand corner of the page, perhaps subtly alluding to the biblical—as well as Goethean (*Faust*) and later Freudian (*Totem and Taboo*)—"Im Anfang" ("In the beginning").

The text encourages an interpretation that moves from the literal to the metaphorical plane by telling us that the young girl's imagination surpasses the young man's by leagues, or in this case, eight or ten flights of stairs. The tower, which once served a defensive purpose, can metaphorically be read as a phallic symbol and generative weapon of assault—in it, the "primal crime of procreation" ("Urverbrechen der Zeugung"), as Bernhard later terms it in numerous interviews and writings, takes place. The tower is also a variant of a watchtower, which allows a controlling gaze from a raised perspective onto an incalculable expanse of land. The view focalizes our attention on the outside environment that stands in opposition to the young, who seek out knowledge that has been beyond their ken. It also lets us ponder the constraints within: the limited male understanding as opposed to the speedy female imagination; the view from above and its impossibility; the hostile cold that becomes a precursor for darkness, itself a precondition for "Erkenntnis" or "knowing" in the biblical sense—blindness and insight are dialectically related.

The conical tower may also be read as an attempt to reintroduce a "vertical" difference into the false societal consensus that is beholden to a discourse of "horizontal" similarity and equal opportunity, which society ultimately fails to provide for its younger members. This false consensus only comes into view in later stories, where there is no dearth of allusions to the recent war and the brutal exclusion of society's weakest members. In *Events*, readers find the denunciations and betrayals that rend communities in short texts such as "The Principal" ("Der Schuldirektor"), about a falsely accused schoolteacher who commits suicide, or in "The Caretaker of the Estate's Owner" ("Die Verwalterin der Gutshofbesitzerin"), who is accused of theft and takes revenge by "beheading" the flowers in the garden. Violence is invariably directed at the vulnerable—often younger—members of society, and we also find descriptions of refugees, executions, and illegal coups d'état.[9] The collection itself ends with "Notes from a Survivor" ("Der Überlebende notiert"), who tells of people hiding in tunnels built into the mountainside near the war's end and their traumatic, recurring returns to them after the war is over. These tunnels or "Stollen" serve as a counterpoint to the tower in "Two Young People" with which *Events* begins. The literal vertical ascent ("zur Höhe") becomes a metaphorical descent; the soaring tower is turned into a downward or inward funnel as the skyscraper becomes an earthscraper.

The social frame is occluded from our view in "Two Young People": the narrator's gaze is fixed firmly skyward, even if the story's as a whole is not. The path up- and outward reveals itself to be stagnation.[10] Although the text is marked as a beginning, it is a thwarted beginning, trapped in a strange middle ground. Many elements allow us to read the text as the description of an arrested stage in a process: the two young people stop midway, "in mid-height" ("in halber Höhe"), which echoes their "half-true" ("halbwahr") gestures. The young man is at a midpoint between the girl, who is literally behind, but metaphorically ahead of him. These two young people flee into a tower, in which they walk upward as if into higher regions where the temperature drops. Bernhard uses the German verb "besteigen," which means both to ascend a mountain or, more vulgarly, for an animal to mount another. The bestial aspect of "besteigen," of animalistic coitus, further undermines the text's efforts to arrive at something approaching consciousness. The two young people move with "thoughtless haste," and their idea—that their gesture of extending their arms could somehow decrease the distance they have to traverse—is shown to be insufficient, only "half true," on the path to knowledge or "Erkenntnis." In contradistinction to an artful ("künstlerisch") approach, the prominent narratorial voice stigmatizes theirs as an "artificial" ("künstlich") attempt. The text also turns back on the openings it at first suggests; the limited view is abrogated in the second to last sentence, when the narrator claims that there are no windows after all. In this heterotopian space, there can be no new beginning as the young people plan. Over time, other cones come into existence in Bernhard's writings, perhaps more congenial to young people's attempts at development.

Chapter 1

✦

Visionary Architecture of the 1960s in "Plain/Plane" (1973)

Bernhard's complex structures, rigid hierarchies, overlapping geometries, and own strategic positioning cannot be fully grasped without an understanding of the Austrian architectural scene of the late 1950s and especially the 1960s. The advent of the "Austrian phenomenon"—in the memorable phrase of the English architect Peter Cook[1]—as a cluster of formally brilliant, linguistically hyperbolic, and radically utopian designers is surprising to outside international observers and internal Austrian commentators alike. The group's emergence infuses the moribund architectural landscape with a neo–avant-gardist rhetoric missing in the immediate postwar period.[2] In demanding a changed building practice, these young practitioners and theorists become vocal spokesmen for a far more dramatic building style: no more watered-down functionalist modernism, but rather highly theatrical spaces, where a creative élite imposes its will and ethical superiority on others. Their counterspaces of the early 1960s, intentionally unbuildable, are meant to initiate a break with the compromises of the previous frugal utilitarianism. They enable complete isolation as well as total concentration. As the decade progresses and we move into the 1970s, the designs gradually become more permeable and pragmatic in orientation, without losing a fanciful, high-tech element.[3] The designs, sketches, and sculptures comment on an envisioned synthetic lifestyle of the future, one marked by a high degree of exchange and interpenetration via television, telecommunication, and even teleportation.[4]

Bernhard, with his ear to the trembling ground, assimilates some of the visionary architects' programmatic statements. He incorporates their palpable moral outrage when they call for new architectural paradigms. Two figures stand out in this context: the architect Hans Hollein (1934–2014) and his early collaborator, the architect and sculptor Walter Pichler (1936–2012). Hollein's domineering, vertical conceits and Pichler's sculptural fortresses animate the up and down, back and forth movement in Bernhard's earliest texts, allowing him to link directionality and upward or downward mobility to *Bildung* and a split with the status quo. A brief epilogue that Bernhard pens for a collection of Pichler's drawings in 1973, entitled *111 Drawings* (*111 Zeichnungen*), makes explicit the surprising interconnections between hermetic enclosures à la Pichler and a young person's emotional and intellectual development.

The Visionaries' "Aufbruch": Breaking out and into the Open in the 1960s

As a number of architectural historians have pointed out, there is much for young artists and architects to deplore after 1945; Bernhard is, in this sense, only one of the many fed-up children of his time.[5] A number of writers, historians, theorists, and practicing architects bemoan the profit-oriented, over-hasty development of both rural and urban areas. The renowned architect Josef Lackner and the architectural historian and writer Friedrich Achleitner lament the humdrum nature of prestige projects such as the Olympic Village in Innsbruck in 1964 and of more mundane ventures, important after World War II.[6] This is the period in which Bernhard comes into contact with architects of stature, such as Clemens Holzmeister (responsible for the expansion of the Salzburg Festspielhaus),[7] and Holzmeister's student Viktor Hufnagl (associated primarily with new school design and perhaps a figure in Bernhard's novel *Yes* [*Ja*, 1978]).[8]

A watershed year is 1958, when the festering dissatisfaction is first articulated. At the 4th International Art Conference in Styria titled "Situation-Konfrontation," the artist Friedensreich Hundertwasser goes so far as to claim that the "material uninhabitability" of slums ("die materielle Unbewohnbarkeit der Elendsviertel") is preferable to the "moral uninhabitability of functional, utilitarian architecture" ("der moralischen Unbewohnbarkeit der funktionellen, nützlichen Architektur"). In his polemical speech, "Moldering Manifesto against Rationalism in Architecture" ("Verschimmelungsmanifest gegen den Rationalismus in der Architektur"), Hundertwasser seeks the confrontation for which the Catholic organizers of the conference called. Rebelling against the human measure that has been used since Vitruvius to determine the proportions of architecture, Hundertwasser excoriates this measure as mass deception or criminal fraud ("ein verbrecherischer Betrug"):[9] architecture takes a fictive average person as its basis, thereby losing sight of the individual and his need for personalized, unique expression. Hundertwasser further criticizes the distinction made between the architect, builder, and inhabitant. In his view, only a recombination of these currently separated activities in a single individual can lead to the creation of buildings that deserve the name of architecture.[10] With his romantically tinged organicism, the artist believes that a building's growth parallels a child's—hence also his preference throughout the speech for the term "Gebilde," with its overtones of imagination, structure, and body, rather than the more clinical "Bau" or "building."[11] Bernhard shares this conceptualization of drafting, constructing, and inhabiting with theorists of Hundertwasser's persuasion: for the writer, a singular dwelling speaks directly to a singular human being's character. As a further sign of his indebtedness, Bernhard echoes Hundertwasser's resuscitation of man's "critical-creative function" ("kritisch-schöpferische Funktion") with his own "practicing and creative critical artist" ("ausübender und schöpferischer kritischer Künstler," *AM* 107)—nearly three decades after Hundertwasser's talk.

Other manifestos reach for comparable hyperbole, while maintaining a refreshing belief in the possibility of change. Günther Feuerstein, an instructor at the Technical University in Vienna from 1961 to 1968 and the founder of the important theory group "Klubseminar," pens his "Theses on 'Incidental Architecture': 1958 Manifesto" ("Thesen zur 'Inzidenten Architektur': 1958 Manifest") in the same year as Hundertwasser's speech in the Sekau Abbey in Styria.[12] Hans Hollein and Walter Pichler produce clipped statements about the necessity of architectural revolution five years later, on the occasion of their first gallery exhibit in Vienna and the publication of a brochure entitled *Architecture* (*Architektur*).[13] As gifted exaggeration artists—the public epithet given to Bernhard in his later years—these architects are all united in their effort to overcome what they see as the empty formalism and utilitarian character of modernist architecture.[14] Recuperating the historical avant-garde's desire to destroy the distinction between theory and practice in a non-bourgeois way of life, Feuerstein, like Hundertwasser, necessarily stresses the accidental, ancillary, anti-aesthetic, irrational, and non-rectilinear as opposed to the purposive, major, aesthetic, rational, and linear in his "Theses." His ten-point list on "Incidental Architecture" largely manages to steer clear of the pathos of progressiveness characteristic of the historical avant-gardist moment,[15] but poignantly emphasizes a contemporary ethical thrust. It is of central importance to all the works under discussion here, and the architectural discourse of the era may be one of the wellsprings for Bernhard's insistence on an artist's moral behavior in his prose. "Incidental architecture," Feuerstein's seventh thesis states, "does not only judge according to beautiful and ugly, but also according to good and evil. *The ethical is decisive*" ("Die inzidente Architektur wertet nicht nur nach schön und häßlich, sondern auch nach gut und böse. *Das Sittliche ist entscheidend*," [Feuerstein, *Thesen*, 375]). As if to underline its point performatively, Feuerstein's mimeographed sheet of ten typed theses eschews any attractive typographic design; instead, it favors the visual poverty, rawness, and roughness the manifesto embraces on a theoretical level.[16]

The new architecture requires master builders: its elect determine the foundations and stakes of a novel building practice, clearly demarcating an expanded moral domain. Indeed, in light of Hollein's programmatic writings from 1963 onward, it is appropriate to speak of a totalizing architectural conception that involves all aspects of life and that is articulated in the journal he edits with Pichler, Gustav Peichl, and Oswald Oberhuber entitled *Bau*.[17] Reading Hollein's definition of architecture in the pages of the booklet *Architecture*, the essay accompanying the legendary exhibit in the Galerie nächst St. Stephan in 1963 and reprinted in *Bau*, I am struck by his radically formulated purpose. Hollein articulates his ideas in a more extreme fashion from those he presented at a talk in the same gallery only a year earlier, with the title "Back to Architecture" ("Zurück zur Architektur"). The newer document swerves away from the focus on Mies van der Rohe's dictum "form follows function"—with which Hollein takes issue, arguing that function follows form—instead concentrating on the original aspects of any new architectural instantiation and the violence implicit therein. Had the "return" to architecture in the first essay from 1962 sought to position Hollein's work in relationship to modernist architectural tenets as well as to an older historical lineage deriving from the nineteenth century, the 1963 essay does away with any anchorage in the past. While the one-page essay is still at pains to note architecture's sensibility for recording fine perturbations and materializing spiritual yearnings, Hollein emphasizes man's ability to dominate over the environment through built forms in "Architecture." In the radicalized program, architecture's "Gestalt," or "form," is less important than its "Gewalt," with all the German implications of "violence," "authority," "force" or "control"[18] inherent in the noun. Architecture's "Gewalt" enables the material expression of man's dominion over his environs. Architecture arises through an originary violence loosed from historical circumstance. The individual's violent creative expression calls forth structures that defy generic conventions. No backward glance through the annals of time is necessary for such an artistic expression to occur. Hollein summons up the cultic, mythic, and irrational to justify (and, by extension, excuse) his harsh conception of architecture.

From metropolis to "mediocropolis"—like Hundertwasser, Hollein is against anything that smells of mediocrity or conformity, and in the urban development of the 1950s he derides the spread of an attenuated modernism that propagates everything middling.[19] The problem is "Mittelmäßigkeit"—literally, a measurement taking into account the mean, the measure of the middle. For the élite that is supposed to create architecture, their imperative is to build an architecture freed from the constraints of bourgeois (middle-class!) compromise, capitalist financial imperatives, and modern functionalism. The elementary, sensual, primitive, brutal, and domineering are its watchwords.[20] As an expression of irrational, cultic currents at work in an individual, architecture facilitates human mastery:

> Architecture masters space. Controls it in shooting upward, carving out the earth below, protruding over the land, spreading in all directions. Controls it through mass and through emptiness. Controls space through space.

> This architecture is not about beauty. If we do want beauty, then it is less a beauty of form, of proportion, but rather a sensual beauty of elementary power [violence/force/authority].

> Architektur beherrscht den Raum. Beherrscht ihn, indem sie in die Höhe schießt, die Erde aushöhlt, weit auskragend über dem Land schwebt, sich in alle Richtungen ausbreitet. Beherrscht ihn durch Masse und durch Leere. Beherrscht Raum durch Raum.
>
> In dieser Architektur geht es nicht um Schönheit. Wenn wir schon eine Schönheit wollen, dann weniger eine der Form, der Proportion, sondern eine sinnliche Schönheit elementarer Gewalt.[21]

In turning against modernism on the surface, the manifesto resuscitates problematic aspects inherent in certain strains of modernism itself: a glorification of violence, mastery, and domination. It furthers the subjugation of the natural world through the hypertrophy of rationalism, which has mankind sinking back into mythic irrationalism.

Hollein's drawings and collages in the small booklet accompanying the 1963 show in Vienna depict agglomerations of what look like massive, irregular boulders, stacked on top of one another to form asymmetrical structures. They suggest high-density, erratic, organic excrescences that are both part of the desert landscape where they are located and foreign to it like man-made foundlings. One subtitle to "Controlling City" ["Beherrschende Stadt"] from 1960 emplaces the photocollage of stones in the Southwest of the United States, giving the reader some idea of Hollein's probable inspiration, namely the geological formations of the American West ["Architektur," 23]). On the following spread, Hollein creates a montage of a rocket ship, turbine, oil drilling rig, flak tower, nuclear explosion, aircraft carrier, and so on, while suggesting that architecture of contemporary society has yet to come into existence: "Architects have nothing to do with the great structures of our time. The architecture of today does not yet exist" ("Architekten haben nichts mit den großen Bauwerken unserer Zeit zu tun. Die Architektur von Heute gibt es noch nicht," "Architektur," 29). As things stand, architects have implicitly abdicated their responsibilities to engineers. The problem also seems to be an American-coded modernity and its infinite belief in the machine. In 1962 Hollein had traced this fascination back to the Industrial Revolution of the nineteenth century.[22] By contrast, the 1963 text does not comment on the provenance of this enthrallment. The images imply that the belief in the machine is still not utilized in combination with architecture to inspire better ways of living.

Hollein and Pichler—to whom I turn in the following section—are greeted with international acclaim, and just a few years after the show in the Galerie nächst St. Stephan, the Museum of Modern Art (MOMA) acquires and displays their works on paper. The 1967 exhibition with the title "Architectural

Figure 3. Hans Hollein, *Highrise Building, Sparkplug, Project. Exterior Perspective.* 1964. Cut-and-pasted printed paper on gelatin silver photograph, 4 3/4 × 7 1/4 in. Digital image © The Museum of Modern Art / Licensed by SCALA / Art Resource, NY.

Fantasies" shows structures that are inhuman in scale and intentionally unbuildable; they invoke the National Socialist architectural past as well as space-age visions for the future.[23] Arthur Drexler, the curator and head of the MOMA's Architecture Department, summarizes the nightmarish aspects of their technoid, monumental drawings: "The absence of human beings from most of the pictures, together with what seems to be functional detail, implies a highly organized world in which a planned environment pursues some purpose of its own." For Drexler, the fantastical and phantasmic creations have a discernible playfulness; he suggests that the diminishing distance between art and life may have already brought to fruition some of their utopian aspects. In the curator's view, these "visual poems" bring together "poetry and prophecy": "Recent announcements that New York City may purchase the Queen Mary for use as a school, rather than put up a conventional building, suggested that where these dreams break into real life the outcome could be quite cheerful."[24]

One of Hollein's drawings evincing this playfulness is now in the MOMA's permanent collection. In *Highrise Building, Sparkplug, Project* (1964, figure 3), he has cut and pasted a printed image of a sparkplug on a gelatin silver photograph depicting rolling hills with roads, fields, small houses, and patches of trees. The sparkplug as high-rise literally towers over the bucolic scene, "mastering" the surrounding space through its magnitude. It "controls it in shooting upward" and "protruding over the land," to borrow from Hollein's 1963 program. The metallic form suggests heaviness. It has a material quality absent from the other man-made elements in the photograph such as streets and buildings, and thus is a disruptive, massive presence. The tower does not permit the emptiness around it to coexist as an equal element in the composition; rather, the negative space is emptied of meaning and turned into a gray expanse of nothingness. Nowhere in this horizontal landscape can we escape the vertical thrust of this architectural construct. As a neo–avant-gardist counterspace, the tower defies convention's gravity and develops a pull of its own, leading the eye away from the undulating horizontals and drawing the gaze upward along the metal's exterior toward the strangely peaceful sky, dotted with clouds. Any movement upward is necessarily also outward. Breaking open the homogeneity of the "Kulturlandschaft," the carefully tended and sculpted landscape submitted to previous, slower development, the "highrise" suggests an exclamation mark or slash, rending the gradual accretion of time and its architectural give-and-take with the countryside. Of course, this sparkplug is hardly just a solid, sinister thing, perched like an alien in a landscape it threatens. It is also quite humorous, and we can smile at the vital mental spark that gave rise to this cut-and-paste brainchild. Its visual rhetoric is as ambivalent as Bernhard's prose: frightening and funny at once.

Walled In: Walter Pichler

Pichler, less likely to express his opinions on architecture in written form than his colleague, nonetheless also pens a brief manifesto for the brochure accompanying the 1963 gallery show. The one-paragraph statement is even more apodictic and exclusivist than Hollein's. For Pichler, architecture springs forth from the minds of a small clique for use as a "weapon" ("Waffe") against humanity, rather than for it. New architecture embodies the power and desires of these few, who use whatever means necessary. The adjective "strong" recurs twice in a superlative form, to characterize not only the ideas from which architecture emanates, but also the force it must expend to reach its goals. For the many weak-willed people under its sway, there are two options, an either-or characteristic of Bernhard's texts: suffocate or live profoundly. Architecture becomes "Zwang" or "coercion," threatening to "crush" ("erdrücken") those who cannot tolerate its brutality ("brutale Sache") and strong-arm tactics ("stärkste [. . .] Mittel"). In seeking to liberate architecture from any deferential function Hegelian philosophy might have envisioned for it, Pichler's architecture neither "avails itself of" ("sich bedienen") other arts nor is "subservient" ("dienen") to them. Its strength, however, is dependent on a symbiotic relationship with machines, which have taken hold of it. "And humans are only tolerated in its domain" is the closing

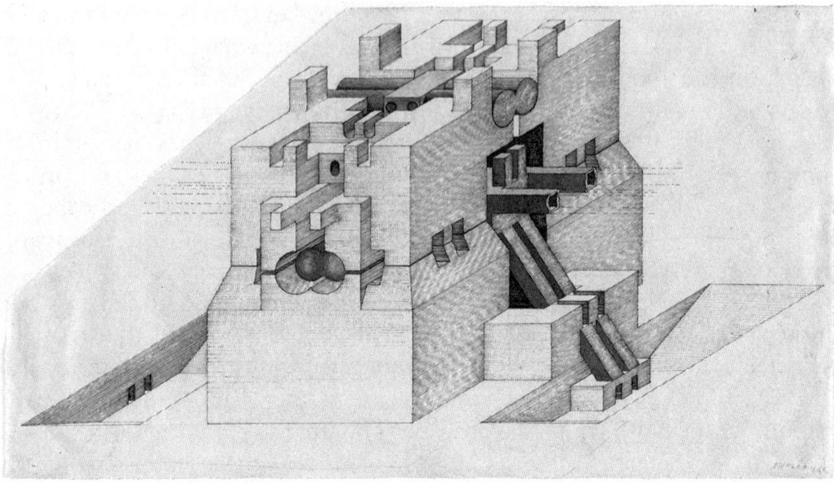

Figure 4. Walter Pichler, *Underground Building, Project, Isometric.* 1963. Ink and graphite on paper, 15 × 27 1/4 in. (38.1 × 69.2 cm). Digital image © The Museum of Modern Art / Licensed by SCALA / Art Resource, NY.

clause of Pichler's admittedly humorless text ("und die Menschen sind nur noch geduldet in ihrem Bereich").[25]

Pichler's sketches take this pact with machines seriously, vacating and even erasing the space surrounding the structures. His "compact cities" on the following pages of "Architecture" are less free-flowing than Hollein's. Rather than draw their inspiration from inorganic nature, the rectilinear and cylindrical agglomerations suggest an engine and its pistons.They are closer to the oil rigs or aircraft carriers than the rock formations of the southwestern United States present in Hollein's drawings and collages.[26] Most of Pichler's multi-leveled structures float freely in an empty landscape. Only rarely is a horizon line drawn in the background. The "pneumatic structures"—large synthetic bubbles that can be blown up and inhabited—that Pichler and Hollein design two to three years later are very different from these hard-edged sketches. Nonetheless, both the compact machine-cities and inflatable constructs suggest hermetic enclosures meant to seal off humans from their outside world.[27]

One typical drawing of this period, entitled *Underground Building* (*Unterirdisches Gebäude*, 1963, figure 4) depicts an isometric plan for what looks to be a heavily fortified building. It could be taken as a fortress, replete with battlements, embrasures, crenellations, and balistraria, through which cannon barrels peek. The hard edges of the structure suggest poured concrete; the rectangular barrels of the "cannons," with emergent dotted lines indicating the line of fire, lack the striations and could be made of metal. The surrounding space is an undifferentiated expanse. Ramps leading to what look like two doubled entrances carry us from the flat ground level toward subterranean entrances. These entryways are hidden from any approaching visitor's sight and lend the building something surreptitious, clandestine: no one is really invited to approach and enter. While the building does connect via underground routes to an elsewhere, the parallel entryways behind another gulley suggest that only the current isolated inhabitants know of these passageways. In sculptures that accompany sketches such as this one, Pichler casts the outer surface in cement, the inserts in metal.[28] The materials' high density carries over the drawings' forbidding aspect into the three-dimensional sculptures. The art historian Günther Dankl plays on the German word for concrete, "Beton," to argue that the casting serves a self-dramatizing, re-auraticizing function: the exaggerated use of cement leads to an overemphasis or "Über*beton*ung" that closes off, amounting to too much concrete ("Über*beton*ierung").[29] Walking around the structures, the meticulous craftsmanship draws the viewers closer; however, there is something literally repulsive about the ostentatious display of self-sufficiency and the forbidding material. The fortress buildings are meant for fortress denizens: fully Cartesian selves, whose willingness to recognize their own imbricated and implicated nature in their environment is nil. They do not sense their connection or responsibility to the landscape or to others.

Occasionally designs and sculptures hint at a more porous relation to the outside world. Ramps may augment a building sketch, as in the *Building with Ramps* (*Gebäude mit Rampen*) from 1963.[30] But the inclines often lead to encased circular openings or otherwise come to a dead end. Even the sketch of the *Sacred Building* (*Sakrales Gebäude*, 1961) hardly beckons upward or outward. This is not the kind of building that can revitalize the connection with the divine or reconstitute a wavering community, the public function ascribed to the vital sector of church construction at the time.[31] In Pichler's design, funnels emerge from a cube's sides, suggesting a prophetic beacon, but the strong underground pylons securing the ground countermand their outward orientation.[32] Although Pichler designs some underground cities with explicit reference to their embeddedness within the environment, with the titles alluding to an exchange between in- and outside (e.g., *Estuary of an Underground City* [*Mündung einer unterirdischen Stadt*, 1963]),[33] it is hard to shake the sense that these structures do not open onto anything. They offer only faux exits and entries.

While Pichler sometimes makes a greater effort to insert his buildings within a particular landscape, the powerful structures generally trump the adjacent environs. This independence from the environment, even where the surroundings assert themselves more strongly than in *Underground Building*—with undulating hills, wide meadows, or craggy boulders—is evident in all of Pichler's architectural renderings from this period. *Entrance to an Underground City* (*Eingang in eine unterirdische Stadt*, 1963; see figure 5), *House Built into a Rock* (*Oggau, Burgenland*) (*Haus an einem*

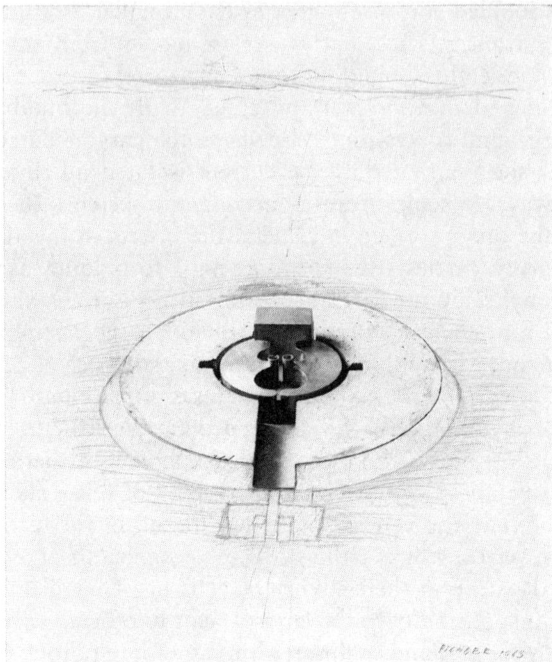

Figure 5. Walter Pichler, *Entrance to an Underground City, Project, Perspective.* 1963. Photomontage and graphite on paper, 13 3/4 × 11 3/4 in. (34.9 × 29.8 cm). Digital image © The Museum of Modern Art / Licensed by SCALA /Art Resource, NY.

Felsen, 1964); *Underground House of Silo-Elements* (*Unterirdisches Haus aus Siloelementen*, 1965), *Building on a Street* (*Gebäude an einer Strasse*, 1965) share the same structural components of cylinders, spheres, and hyper-rectangles sunken into the land.[34]

Calling forth technological associations to nuclear reactors and shelters as well as to the Soviet Union's Luna 2 space mission from 1959 (a futuristic metal sphere catapulted onto the moon), Pichler's structures embody two conflicting impulses—a fear of the imagined future and a desire to transcend this paralyzing fear.[35] Ultimately the paralysis seems to dominate.[36] All sketches convey a similar sentiment: isolation from the adjacent countryside, self-sufficiency, retreat into the underground as an answer to the problems of the day rather than engagement with the neighboring natural and man-made forms.[37]

The Austrian architect Richard Neutra, mentioned in Bernhard's novel *Correction* (1975), argues in *Building and the Sensory World* (*Bauen und die Sinneswelt*, 1977) that an astronaut's constrictive interior is only bearable if he remains connected with the outside through the rocket's windows. Unlike Walter Pichler's empty underground bunkers for an atomic age, the man in

Neutra's space capsule requires the view onto the immensity of outer space (to be sure, Pichler's 1970s sculptures, *Prototypes/Prototypen*, are no better in connecting exterior and interior than his earlier designs). For Neutra, the view saves the enclosed astronaut from the madness resulting from his restrictive sensory environment:

> In the tiny inner-space of a rocket ship the human anatomy of the astronaut can just barely be housed. In his constricting position with the tactilely felt limitations on space he is helped psychologically through his encompassing view of the planetary system! Skin-tight narrowness feels completely different in a closed cell *without* such "loans" from the outside.
>
> Without "borrowing" from the optically soul-stirring, dynamic exterior space the small chamber or room shrinks, not only spatially. It quickly becomes a literal strain for the heart through the tiring package of permanent, static inner impressions.
>
> Im winzigen Innenraum einer Weltraum-Raketenkapsel läßt sich die menschliche Anatomie des Astronauten gerade noch unterbringen. Ihm wird in seiner bedrückenden Position mit taktil erfühlten Raumbegrenzungen psychisch außerordentlich geholfen durch den umfassenden Blick auf das Planetensystem! Hautnah knappe Enge wirkt ganz anders in einer geschlossenen Zelle, *ohne* solche anregenden "Anleihen" von Außen.
>
> Ohne "Borgen" von optisch gemütsbewegendem, dynamischem Außenraum schrumpft ein Gelaß oder Zimmer nicht nur räumlich. Schnell wird es buchstäblich herzbelastend durch ein ermüdendes Paket permanenter, statischer Inneneindrücke.[38]

To avoid what Neutra terms the "torture chamber" ("Folterkammer") of constrictive space, educational spaces, too, must allow vistas and perforate closed spaces, infusing the interior as well as the exterior with energy.

Bernhard's Pichlerianism

It stands to reason that Pichler's conflicted art comments on international geopolitical problems, given Austria's geographical location as the furthest Western outpost during the Cold War and Pichler's strong ties to the eastern province of Burgenland, directly adjacent to the Iron Curtain (he owns a farmhouse, outbuildings, and grounds in the isolated village of St. Martin, close to the Hungarian border, which become his full-fledged studio in 1972).[39] Pichler's works of the 1960s are at once supremely local in their effort to end Austria's artistic isolation after National Socialism and work through some of modernism's unresolved tensions, as well as intensely international in refracting anxieties about nuclear armageddon and the Space Race. His ability to speak to audiences both within and outside the country perhaps accounts for his quick rise on the international art scene as well as his desire to withdraw from its distractions.[40] In his works, the politicized, utopian 1960s give way to a more sober assessment of the potentialities inherent in any neo–avant-gardist undertaking, the pitfalls of stardom, and the neutralization of oppositional energies through absorption into the art market. In the 1970s, Pichler's drawings lose some of their extreme rigidity. Although they are no more optimistic in their outlook than his earlier designs, they do allow the human form to emerge.

In the works collected in *111 Drawings* (*111 Zeichnungen*, 1973), Pichler starts to pay attention to the singular human being in the landscape, and Bernhard pens an essay for this compendium of works on paper. While the symmetry and hermeticism are still in evidence, man is now more implicated in his environment. In some images, Pichler draws rudimentary structures to encase the figure or prostheses that otherwise hinder his or her movement. The titles of his drawings evidence the constraints placed upon the figure: *Man with Sticks* (*Mann mit Stöcken*); *When One Has Legs of Marble, One Needs Aids* (*Wenn man Beine aus Marmor hat, braucht man Hilfsmittel*); *Humans with Bad Feet* (*Menschen mit schlechten Füßen*) are but some examples.[41] The horizon line is the dominant axis in these drawings. Efforts to move upward are thwarted, as in the case of the angels and birds with clipped wings (*Fly, Angel, Fly* [*Flieg, Engel, flieg*]; *Angel* [*Engel*]; *Bird and Butterfly* [*Vogel und Schmetterling*]).[42] The ground, as in his earlier drawings, is presented as a homogeneous, empty expanse.

In this collection, Pichler for the first time makes explicit the connection between architecture and man's mind, between the structures he draws and the thought structures man creates. In some drawings, we see a human skull from above, as if from an aerial viewpoint. Where the cranium is drawn in a technical manner, it could be confused with an isolated bunker or one of Pichler's self-sufficient fortresses. The skull's shape is a house, depicted with the same isometric lines as the architectural renderings of the 1960s. In more vibrant sketches, done with quicker strokes, the skulls might be confused with rock formations. These many "skull houses" ("Schädelhäuser") or "head houses" ("Kopf-Haus"), as Pichler labels them when there is a profile, imply a structural analogy: the skull houses the mind in the way in which a building shelters—and perhaps insulates—the man. (See, for example, figure 6.) The mind within it is an isolated outpost in an undifferentiated and undifferentiating world; the thought structures man creates may be as solitary and isolating.

Architecture and individual are completely interconnected here, in ways that are more humic than before, at times even suggesting a natural cycle of organic development and decay. In the midst of flat land, a head protrudes

Figure 6. Walter Pichler, *Schädelhäuser* (1972), from *111 Drawings* (*111 Zeichnungen*). © Anna Tripamer.

from the ground. In turn, it is connected to the earth through the tears streaming in rivulets down the face.[43] Where pylons anchored Pichler's earlier structures, roots or arteries now bind to the soil, fixing the cranium in place. The skull is connected to the head shown in profile via lines suggesting either further interconnectors or rotational axes, as if it were the same skull from a different perspective. A phallic projectile pierces through and above the eye socket; the head shown in profile sends its effluvium running to the ground through eye, nose, and mouth. A cavernous hollow in the earth absorbs the discharge, closing a cycle going from dark to light and, presumably, back. No apparent connection to a larger community or direct source for the wound exists; light shading above the horizon line does not draw attention to any distinguishing features of the landscape or other points of reference.

In his epilogue to *111 Drawings* entitled "Plain/Plane" or "Ebene," Bernhard thinks through the implications of humans' imbrications with their built environment. He never explicitly mentions Pichler's works, but alludes to this parallelism between mind and house to reflect on the relationship between form and formation, between being emplaced or isolated, and being instructed or formed ("gebildet"). He presupposes that the conditions of enclosure, separation, and insulation that Pichler conjures up hold true. However, Bernhard inflects Pichler's totalizing conception of architecture with his own interest in *Bildung* and its extension into the moral domain, via edification or *Erbauung*. The author stresses the failure of conventional lessons ("Unterricht"), enlightenment as well as elucidation ("Aufklärung"), and communicativeness or self-unfolding ("Aus-sich-Herausgehen"). We can see how Bernhard takes the neo–avant-gardist gesture of breaking with the past in Hollein and Pichler's manifestos and leads it towards its own aporia: violently rending the links to the past turns out not to have been a definitive cut; having gone away is ultimately not an exit strategy. This is the case for Pichler's compact underground cities and encumbered, solitary figures as well as for Bernhard's spaces and characters in his early work. What remains is the impotent anger inherent in the desire to shatter the bonds of tradition and historical succession, to reconcile life and art. Bernhard, particularly through the mid-1970s, also sets his characters' "Erregungen" (the subtitle of his novel *Woodcutters* [*Holzfällen*])—their excitations and agitations—in airtight spaces, often located somewhere above. Only later does he hint at the option of going down and especially outward, in this way freeing oneself for another condition: a state of receptivity for learning and openness to experience. This possibility is excluded in the early essay, where movement downward and outward is attempted and foiled. Taking his cue from Pichler's horizon lines, Bernhard entitles his piece "Ebene," meaning both plain, as in the flatlands of eastern Austria and western Hungary, and the geometrical plane. His title already forecloses any vertical movement from the outset. How could one move up or down if there is only the possibility of going sideways?

Children's first teachers, Bernhard's afterword to *111 Drawings* makes clear, are within the family, where physical and emotional proximity are greatest. Parents are failed teachers, however, since they leave their children in the dark about the dismal aspects of life itself. They have thereby abdicated their responsibility for the children's formation in a wider sense. Bernhard couches his reflections in an inclusive third person, placing readers in his own position as a member of the children's group. Had our parents told us the primary fact of life, namely that it is nothing but a "process of illness" ("Krankheitsprozeß"), Bernhard writes in "Plain/Plane," "we" would have been able to construct a different relationship to our environment or "Umgebung":

> If we had been informed that our life's process is in truth nothing other than the process of disease, and thus been enlightened in an exceptional manner, we say and we ask ourselves, what or, more importantly, who has not informed and not enlightened us in the slightest, over and over again and, to be sure, with the same, always the same remonstrations against our parents as against our whole environment, in which we, as we now see, have been forced to exist and this for decades, without actually seeing and thus without actually thinking for decades.
>
> Wenn wir über die Tatsache, daß unser Lebensprozeß in Wahrheit nichts anderes ist als ein Krankheitsprozeß, unterrichtet und dadurch in ungemeiner Weise aufgeklärt worden wären, sagen wir und wir fragen uns, *was*, vielmehr *wer* uns nicht unterrichtet und darüber

> überhaupt nicht aufgeklärt hat, immer wieder und zwar mit den gleichen, den immer gleichen Vorhaltungen gegen unsere Eltern wie gegen unsere ganze Umgebung, in welcher wir, wie wir jetzt sehen, jahrzehntelang, ohne tatsächlich zu sehen und also jahrzehntelang, ohne tatsächlich zu denken, zu existieren gezwungen waren. ("Ebene," 245)

With the benefit of hindsight, the textual "we" can see the environment's relationship to the malleable young as one of coercion ("gezwungen"). For readers sensitized to the analogical relationship between architecture and thought through the visionary architects' 1963 statements, it is hard not to interpret Bernhard's 1973 text as both a homage to and mitigation of those earlier totalizing and intimidating views.

Education, understood in an encompassing sense of being shaped for life, is aligned throughout the text with edification: existence in a particular edifice determines the kinds of questions one can ask and the kinds of answers one can formulate. Bernhard seems to envision a vertical structure, and he mobilizes a slew of up-down metaphors to describe the motion that would be useful for youths' development. The structure in which "we" are trapped, which does not allow this mobility, is like Pichler's fortress: a place of faux exits and limiting constraints. The text shifts to the subjunctive to intimate what an ideal situation might have been, had the process of education taken a more positive turn. Bernhard closes the if-then clause that I cited above:

> We would have, under these informed and enlightened circumstances, given up everything much earlier and would have left everything and in fact for ever left it behind; we would have gone away and down—and also out of ourselves—and gone down and would have given up everything and left and left behind and extinguished everything decades ago.
>
> Hätten wir unter diesen unterrichteten und aufgeklärten Umständen schon viel früher alles aufgegeben und alles verlassen und tatsächlich für immer zurückgelassen; schon vor Jahrzehnten wären wir weg— und hinunter—und auch aus uns selbst heraus—und hinunter gegangen und hätten alles aufgegeben und verlassen und zurückgelassen und ausgelöscht. ("Ebene," 245–46)

Such an intellectual and emotional expansiveness is not possible, and "we" are not able to leave behind the victimizing constraints and go downward—note the doubling of the "hinunter" or "down" for emphasis—and outward. The parents and the environment conspire to trap and confine the young in a claustrophobic space. As a result of this imprisonment (the text mentions our being "gefangen" or "trapped"/"imprisoned"), life has now become "demeaning" or "erniedrigend," literally brought low, to which the "niedrig" or "low" in "erniedrigend" alludes:

> Then we would have, we think, gone outside of ourselves and down and would have left everything and left behind everything, since what we are now doing should have been done by us decades ago: go away, abandon, leave behind, extinguish that wherein we are now strained and overwhelmed in the most extreme and demeaning manner, we could have tolerated and gotten over decades ago without effort.

> Dann wären wir, denken wir, schon vor Jahrzehnten aus uns heraus- und hinuntergegangen und hätten alles verlassen und alles zurückgelassen, da, was wir jetzt tun, von uns schon vor Jahrzehnten hätte getan werden müssen; weggehen, verlassen, zurücklassen, auslöschen, daß, worin wir jetzt auf das äußerste und auf die erniedrigendste Weise angestrengt und überfordert sind, wir vor Jahrzehnten mühelos ertragen und hinter uns bringen hätten können. ("Ebene," 246)

Bernhard's directionalities—down, in, out—are nonsensical if Pichler's hermetic structures are not kept in the mind's eye. The subjunctive use and the doubled temporal perspective are noteworthy: the "we" reflects from the present moment on a past that has determined the present's course. The spatial segues into the temporal register. This allows a reckoning to take place, and the judgment is devastating. Moving down and outward, away from the past, would have been necessary to take leave of the presumed culprits, the parents. The older generation is associated with antiquated social structures and the unquestioning acceptance of and submission to a tradition passed on through the generations. With Bernhard's artful variations, intoning the same series of nouns, verbs, and prepositions with slight modulations, and his collusive "we," he manages to deepen the readers' sense of entrapment in the course of the essay.

The repetitions intensify the magnitude of the coercive force exerted on the children within these walls, so that when death comes into "Plain/Plane" as the ultimate signified, readers are prepared for its arrival. Indeed, everything has led inexorably toward it, as the final outcome of disease. Neither "development" ("Entwicklung") nor "education" or "upbringing" ("Erziehung") are possible, and "our" demise is again linked to the structures in which "we" remain ensnared. "We" should have gone away and left

> our walls and our pieces of furniture and the air in these walls and in these pieces of furniture and our books and our writings and the air in these books and in these writings, which have always been our books and our writings and that has always been our air and,

> as we now see, are deadly walls and deadly pieces of furniture, and deadly air.
>
> unsere Mauern und unsere Möbelstücke und die Luft in diesen Mauern und in diesen Möbelstücken und unsere Bücher und unsere Schriften und die Luft in diesen Büchern und in diesen Schriften, die immer unsere Bücher und unsere Schriften gewesen sind und die immer unsere Luft gewesen ist und wie wir jetzt sehen, tödliche Mauern und tödliche Möbelstücke und eine tödliche Luft. ("Ebene," 246)

"Plain/Plane" maintains this then-and-now perspective, which is especially characteristic of Bernhard's mid- to late fiction, to the end. In the final lines, Bernhard carefully circles back to the opening subjunctive tense with its missed opportunities: "Decades ago we could have easily left these walls" ("Vor Jahrzehnten hätten wir ruhig diese Mauern verlassen [. . .] können"). At this juncture in the text, this anterior moment and missed opportunity give way to an unusual preterit, the simple past tense, when the looping consciousness can precisely define the location of the "we's" failure. Note the incorrect capitalization of the adverb of place in the original German in *111 Drawings*, which gives the locative adverb the status of a noun and underscores its relevance. This is a telling error that has been "corrected" and made lowercase in the reprinted version in *Werke* (vol. 14, 397): "We were Above, under the parents, locked in our walls and in our rooms and in our books and writings and everything around and in us was nothing other than deadly" ("Wir waren Oben, unter den Eltern, in unseren Mauern und in unseren Zimmern und in unseren Büchern und Schriften eingeschlossen und alles um uns und in uns ist nichts als tödlich gewesen," "Ebene," 247). The paradoxical positioning—above and below at once—is a symptom of Bernhard's Pichlerianism: we can be above physically, but still be metaphorically below, subjugated and coerced. In Pichler's underground city, we might be simultaneously above and below, but imprisoned and isolated regardless.

Knowing where one is, as paradoxical as this positioning might be, also enables a final verdict. By exactly pinpointing the emplacement "Above," the textual "we" has moved into a position associated with authority and can judge from the raised moral ground it has arrogated. Nonetheless, the condemnation of what went before changes nothing about the unbearable nature of the present, which shifts the "we" to the position it has sought out below. The final sentence segues from the present perfect ("ist gewesen") to the present tense ("sind"), actualizing the relevance of the analysis: "and we are down here, without the parents, again trapped in these our walls and in our rooms and in our books and writings and everything around us and in us is nothing but deadly" ("und wir sind herunten, ohne die Eltern, wieder in diesen unseren Mauern und in unseren Zimmern und in unseren Büchern und Schriften eingeschlossen und alles um uns und in uns ist nichts als tödlich,"

"Ebene," 247). Bernhard's use of the present tense is the moment when definitive judgment is also passed on the living: the hermeneutic loop through the past, reflecting on the conditions that have given rise to the present, is closed. Bordered by walls, crushed by what came before, the textual "we" cannot but experience its sequestration as life-negating. In the 1973 essay, any downward direction is ultimately deceptive. No heights of development can be reached when the constraints placed on the children are so powerful.

Bernhard's *Gargoyles* (*Verstörung*, 1967) can be interpreted as an elaboration of some of the ideas I have been outlining. In closing, let me tease out a few of the implications of Bernhard's engagement with the visionary architects, especially for the first half of the novel. The narrating son, following on his father's heels as the elderly doctor makes his rounds, is taught the necessity of distance from inherited structures and the beneficial aspects of isolation. He is introduced to the difficulties of *Erziehung* and its relation to landscape. The father claims that his children "seemed . . . the children of the landscape" to their deceased mother, not subject to parental influence (G 17; "wir seien . . . *Kinder der Landschaft*," V 21). In *Gargoyles*, there is a tension between the heights the nameless student tries to reach with his university studies—much is made of his enrollment at the Montanistische Hochschule (literally, the "high" school)—and the downward movement toward independence from inherited or otherwise confining structures. His father repeatedly presents his own life as a foil for his child's development. The so-called intelligentsia of the doctor's generation is "exiled in deep, sunless valleys" ("tiefe, sonnenarme Täler"). The intellectuals' "high point," or "Höhepunkt," lies in past university studies. They entered the "hollow space" between *Bildung* and working life, only to fall into "horrible familial and consulting-room apathy" (*G* 23; "grauenhaftesten Familiär- und Ordinationsstumpfsinn," *V* 26). These heights cannot be recuperated in the present.

These people's "total submergence" parallels the descent dominating the first half of the novel, where the son enters darkened inner spaces and ravines. Characters burrow downward and inward in closed-off spaces meant to protect them from the vicissitudes of life. At the same time, their homes structure their thought processes, often limiting their perspective. In German, Bernhard uses various verbs to denote this exploring ("sich versenken," "eintauchen," "sondieren") and penetrating ("eindringen," "durchdringen"), which make possible a thorough analysis and dissection ("zergliedern") of issues. In the darkened bourgeois Ebenhöh home—the name itself a compound of the words "Ebene" and "Höh[e]" or "height"—the characters comment on the deceased head teacher and his widow's penchant for erudition and high culture. Their conversation suggests that the couple sought a compromise between the limiting constraints of a flat horizon and the desire for heights. In the Fochler Mill in a ravine, the son learns about the processes of physical and mental degeneration, about life as illness or "Krankheitsprozeß." In the industrialist's hunting lodge, located at the base of a mountain, the young man hears about the spatial reduction needed to follow an idée fixe. A serious course of study requires solemn concentration, and this can only take place in minimally furnished and unadorned rooms. The son's movement from Ebenhöh's gardens to the ravine, and on to the mountain's base goes hand in hand with his reflections on studying the earth's interior (mining, metallurgy, etc.) and exterior (the "earth's surface" or "Erdoberfläche") and his life in a quasi-monastic cell that offers no distractions.[44] The discussions with the Prince, which read like verbatim transcriptions in the second half of the novel, take place high up in Hochgobernitz Castle; the three men circle the castle along its outer walls, as the Prince reflects on many things, including the ability of place to determine and occlude thought (*G* 81, 151; *V* 83, 152).

The dialectical relationship between absolute concentration and necessary isolation on the one hand and insanity or eccentricity on the other is described repeatedly. At any moment, mental collapse threatens intellectual achievement within such confining spaces. The malleable youth engaged in *Bildung* must navigate this dangerous dialectic. The fundamental architectonic impulse underlying *Gargoyles* is clearly expressed in the youthful narrator's claim about his university studies as a process of construction and obliteration: "Every day I completely built myself up [at the university], and completely destroyed myself (*G* 41; "An jedem Tag [an der Hochschule] baute ich mich vollkommen auf und zerstörte ich mich vollkommen," *V* 41). Bildung becomes "Erbauung" (literally "building up") or "edification" when education and moral uplift coincide (one of the things his father teaches the student is empathic identification). Both require a measure of creative destruction.

There is, as I have intimated, a fine line between a learner's necessary isolation and the suffocation of any openness to new insights. The curator Arthur Drexler alludes to this risk when discussing the designs of the visionary architects: there is the danger that the formally edgy, exactingly designed spaces follow purposes of their own. They might refuse to be subordinated to the people living and working in their confines; they may actualize Pichler's threatening manifesto and overpower the humans in their domain. I can well imagine these "severe structures" engendering a sense of claustrophobia and a desire to escape them.[45] In *Gargoyles*, Bernhard's spaces exceed the salutary aspects of control. The heights of the castle turn out not to be heights at all: indeed, Hochgobernitz is damp and dank like a basement, and the "spirit of the walls" pervades the people living within them (*G* 194; "Geist der Mauern," *V* 194). Nearly every statement of the Prince's can be mapped onto the Cartesian coordinates determining Pichler's constructions; however, "Grundstücksmenschen" (untranslated in English) like the Prince cannot reground themselves in their society via edification. Education is closed off; communication is closed down. The relationship between Prince Saurau and his son, studying in England (and failing to concentrate on his dissertation), makes this clear: the exchange has been cut off, because the son has cut off communication—"No entry" (*G* 183; "Eingang verboten!", *V* 183). Entry to his grounds, the Prince states, is forbidden: "*No trespassing*" ("*Zutritt verboten*"; *G* 136; *V* 137). We are back to the fortified structures that Walter Pichler designs in the 1960s and that Hollein lauds as pure architecture.

How bracing to visualize a catapult that would shoot a person up and outward, across the crenellations of the castle keep in the *Underground Building*, away from the "deadly walls," or out of the "stinking atmosphere" of the London apartment: "I suddenly had the refreshing idea of catapulting myself out of my morgue at the last moment," says the narrator of *Concrete* (*Beton*, 1982).[46] But seen against the backdrop of the aerial bombardments during the war and the destruction of buildings, it becomes comprehensible why the austerity of a "monastic" life of learning within tightly circumscribed confines is appealing to a youngster who has just lived through the intellectual and material deprivations of World War II. A kind of capsule can be found in the description of Bernhard's first high school in *An Indication of the Cause* (*Die Ursache*, 1975). I quote this passage at length:

> What revealed itself upon inspection here as in other grammar schools, especially to the pupil, the victim of the system, was the spirit of bygone centuries. This building with its long corridors and whitewashed arches, which had been the old university and was more like a monastery than a school, inspired awe and reverence in me when I first entered it—that is to say, when I first moved up from the main school, the Andräschule, to this superior secondary school and was suddenly admitted to the higher orders which had always been associated with this *venerable house*. It was borne in upon me that now, as I entered the school and climbed the marble staircase every day, I too, like the building, belonged to a higher plane of existence. And indeed what young person would not, upon entering this building from the surrounding streets, or, like me, from the woods and the countryside, have felt a certain pride as he took his first official steps in this austere pile, which (so one is constantly told) has always supplied the nation's élite?
>
> Es war naturgemäß wie in allen andern Gymnasien auch der Geist vergangener Jahrhunderte gewesen, welcher sich hier dem Betrachter und vor allem dem Schüler einer solchen Schule als Opfer ihres Systems in jedem Augenblick und unter allen möglichen Gesichtspunkten dokumentierte. Dieses Gebäude also, welches einmal die Alte Universität gewesen war, mit seinen langen Gängen und weißgekalkten Gewölben mehr ein Klosterbau als eine Schule, hatte tatsächlich bei meinem Eintritt in das Gymnasium, also in dem Augenblick meines Aufstiegs von der Hauptschule, der sogenannten Andräschule, in diese höchste

> Mittelschule, Ehrfurcht und Staunen in mir hervorgerufen und mir aufeinmal, aufgenommen in diese mit dem *altehrwürdigen Hause* immer schon verbunden gewesenen höheren Weihen, die Erkenntnis vermitteln und fühlen lassen, daß ich selbst jetzt, tagtäglich in diese Schule eintretend und in ihr die Marmortreppen emporsteigend, wie sie etwas Höheres sei. Und welcher, ganz gleich, ob aufeinmal nur aus den umliegenden Gassen oder, wie ich, aus den Wäldern und vom Lande in das Gebäude hereingekommene junge Mensch wäre nicht stolz gewesen bei seinen ersten offiziellen Schritten als Schüler in diesem strengen Bauwerk, aus welchem, wie es immer wieder heißt, seit Jahrhunderten die Elite des Landes hervorgegangen ist.[47]

The desire for heights and social improvement is apparent in every aspect of the student's approach. Climbing a staircase, he ascends into the halls of higher learning ("moved up"/"Aufstieg," "climbed"/"emporsteigend"). The lure of such higher or highest education and the attractiveness of elitism are coupled with adjectives denoting the high school's upward-positioning and its promise of the better, because "higher," things in life ("higher orders"/"höheren Weihen," "higher plane of existence"/"etwas Höheres"). Let me here draw attention to Bernhard's typical superlative, which makes out of "high school" the "highest school" in a neologistic locution ("superior secondary school"/"höch*ste* Mittelschule," my emphasis). The desire for advancement up the social ladder through education stands in a direct relation to the imposing nature of the building itself ("*venerable house*"/"*altehrwürdige[s] Hause*," "austere pile"/"strenges Bauwerk"). The somber structure makes a magnificent impression on students from the surrounding rural countryside ("from the woods and countryside"/"aus den Wäldern und vom Lande"), as well as those coming from the abutting gutter ("surrounding streets"/"umliegende Gassen"). Replacing the Gothic cathedral in function, the high school draws people toward it. Inspiring respect, the building reconciles various social strata in their aspirations for a better, more educated life.

The young Bernhard, passing over the threshold into these halls and then moving upward on the marble staircase, perceives his entrance and first steps as an initiation into a small circle—all the more so since entry into the Gymnasium is the German-speaking world's equivalent of university admission, which the mention of the school's former function as university emphasizes (over and beyond the mention of the "main school," which does not). The fantasy of a space in which every aspect of life is regulated, controlled, and far away from the messy quotidian combines with an attraction to educational progress, intellectual superiority, and the upward movement that the different forms of the adjective "hoch" or "high" indicate. Even though the student eventually comes to see himself as the victim of the repressive and constraining model of education this building signifies, he nonetheless participates in it because of the structure itself. Architecture mediates ("vermitteln") knowledge and cognition or "Erkenntnis," with "Erkenntnis" occuring on an intellectual and a somatic level ("fühlen"). The building reveals its full, ephemeral beauty when a bombing raid shatters it. The burst-open innards of the Gymnasium during aerial bombardments may have suggested surprising views and instantaneous shifts in positioning to Bernhard, which the postwar period and its cold peace might otherwise not have.

Way Station 2

✦

Elementary Structures and Perforated Space

The Austrian architect Raimund Abraham (1933–2010) uses somewhat milder phrases than his colleagues in his 1963 book *Elementary Architecture* (*Elementare Architektur*). Although he is grouped with Walter Pichler and Hans Hollein as one of the visionary architects and his drawings share many of their hyper-urban, machinic characteristics (see Chapter 1), his treatise takes a different tack. In lieu of the rhetoric of rupture, mastery, and totality in the others' neo avant-gardist manifestos, he postulates a less conflictual approach between tradition and modernization. Like Pichler and Hollein, Abraham also seeks to resuscitate the theoretical discussion surrounding architecture, intoning the benefits of the "elemental," "simple," "root[ed]," "ordered," "pure," "original," and "authentic" in his short text. However, he does so to conjure up a vision of a modern, technological future in harmony with an archaic past.[1] In his introduction to *Elementary Architecture*, he construes contemporary architecture as arising organically from agrarian antecedents divorced from their "blood and soil" stylization under National Socialism. In short, what Abraham tries to do is to revitalize architectural discourse through a rethinking of its basic elements, stressing the necessity of a dialogue with rural forms.[2] Architects, in his view, should work in tandem with the technology at their disposal, but be mindful of the anonymous builders of yore and their innovations. Only through such an exchange can contemporary architecture provide a working order and a workable grammar, Abraham contends, imparting structure to human life and thought.

We can imagine why such a re-situation of architecture within a discourse of grounding and re-foundation takes on such urgency in the early 1960s. The very *life form* Thomas Bernhard begins to interrogate simultaneously in his literature—the life form of a Central European *Bildungsbürger* with a certain claim to cultural competence and ethical uprightness, handed down through time—has been eroded through fascism. Abraham, like Bernhard, wants to evaluate what remains of tradition in light of this historic caesura. What kind of new ground could elementary architectural forms drawn from prior models establish—what "grundlegende Ordnung," as Abraham writes in *Elementary Architecture*, literally lays the groundwork? What foundations would elementary constructions guarantee for the people who circulate around them? Would or could these buildings and people become coextensive, avoiding isolation and confinement and turning into a more positive type of humic architecture, a Pichlerian *Schädelhaus* without tears (chapter 1)? In other words, could a synthetic architecture arise, where there would be no schism between the landscape, the built environment, and the experiencing self, no break between the architectonic schema, its built incarnation, and the person the building expresses and upon whom it impresses itself?

Structure and structuring stand at the forefront of Abraham's attempt to establish a new foundation for building and hence humanity: "Structure means more than a sum of constructive solutions; rather, it is a necessary and foundational order for architecture as well as for man. In the structure every last detail appears determined by the whole, captured and imprinted by one and the same idea" ("Struktur bedeutet mehr als eine Summe konstruktiver Lösungen, sie ist vielmehr eine notwendige und grundlegende Ordnung für die Architektur wie für den Menschen selbst. In der Struktur erscheint noch das letzte Detail vom Ganzen bestimmt, erfaßt und geprägt von ein und derselben Idee").

Abraham begins his *Elementary Architecture* by positing an unusual and unusually authoritative definition of architecture. It expresses ideas with the most basic elements, dependent as these are on whatever technology is at man's disposal at the moment of building. The first sentence of his text is apodictic: "Architecture is elementary in the realization of ideas about building with the simplest means" ("Architektur ist elementar in der Verwirklichung von Baugedanken mit den einfachsten Mitteln," *Elementare Architektur*, n.p.). The German word "elementar"—far less common than its English equivalent—carries overtones of rudimentary power, vitality, and strength. Abraham's definition also suggests that building is a primal form of expression in a language self-evident to everyone. In contemporary bridges and dams (which play a significant role in Bernhard's work *Frost* from 1963), Abraham sees the same immutable laws at work as in the purportedly crude wooden barns and stables dotting the central and southern European landscape, which are depicted in the accompanying photographs by Joseph Dapra. Abraham's goal is to liberate the "taken-for-granted results of primitive methods of building" ("selbstverständliche Resultate primitiver Baumethoden") and redefine these as "pure constructions" ("reine Konstruktionen"), liberated from the isolating effect of anonymous traditions and geographically limited customs. As Abraham contends:

> Cone, cube, and cylinder are those ever-recurring elements of architecture that obey a timeless order. [. . .] These objects are by no means inhabitable buildings, but barns and stables, in which the constructional conception is expressed most purely. They are untouched by outer influences, having grown organically in the process of building. Without the attributes of a particular epoch, they have already stood

> for half a millennium and have lost nothing of their original vitality [power/strength/energy].
>
> Kegel, Würfel, Zylinder sind jene immer wiederkehrenden Elemente der Architektur, die einer zeitlosen Ordnung gehorchen. [. . .] Es handelt sich bei diesen Objekten keineswegs um bewohnbare Gebäude, sondern um Scheunen und Ställe, in denen die bauliche Konzeption als am reinsten verwirklicht zum Ausdruck kommt. Sie sind von äußeren Einflüssen unberührt, im Bauprozeß organisch gewachsen. Ohne Attribute einer bestimmten Epoche stehen sie schon ein halbes Jahrtausend und haben nichts von ihrer ursprünglichen Kraft eingebüßt. (*Elementare*, n.p.)

Conceiving of the elementary as atemporal by stressing the "timeless order," Abraham reclaims the countryside's architecture from its fascist instrumentalization. In this manner, he removes the rural from the historical catastrophes of the twentieth century, making agrarian architecture available to present-day practitioners as a repository of valuable abstract forms (cones, cubes, and cylinders).[3] Further along in the essay, temporality is again suspended; the repetition of such unadulterated structural elements in the landscape places them outside of time's march. The "timeless order" imagined here is almost Edenic, one of purity and harmony, organicism and higher truth—but devoid of people, since no human habitation is discussed and no human being is ever shown in the images.[4] Abraham quotes from Mies van der Rohe to underline the fact that modernism, functionalism, and rural architecture are not in antagonistic competition with one another for exclusive dominance, since they behave according to the same principles. Abraham cites van der Rohe's dictum to establish his modernist credentials and thereby stress his own anti-elitist conception of architecture: "Architecture begins there where two stones are meticulously placed one on top of the other" ("Architektur beginnt dort, wo zwei Steine sorgfältig übereinandergelegt werden").[5] A feeling of care, expressed in the "Sorge" of "sorgfältig," binds the anonymous architects of yesteryear to the current generation seeking to make its mark. A "natural feeling" ("natürliches Gefühl") for the possibilities and limitations of a specific material and type of construction guide the primitive builder's hand and the contemporary architect's.[6]

Abraham's essay describes how human building activity transforms the landscape. Buildings penetrate the countryside, endowing it with a rhythmic potential and giving it the structure upon which both architecture and man depend. The photos in Abraham's volume are of simple stone and wooden edifices in Austria, Germany, Italy, France, and Switzerland. Pictures are grouped together based on structural similarity; repetitive images of wooden doors and door frames, window shutters, sheds, and stone shingled roofs relay regularity and rhythm. The buildings impart to the landscape around them a musical beat and a geometric order via vertical and horizontal lines. Abraham writes: "The rhythm of this structure results from the type and use of tools, it penetrates the cultivated countryside and is staunched in the compact arrangements of buildings. The geometric order of the fields, paths, and walls continues in the horizontal and vertical lines of the buildings" ("Der Rhythmus dieser Struktur resultiert aus der Art und dem Gebrauch der Werkzeuge, er durchdringt das bebaute Land und staut sich in der kompakten Gruppierung von Gebäuden. Die geometrische Ordnung der Felder, Wege und Mauern setzt sich in den Waagrechten und den Senkrechten der Bauten fort," *Elementare*, n.p.). The built environment syncopates the natural one, drawing it together around certain structures, and radiates outwards in a reciprocal relationship with the cultivated fields. Had Bernhard's text "Plain/Plane" ("Ebene") and Walter Pichler's drawings focused our interest largely on the up-down movement and vertical contraction within an empty, desolate landscape (chapter 1), Abraham's introduction turns our attention to the interplay between concentration ("dammed up," "compact") and outward, horizontal extension.

One central presupposition underlies this conceptualization of the built landscape as both a musical and mathematical pattern, as an intensification and extensivity: Abraham assumes that the architectural structuration of the environment functions like a language with an inherent grammar. The ubiquity of architecture is related to language and its creative potential as well as its constraints. While both architecture and language allow for individualistic use and expression, they nonetheless remain generalizable phenomena. The particular is always subsumed under the general, and Abraham again relies on Mies van der Rohe to endow his argument with respectability and the appropriate historical lineage. Abraham quotes the entire paragraph from an unspecified Mies van der Rohe source:

> The characteristic of language consists in the fact that it contains different possibilities for use, but it always stays the same language. When the physicist Schroedinger says: "The creative power of a general principle lies in its generality," then this is what I understand as structure in architecture. It is not a specific solution to different problems, it is a general idea. And even though every building is an individual achievement, it was not motivated to be one.
>
> Das Charakteristikum der Sprache besteht darin, daß sie verschiedene Verwendungsmöglichkeiten in sich birgt, doch sie bleibt immer dieselbe Sprache. Wenn der Physiker Schrödinger sagt: „Die schöpferische Kraft eines allgemeinen Prinzips besteht in seiner Allgemeinheit", so ist es das, was ich in der Architektur unter Struktur verstehe. Es ist keine spezifische Lösung von verschiedenen Problemen, es ist eine allgemeine Idee. Und obwohl jeder Bau eine Einzelleistung ist, ist er nicht als solcher motiviert. (*Elementare*, n.p.)

Architectural structure, like language, serves the multitude and not solely the individual.[7]

For Abraham, basic architectonic elements provide an ordering, protolinguistic principle. They thereby avoid the vagaries of chance, bringing together human agency but setting up limits: "Determined equally in its logical composition by self-supporting, superimposed elements and in its rhythm by openings and compact parts, a 'grammatical' order becomes visible in the structure itself, which is based on an indispensible corporeality and never allows the fiction of the façade to arise" ("Im logischen Aufbau von selbsttragenden, übereinandergeschichteten Elementen, im Rhythmus von Öffnungen und kompakten Teilen gleichermaßen bestimmt, wird eine 'grammatikalische' Ordnung im Bauwerk sichtbar, der das unerläßlich Körperhafte zugrunde liegt und die nie die Fiktion der Fassade aufkommen läßt," *Elementare*, n.p.). Architecture is a text with a particular "composition" ("Aufbau"), punctuation marks ("Öffnungen"), and intrinsic realism ("nie [. . .] Fiktion"). Since it avoids "fictions," it acts as a guarantor of authenticity and groundedness ("zugrunde"). Indeed, it can only be true to life—to the immutable laws of form, material, and structure Abraham evokes—if it studiously avoids the fictionality and superficiality equated with the exterior façade. When it functions in this manner, architecture is the visible expression of a deeper, inner corpus of ideas.

No elementary architecture is more functional than another, and none is the same as another in relating particular to general. Abraham bookends his short introduction with reference to another émigré to the United States besides Mies van der Rohe, namely the architect and theorist Konrad Wachsmann. In Wachsmann's essay "A Turning Point in Building" ("Wendepunkt im Bauen"),[8] the German architect offers yet another model for the interaction between built and human environment, where the very environment man produced produces him in turn. Wachsmann, who taught in summer in Salzburg while Bernhard was a student in the city, had a great influence on the Austrian architectural scene with his ideas about mass production in architecture and prefabricated components. In "A Turning Point in Building," Wachsmann argues against using man as the timeless measure for building: "The human being in his relationship to his environment is subject to processes of reshaping in the same measure as it is. Inevitably, he cannot be used to determine the law of measure permanently. Man will always adapt to his environment in the way in which it permanently adapts itself to be useful to him" ("Der Mensch in der Beziehung zu seiner Umwelt ist in demselben Maße wie diese Umformungsprozessen ausgesetzt. Durch ihn kann also notwendigerweise nicht das Gesetz des Maßes permanent bestimmt werden. Der Mensch wird sich immer seiner Umwelt ebenso anpassen, wie diese sich andauernd umformt, um ihm nützlich zu sein").[9] By referring to Wachsmann at the end of his introduction, Abraham rescues the primitive agrarian structures from the timelessness in which he originally situated them. Humans are only relationally a measure for things, and even their most untouched seeming buildings cannot withstand the pressures of technological modernization and the revolution in building styles. As the processes at work in the world change people, they must take this alteration into account when determining any architectonic standards; they must negotiate their ties to the present while being mindful of the past, without glorifying or reifying it.[10]

Bernhard finds a literary solution for the regularity and generality implied in Abraham's conception of simple buildings radiating across a landscape and their effect on humans. In his works, Bernhard envisions a human-architecture interface that might make people receptive to thought outside of societal constraints and disciplinary boundaries. He carries over this idea to the level of sentence structure. If we extrapolate from Abraham's essay, we might begin to see Bernhard's texts as architectural counterspaces in which two competing tendencies jostle for advantage. On the one hand, there is the imagistic use of architecture to suggest a concentration or reduction, with the etymological overtones of "leading back" and "restoration" present in the latter term (from the Latin *reductio*). Architecture creates spaces where people withdraw from a world they perceive as hostile to their thought processes, in the hope of bringing structure to them. These spaces evoke similarities to Abraham's "staunching" and "compact parts," as well as Pichler's fortified structures. On the other hand, we find the linguistic use of structural grammatical elements to suggest an Abrahamian concatenation, a rhythmic interlinking through the landscape. Over and over again, repetitive grammatical elements, italics, and punctuation marks either interrupt a narrative's flow or rhythmically invigorate the prose.[11] These competing aspects give rise, in an interesting interplay of up-down and in-out, to the model of perception Bernhard envisages in *Amras* and *Old Masters* as a necessary precondition for thought (chapters 2 and 3).[12] Furthermore, the simultaneous complexity and non-exclusive nature of elementary architectures is brought to the fore in Abraham's essay. With Wachsmann as his guarantor, elementary architectures become relational structures—ones involved in a multifaceted, developing relationship with people and the landscape.

To make the architectonics of Bernhard's writing clearer, let us take as an example the tower of *Amras*—one of the many elementary architectural forms in Bernhard's early to mid-career works and a predecessor of the cone in *Correction* (*Korrektur*, 1975). Here we find the "pure" and "elementary" shape Abraham lauds, a cone with a protective function described in the second paragraph: "The tower, which belongs to our uncle, was a refuge to us during those two and a half months, protecting us from the clutches of people, sheltering and concealing us from the eyes of a world whose actions and perceptions are forever determined by evil" ("Der unserem Onkel gehörende Turm ist uns in diesen zweieinhalb Monaten eine vor dem Zugriff der Menschen schützende, vor den Blicken der immer nur aus dem Bösen handelnden und begreifenden Welt bewahrende und verbergende Zuflucht geworden").

There are a slew of participial adjectives in German ("protecting"/"schützende," "acting"/"handelnde," "understanding"/"begreifende," "sheltering"/"bewahrende," "concealing"/"verbergende"), to cite the examples from this paragraph. There are also participles used as nouns ("apprehended"/"Entdeckten," "condemned"/"Verurteilten," "disfigured"/"Entstellten," "deranged"/"Zerrütteten," "shattered"/"Zerschlagenen"), all from the following one-sentence paragraph. Extended participial constructions litter the first pages (e.g., "der immer nur aus dem Bösen handelnden [. . .] Welt" and "in den uns von allen Seiten nur in Bruchstücken schamvoll beschriebenen, dadurch so dunkel gebliebenen Tagen kurz auf die Selbstmordnacht").[13] Words in which the prepositions "over" and "under" often serve as prefixes are to be found throughout the first few pages.[14] There are also many ellipses. They bring the novella to brief stops, suggesting a narrative style befitting the protagonist's youth and precarious mental state, with his traumatized thoughts. The interplay between the punctuation marks and grammatical forms creates a stop-and-go rhythm. We readers are alternately propelled forward and brought to a momentary rest.

What the architectural historian and theoretician Christian Norberg-Schulz has written about prepositions might be applied to all of Bernhard's stylistic particularities. For Norberg-Schulz, human identity presumes the identification with and orientation within specific places. In this sense, prepositions are important on a grammatical and phenomenological level. As indeclinable particles expressing relations between humans and places, they *pre-position* us. Such words denoting emplacement are not indifferent markers of place; instead, they qualitatively determine our position in relation to other things.[15] Furthermore, the prepositions serve as *pre-fixes*. They fix one thing to another briefly, tying them together in both expected and unexpected ways. In the case of Bernhard, the pre-positioning and pre-fixing also indicates a kind of probing effort. The positioning is often temporary; it comes before (*pre-*) the firm establishment of definitive relationships and coordinates. The characters in *Amras*, for instance, examine the tower's suitability to see if it can fulfill their need for shelter and protection. As an alternative site for study, the tower needs to guarantee them both a place "above" the fray of malevolent human society and "below" the pernicious influence of family. It thereby makes possible their receptiveness to new ideas and impressions. Finally, Bernhard's structural order pre-positions and prepares the reader—through repetition, alliteration, restarts, and rehearsals—for the repeated attempts that are an indispensable part of learning and which often make orientation along the path of *Bildung* (the *Bildungsweg*) or in the edifices of learning befuddling, arduous, or unmanageable.

Ultimately, the pre-positioning that readies the characters and readers for something to come defers the completion of their—and our—task. The spatialization of time, which seems to rise up from the page's unending sentences like an unconquerable impediment, helps account for the text's anti-narrative stance and non-progression. Information is "dammed up" in narrative blocks, retarding the plot's flow.

However, where ellipses perforate *Amras*, they break up this obstruction, endowing the prose with openings.[16] These ellipses allow the mind to rest from the onslaught of information and difficult hypotactic sentences.[17] The different genres, with the alternation of letters, descriptive passages, allegories, propositions, and aphorisms, also structure the text like signposts, concentrating the information in certain passages and letting other, more poetic or atmospheric sections segue into one another with a kind of narrative drift. The diverse strains are separated from one another through careful spacing, visible in the typescripts in the Thomas-Bernhard-Archive as well as on the printed page itself (see figure 7). The ellipses, moreover, are like slashes in Bernhard's hand, providing respite from what seems to be an impossibly bleak continuum and perhaps giving lie to Abraham's idea of a temporal continuity between past and present. The prose and punctuation variations mirror the excitations of the narrative's protagonists; the rhythmical motion of these different elements enlivens the text's body, as it were. The grammatical and generic features work against the structural concentration, which the text's central metaphor of the tower implies. They disperse the text outward, pulling the reader forward and out of the cone.

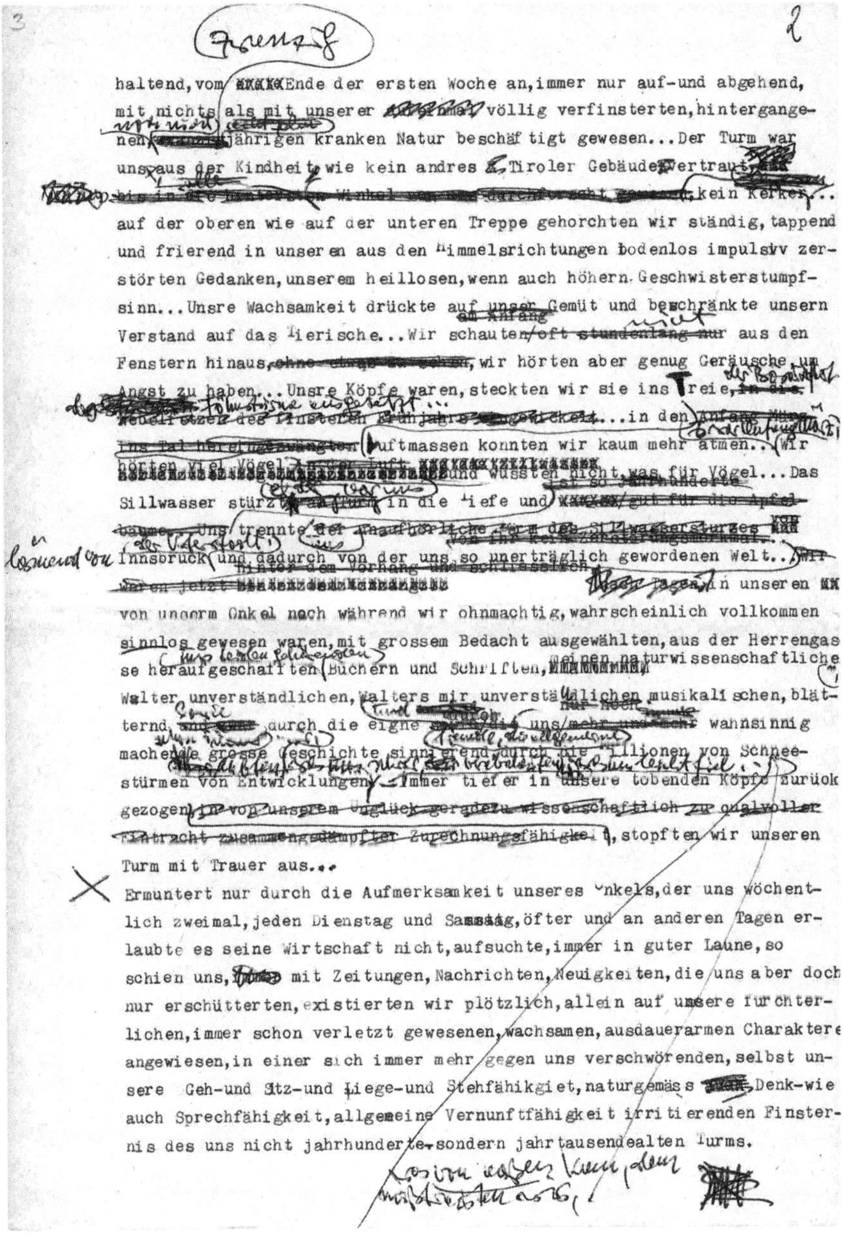

haltend, vom [illegible] Ende der ersten Woche an, immer nur auf-und abgehend,
mit nichts als mit unserer [illegible] völlig verfinsterten, hintergange-
nen [illegible] jährigen kranken Natur beschäftigt gewesen... Der Turm war
uns aus der Kindheit wie kein andres Tiroler Gebäude vertraut, [illegible]
[illegible] kein Kerker...
auf der oberen wie auf der unteren Treppe gehorchten wir ständig, tappend
und frierend in unseren aus den Himmelsrichtungen bodenlos impulsiv zer-
störten Gedanken, unserem heillosen, wenn auch höhern Geschwisterstumpf-
sinn... Unsre Wachsamkeit drückte auf unser Gemüt und beschränkte unsern
Verstand auf das Tierische... Wir schauten [illegible] aus den
Fenstern hinaus, [illegible] wir hörten aber genug Geräusche, um
Angst zu haben... Unsre Köpfe waren, steckten wir sie ins Freie, [illegible]
[illegible] ...in den [illegible]
[illegible] Luftmassen konnten wir kaum mehr atmen... Wir
hörten viel Vögel [illegible] und wussten nicht, was für Vögel... Das
Sillwasser stürzt [illegible] in die Tiefe und [illegible]
[illegible] trennte [illegible] des Sillwassersturzes [illegible]
Innsbruck und dadurch von der uns so unerträglich gewordenen Welt... [illegible]
[illegible] in unseren [illegible]
von unserm Onkel noch während wir ohnmachtig, wahrscheinlich vollkommen
sinnlos gewesen waren, mit grossem Bedacht ausgewählten, aus der Herrengas
se heraufgeschafften Büchern und Schriften, meinen naturwissenschaftliche
Walter unverständlichen, Walters mir unverständlichen musikalischen, blät-
ternd, [illegible] durch die eigne [illegible] uns [illegible] wahnsinnig
machende grosse Geschichte sinnierend durch die Millionen von Schnee-
stürmen von Entwicklungen, immer tiefer in unsere tobenden Köpfe zurück
gezogen, [illegible]
[illegible], stopften wir unseren
Turm mit Trauer aus...
Ermuntert nur durch die Aufmerksamkeit unseres Onkels, der uns wöchent-
lich zweimal, jeden Dienstag und Samstag, öfter und an anderen Tagen er-
laubte es seine Wirtschaft nicht, aufsuchte, immer in guter Laune, so
schien uns, [illegible] mit Zeitungen, Nachrichten, Neuigkeiten, die uns aber doch
nur erschütterten, existierten wir plötzlich, allein auf unsere fürchter-
lichen, immer schon verletzt gewesenen, wachsamen, ausdauerarmen Charaktere
angewiesen, in einer sich immer mehr gegen uns verschwörenden, selbst un-
sere Geh-und Sitz-und Liege-und Stehfähigkeit, naturgemäss [illegible] Denk-wie
auch Sprechfähigkeit, allgemeine Vernunftfähigkeit irritierenden Finster-
nis des uns nicht jahrhunderte-sondern jahrtausendealten Turms.

Figure 7. Typescript page of *Amras*, 15/2, p. 3. © Thomas-Bernhard-Archive, Dr. Peter Fabjan.

Chapter 2

✦

Middle Positions and Mystical Moments in *Amras* (1964)

The tower of *Amras* (1964) is an elementary architecture of the first order. It is not unlike the vertical structures to which Bernhard alludes in his discussion of Walter Pichler's works and which animate Abraham's resuscitation of past architectural forms. Modeled on the tower of Ambras Castle in Innsbruck and thus located on a multiply resonant site, Bernhard's structure functions as a microcosm of Austrian and Renaissance history.

The opening of the short novella immediately situates us in this disorienting space, which is far more complicated than its cylindrical shape would have us believe:

> After our parents' suicide, we were shut up for two and a half months in the tower, a landmark of our suburb of Amras, accessible only by traversing the large apple orchard, years ago still a property of our father's, which leads up in a southerly direction to the primary rocks.
>
> The tower, which belongs to our uncle, was a refuge to us during those two and a half months, protecting us from the clutches of people, sheltering and concealing us from the eyes of a world whose actions and perceptions are forever determined by evil.
>
> Nach dem Selbstmord unserer Eltern waren wir zweieinhalb Monate in dem Turm eingesperrt, in dem Wahrzeichen unseres Vorortes Amras, das nur durch den großen, in südlicher Richtung hinauf an das Urgestein führenden Apfelgarten, vor Jahren noch ein Besitztum unseres Vaters, zugänglich ist.
>
> Der unserem Onkel gehörende Turm ist uns in diesen zweieinhalb Monaten eine vor dem Zugriff der Menschen schützende, vor den Blicken der immer nur aus dem Bösen handelnden und begreifenden Welt bewahrende und verbergende Zuflucht gewesen.

The tower is simultaneously sanctuary and prison, pre- and postlapsarian space, public landmark and private refuge; it is temporally both after ("nach") and before ("vor Jahren," "Ur-").[1] Indeed, its in-between spatial and temporal locations already hint that it cannot entirely fulfill its function as an alternative site of *Bildung*. Nonetheless, this tower becomes, at first, a *pre-positioning* counterspace, the prerequisite for independent learning in Bernhard's evolving pedagogical model. In the 1964 text, the guide who shepherds the students is lacking, and the architecture does not entirely facilitate the kinds of experiences requisite for a rewarding development. However, the tower initially allows for a more holistic approach to learning, and its detrimental consequences emerge only later in the narrative.

In nuce, *Amras* contains the many themes to which Bernhard returns throughout his writings,[2] long and short: an ideal place and elementary architecture for learning; intimate ties among men engaged in the quest for knowledge; the modern unhomely and uncanniness inherent in sets of two; the architecture of isolation that is the precondition for freedom of thought; mystical communion and a romantic yearning for synthesis. The short novel is essentially a Bildungsroman, a novel of education and formation, both on a formal and thematic level. The book casts doubt on the idea of a ground zero from which to begin after 1945 and provokes skepticism about the neo–avant-gardist gestures of the visionary architects Hollein and Pichler, as well as the mythification of a "zero hour" that artists such as Joseph Beuys (with his "re-birth" after his airplane was shot down during World War II and he was "saved" by Tartars), new German cinema filmmakers (who sought to redefine themselves as children of their Weimar grandparents), and the other young Austrian architects (who construct a lineage to émigré architects such as Frederick Kiesler and Rudolf Schindler)[3] practiced in the 1960s. And *Amras* begins to reflect on the politics of collection and musealization, for lack of a better word, that come to increasingly define the relationship of the state to what it espouses as "high" culture—now no longer linked to territorial aspirations, but to other, less tangible desires for cultural and historical rehabilitation as well as education and edification.

Primary Foundations: Castle and Tower

The rudimentary plot of *Amras* is quickly summarized: two brothers survive their family's joint suicide attempt, but their parents—a heavily indebted father and a neurologically sick mother—die. Their uncle removes the young men from Innsbruck, where the parents' deaths are the subject of murky speculation and bankruptcy proceedings against the family have begun. He sequesters them in a tower on the outskirts of Innsbruck named Amras. From here, the narrating brother K. sends letters and collates material from his younger brother, Walter, who continues to suffer from the "Tyrolean epilepsy" he has inherited from his mother. The weekly visits to the internist are for naught; in the face of his worsening condition, he commits suicide by jumping from the tower window. The surviving brother K. is then sent to

Figure 8. Castle Ambras, Innsbruck. Image © Kunsthistorisches Museum, Vienna.

another Innsbruck suburb, Aldrans, and from here continues his reflections on his brother's mental condition, the environs, their relationship, and his coworkers. The short novel ends very tentatively—with intimations that the fate the brother K. foresaw for himself in the novella's opening pages, namely, incarceration in a Tyrolean mental institution, has actually taken place.

The site of Amras possesses a kind of historical overdetermination, telescoping the Habsburg past, the National Socialist catastrophe, and the post-1945 enterprise regarding *Bildung*. The novel delves into the relationship between this particular place and its historical embeddedness to raise issues of patricidal and fratricidal relationships. The eponymous district of Amras, whose name is believed to derive from the Latin "ad umbras," is today part of Innsbruck in the southeast.[4] The famed Renaissance Castle of Ambras (figure 8), which carries the resonances of "in the shadows" in its name, is located at the southern periphery of this district. It, too, functions as an echo chamber, allowing the novel to allusively raise issues of primogeniture, genealogical politics, and artistic bequests. Archduke Ferdinand II (1529–1595) refashioned the medieval castle for his wife Philippine Welser (1527–1580), a daughter of bourgeois parentage—it was a morganatic marriage that led to the exclusion of the sons from succession (until later interventions on their behalf). Welser is mentioned numerous times in the novel, a cipher for an alternative lineage. The

Figure 9. Print of *Castrum Ameras* in Bernhard's house at Niederpuchheim 13, Ottnang. Image © Thomas-Bernhard-Stiftung, Dr. Peter Fabjan.

last Habsburg owner of the Castle was Archduke Francis Ferdinand (1863–1914), who met his end in Sarajevo in 1914. His death at the hands of the Serbian nationalist Gavrilo Princip was the immediate cause of the outbreak of World War I and hastened the end of the Dual Monarchy in 1918. The "ridiculous pygmy state" or "amputated state," as Thomas Bernhard liked to call the Austria that resulted from the breakup of the multinational Habsburg Empire,[5] is remembered in the novel as well. Furthermore, the district Amras only became a part of Innsbruck in the fateful year of the Anschluss of the First Republic to Germany in 1938. The famous art collection in Ambras was subjected to myriad dispersions and reconsolidations, moved from Prague to Vienna and back to the Tyrol. The problems charted in the book are thus multiple: a family's, a region's, an empire's, and a republic's are equally invoked.

Bernhard always maintained that *Amras* was his particular favorite—he inserts the novella in third place in the German canon in his last published novel *Extinction* (*Auslöschung*, 1986), after Jean Paul (*Siebenkäs*) and Franz Kafka (*The Trial* [*Der Proceß*]), and before Robert Musil (*Die Portugiesin*) and Hermann Broch ("Esch oder die Anarchie," the second part of *The Sleepwalkers* [*Die Schlafwandler*]), as a must-read for the pupil Gambetti. With this positioning, *Amras* functions as a kind of central point along a spectrum of predominantly modern texts. A print on the wall of his house in Ottnang (figure 9), prominently displayed in the living room on the second floor, corroborates the view of *Amras*'s centrality: the inscription on the top left of the print describes "Castrum Ameras" as housing a "Bibliotheca et Musoeum"—it is a well-known place of learning and art. The depicted castle is perched high above the city of Innsbruck, visible in the distance, and bulls frolic in a meadow below.

The castle at Ambras possesses the in-betweenness I noted in Bernhard's opening description of the tower. It was already reputed to be a center of culture in the sixteenth century, so much so that travelers made it a point to stop at the castle on their journeys north and south from and to Italy. An early site plan, less paradisiacal than Bernhard's print, lauds the "air(y) castle" or "Luft-Schloß" for its "wonder-worthy, priceless chamber of armor, art and rarities" ("wunderwürdig, ohnschäzbare Rüst Kunst u. Raritaeten Kammer").[6] Bernhard probably visited Ambras in 1955, as a participant in the now legendary Innsbrucker Youth Culture Weeks (Jugendkulturwochen).[7] The up-down coordinates of the castle, in addition to its architectural magnificence and historical importance, strikingly exteriorize the aspirations of the bourgeoisie as regards "upward mobility." While Archduke Ferdinand II and his wife Philippine Welser lived in the upper castle, the "Hochschloss," the lower castle complex, or "Unterschloss," was devoted to the archduke's holdings. The lower buildings, constructed solely to house his famous collection, became one of the first museums in Western history. In the drawn-out tract, portraits and busts were displayed along with many corals, swords, ivory sculptures, ornate clocks, compasses, handicrafts, armor, and unusual artifacts. For us today, used as we are to the museal practices of the late twentieth century, the lower castle with its mannerist cabinet of curiosities becomes a kind of *prepositioning* space, preparing visitors on their way to the upper castle with the important Habsburg portraits by Teniers, Rubens, Cranach, van Dyck, and so on, which were reinstalled there in 1976.[8] The cabinet of curiosities serves, in this interpretation, as a kind of preparatory space, sensitizing the roaming viewer to the value judgments underpinning the modern museum and the segregations on which it is predicated. These aspects, I think, make it significant that Bernhard framed this particular print and displayed it so prominently. A street sign with the inscription "Niederpuchheim 13" is also to be found in the same house in Ottnang, tucked away on a windowsill. The sign, Bernhard's half-brother Dr. Fabjan told me, was removed because of its connotations. The unlucky thirteen rubbed Bernhard the wrong way; more importantly, he disliked the implications of being "down below" ("nieder") rather than up high, as in the Castle Ambras on its promontory. The spatial underpinnings of his thinking are thus nicely concretized in the two examples of the print and the sign: the emphasis on being *high up*, both in the sphere of high culture and higher education, and the desire to escape the depths were in these instances translated from a metaphorical onto a literal plane. These facets of Bernhard's reflections on how we are positioned to learn in specific spaces are focalized through the gallery, in its early and later permutations, in *Amras*.

Within the echo chamber of history I outlined, Bernhard's *Amras* sets up two confining spaces to play them off against one another. Temporally first is the claustrophobic space of the university; second is the tower of the novel's opening lines with which I began. Unsurprisingly, the portrait of university life is damning. The characters' walk through the university itself is equivalent to moving through a dense Pichlerian space. The brothers deride the depressing "traversal of Leopold Franz University and its institutes adjacent to the Botanical Gardens, stifling our natures arbitrarily no less than radically, the daily passage through a full millennium of our rotten world of learning" ("unterdrückendes Durchqueren der Leopold-Franzens-Universität und ihrer Institute am botanischen Garten [. . .], der tägliche Gang durch ein rundes Jahrtausend unserer faulen Wissenschaftswelt"). They find themselves in architectonic spaces that have come to signify torpor: "in the high-ceilinged and gray and answerless courtrooms of dull curricula, world views, of dusty theories and philosophies, an awakening in the stinking laboratories and auditoriums of our gloomy provincial capital" (*A* 20–21; "hohen und grauen und antwortlosen Gerichtssälen dumpfer Lehrpläne, Weltanschauungen, staubiger Theorien und Philosophien, ein Aufwachen in den stinkenden Laboratorien und Hörsälen unserer düsteren Landeshauptstadt," *Am* 134). The narrator K. speaks often of the brothers' diametrically opposed sciences and arts, in which they can no longer discover commonalities.[9] K.'s interests in cell biology, genetics, and the history of science no longer excite his brother Walter, with his predilection for French and German literature, and vice versa. The inability of their disciplines to provide any solace (which returns, generalized to art as a whole, in *Old Masters*) or coherence should be seen against the backdrop of the increasing specialization various disciplines demand and their inability to communicate with one another in the stagnating halls of academia. We might take Pichler's *Entrance to an Underground City* (1963, figure 5) in Chapter 1 as an emblem of the incarcerating space within a space that Bernhard correlates to the university in *Amras*. The viewer is led inward, navigating the submerged antechamber from the ground-level entrance, guided along a straight groove as toward an inner sanctum—but comes up against a hard, impenetrable core that cannot be breached. There is no exchange, no permeability, no communication, and no further passage upward, downward, or inward.

Bernhard imagines an alternative to this impassable architectonic conceptualization of knowledge within the academy, with the topography of heights so typical of his work. It comes as no surprise that the brothers' effort in *Amras* at intellectual emancipation is articulated via a return to the foundations of learning marked by up-and-down rhetoric. While the text repeats the adjective "higher" in relation to "higher education" in the crucial letter to their friend, the psychiatrist Hollhof—"Hochschulwesen," "Höhere Schulische" (twice), "Hoher Schule und Hohem Schulzwang," "Hochschulmartyrien," "Hochschüler"—these are false heights. Following their

Figure 10. Tower on the grounds of Castle Ambras, Tyrol. Photo © author.

misgivings about institutionalized higher education, the brothers look downward and grab on to "the girders of those research bridges" they themselves have devised ("von uns selber erfundenen Wissenschaftsbrückenträger") to escape the "nauseating subdeliria of academia" ("Unterdelirien des Hochschulwesens"). The five-and-a-half month stint at the university in Innsbruck cannot restitute the ground ("Boden") for self-cultivation, so that they must search for a new grounding: "We could find the wellsprings of our music and our natural science not in the soil [ground] of the state system but only in ourselves" ("Wir konnten die Quellen für unsere Musik und für unsere Naturwissenschaft nicht auf dem staatlichen Boden finden, sondern nur in uns selbst").[10] Their intellectual "unhousedness" is briefly interrupted when they reach higher ground—with the personalized lessons "high up over the terrible, dark city" ("hoch oben über der schrecklichen, finsteren Stadt") in the science professor Nicolussi's "'metaphysical' house" ("'metaphysischen' Hause"); with the enlightening instruction of a botanist named Ratteis, up in the South Tyrolean Alps near Merano in Alto Adige (*A* 58; *Am* 178); and, most importantly, in the tower of the suburb Amras in the first half of the text (see figure 10).

Emplaced within their variant of an ivory tower, which condenses all the attributes and historical properties to be found in the actual Castle Ambras itself, Walter and K. engage in their own metaphorical flights outside the guidelines and structures of formal higher education. The narrating brother K. describes it as a paradoxical flight that returns them to the primeval rock with which the text began. Their sudden independence suggests a new grounding for their thinking and an inner, fundamental transmutation. They allow themselves,

> in obedience to a glorious intuition, blithely unconcerned about higher education and higher educational coercion, relying solely on our innate intelligence, to be abruptly transformed into primeval rock and into family, with our penchant for illuminating, together with nature, every cranny in the gloomy edifice of our thought, in the respective fields of study that seduced us, yes, soaring up and away into higher regions, indeed in the highest, we were out of the woods . . .
>
> Sobald wir uns aber, einer glorreichen Eingebung Folge leistend, ganz unbekümmert von Hoher Schule und Hohem Schulzwang, allein mit dem uns angeborenen Scharfsinn, auf einmal in Urgestein und in Familie, mit der Vorliebe für das Ausleuchten aller Ritzen unseres finsteren Denkgebäudes mit der Natur gemeinsam in unseren beiden uns verführenden Wissenschaften verändern ließen, ja, auf und davon flogen in hohe, ja höchste Regionen, waren wir über die Berge . . .[11]

The belief in the false heights of higher education is left aside; the "gloomy edifice of our thought," or, closer to the original, the "dark thought structure" ("finstere [. . .] Denkgebäude") must be set on new terrain, no less foundational than the tower's location in the garden on primordial rocks. Only then do one's facilities reveal their transformational potential: the "Denkgebäude" turn out to be structures that have no in- or outside, and the brothers can fly outward to new regions—to the highest ones ("höchste Regionen").[12]

The brothers' alternative ivory tower is, however, not only a space up above, with similar dead ends to those noted earlier. The brothers literally move into a "middle ground" or "intermediate floor" ("mittleren Boden") in the tower, which allows them to transcend the up-down movement we saw in "Plain/Plane," where it meant more of the same, or in the short parable "Two Young People," where the social frame's occlusion is the reason for the lack of progress halfway. This middle position in *Amras* suggests the overcoming of the tensions that crisscross the text, getting beyond any simplistic resolution of the thesis-antithesis binaries on which the text relies for much of its rhetorical force with its couplings of up-down, dependence-independence, openness-closedness, and life-death. The tower, where the brothers are both above and in-between, develops into a space of self-cognition and recognition of the external world that dissolves distinctions between in- and outside:

"*in the tower* we had suddenly become fully conscious of ourselves, it was then that we looked at ourselves, for the first time, from the outside *and* from the inside" (*A* 23; "*im Turm* waren wir unser selbst bewusst geworden, da schauten wir uns, zum ersten Male, von außen *und* innen an," *Am* 136–37).

The knowledge they acquire pacing the tower's middle floor is esoteric, sensuous, overpowering, erotic—and fleeting. Strikingly, the section that describes this type of knowledge and the moments of insight is capitalized. The typographic emphasis lifts it out of the mass of fragments from various genres that compose *Amras*. The passage is entitled "FLOORS AND WALLS" ("BÖDEN UND MAUERN"). These become the brothers' physical point of contact with the entire universe. When they press their temples against them, these structural elements suddenly become porous. Through these portals to another way of being, learning, and knowing, the brothers are able to move outward in a kind of Abraham-inspired movement, into a post-Babelian language potpourri and a Genesis-like creation. The two youths sense their interconnectedness with the universe in the ensuing quasi-mystical moments:

> Through the floors and walls, not only the air, we were connected most intimately to all of nature, that is to say to all of nature in a doubly rational way . . . we would listen for hours at the most distant shores . . . we heard the mingling of all imaginable languages, the mingling and droning of all sounds filled our cranial cavities, which at times were completely emptied of flesh, of blood . . . at a certain ratio between our temporal bones and the center of the earth, which we were able to determine for ourselves and for everything, we were privy to the processes of creation, to the willpower of all of matter . . . Thus we were conscious of ourselves as of two double mirror images of the universe . . . we felt and we understood . . . Pressing our temples to floors and walls, we observed the revolution of millions of light years, far away . . . gyrating cones, spherical celestial bodies, the precise elasticity of mathematics . . .
>
> Durch die Böden und Mauern waren wir auf das engste mit der gesamten Natur, und zwar doppelt verstandesmäßig mit der gesamten Natur verbunden, nicht nur durch die Luft . . . wir horchten stundenlang an den entferntesten Ufern . . . wir hörten das Gemisch aller möglichen Sprachen, das Gemisch und Gedröhn aller Laute erfüllte unsere Kopfhöhlen, die zeitweise ganz ohne Fleisch, ohne Blut waren . . . in einem bestimmten Verhältnis unserer Schläfenknochen zum Erdmittelpunkt, den wir uns für uns und für alles bestimmen konnten, waren wir eingeweiht in die Schöpfungsvorgänge, in die Willensstärke der ganzen Materie . . . Wir waren uns dann unser selbst als zweier doppelter Spiegelbilder des Universums bewußt [. . .]

> wir fühlten und wir begriffen [. . .] Unsere Schläfen an Böden und Mauern gedrückt beobachteten wir die Drehung von Millionen von Lichtjahren, weit entfernt . . . konische Kreisel, kugelförmige Himmelskörper, die präzise Gelenkigkeit der Mathematik . . .[13]

The rational is not separable from the irrational; the haptic from the auditory; intuition from consciousness; the body from the mind (note the "cranial cavities"or "Kopfhöhlen" as precursors of Pichler's *Schädelhäuser* and *Gargoyle*'s "Hohlraum"). Feeling, sensing, knowing—the combination enables the moment of "begreifen," necessary to formulate a new concept or "Begriff." They are released from the constraints of place into a *mise-en-abîme* of reflection as "two doubled mirror images," where the abstract forms—dynamic cones and spheres—arise out of the concrete.

Other Conditions à la Musil

In this manner, the novel revitalizes the "Other Condition" that Bernhard's compatriot Robert Musil strikingly formulated in the fragmentary novel *The Man without Qualities* (*Der Mann ohne Eigenschaften*) some thirty years earlier.[14] Musil's work moved into the center of public attention with a new posthumous publication in 1952. The Austrian writer Ingeborg Bachmann's 1954 essay "Ins Tausendjährige Reich" for the first edition of the newly founded journal *Akzente*, which devotes a section to Musil, played a role in the writer's rediscovery.[15] In terms that are recognizable to all Bernhard readers, she alludes to the non-teleological orientation of Musil's utopian thrust, his thinking in potentialities and alternative possibilities:

> The recourse of the *Man Without Qualities* to the idea of the Millenarian Reich, his desire for an "Other Condition," the "unio mystica," is less disconcerting when we see it as Musil does—as a possible utopia, and utopia not as goal but as a direction. Musil's thinking is antagonistic to any goal, it is mobile, it runs counter to the prevailing orders where each and everything is a "congealed isolated case of its possibilities."

> Der Rückgriff des Manns ohne Eigenschaften auf die Idee vom tausendjährigen Reich, sein Verlangen nach dem "anderen Zustand," der "unio mystica," ist weniger befremdend, wenn man sie mit Musil als eine mögliche Utopie begreift und die Utopie nicht als Ziel, sondern als Richtung vor Augen hat. Musils Denken ist ziel-feindlich, beweglich, es rennt gegen die herrschenden Ordnungen an, in denen jedes Ding "ein erstarrter Einzelfall seiner Möglichkeiten" ist.[16]

Bernhard shows Musil reverence in a televised interview in 1971, long before his mention of both Musil and Bachmann in the novel *Extinction*[17]—and so takes part in Musil's ongoing reevaluation and canonization.[18]

The Man without Qualities centers on the dyadic relationship between a brother and sister that transcends boundaries of many sorts, including those of traditional academic disciplines. The beginning of the novel charts the failure of conventional educational means in satisfying a bright young man's sense of self. The army, the technical college, or university cannot fulfill Ulrich's longings. A fulfilling state of being can only be realized in a hyper-rational and sensuous realm—separated from the capital city of Vienna and the provincial town of B(rünn), with their multifarious diversions and strictly segregated institutions. Significantly, Musil creates a *hortus conclusus*, a cloistered garden, and an empty house as the site where communication and communion occurs. Here, the siblings' discussion of mystical writings and their near incestuous relationship give rise to the "Other Condition" ("der andere Zustand"), which removes them from their belligerent society and parochial compatriots.[19] The novel oscillates between outer doublings—when one sibling appears as a kind of gender double of the other—and the internal bifurcations—when the siblings appear bisexual or even hermaphroditic.[20] The passage from gender doubling to interpenetration and/or internal splitting coincides with hints of the utopian "Other Condition," when the momentary experience transitions into a remembered one or the current order crumbles to hint at another, simultaneously present one.[21]

In *Amras*, the siblings Walter and K. also open themselves to a utopian moment that still has its footing in a very real location—the impossible emerges from thinking about what is possible within the confines of a tower in a garden.[22] As in the "Other Condition" in *The Man without Qualities*, the ostensible permanence of spatial and temporal coordinates is undermined. *Amras*'s landscape becomes metamorphotic; linear time loses its validity; sexual orientation becomes fluid; the subject is decentered; sensory perception is synaesthetic. Sight takes on another dimension in the moments when the brothers transcend their confining environment in their thoughts and feelings, allowing them to "see" different temporal moments simultaneously.[23] Knowledge surpasses the fragmented, discontinuous state that the text disparaged, in order to give the brothers an encompassing sense of themselves within universal coordinates. As in Giovanni Batista Fontana's ceiling painting now in Castle Ambras's *Kunst- und Wunderkammer* (ca. 1580/85), illustrating the interrelatedness of zodiac signs, Roman allegories of the planets, and star constellations in both hemispheres,[24] the brothers can conceive of themselves as both microcosmically and macrocosmically significant. The same may be said of a late sixteenth-century painting of a "curiosity" hung in the cabinet, showing the giant *Bartlmä Bon* next to the dwarf Thomele (figure 11).

Figure 11. Anonymous, *The Giant Bartlmä Bon with the Dwarf Thomele.* Late sixteenth century. Image © Kunsthistorisches Museum, Vienna.

Such examples of supposed abnormalities have a place within the larger universe, where nothing is aberrant and everything is "naturgemäß"—"according to nature," to use one of Bernhard's favored phrases. These inclusive aspects of a normalcy defined in this manner are worth emphasizing: the brothers can see themselves as concentrated signs of a universal harmony and linked to all other things and beings, despite their societal stigmatization.

As in Musil's famous unfinished novel, Bernhard subordinates his alternative spatial order to the "architectural uncanny," Anthony Vidler's name for the peculiarly modern architectural manifestations that signal humans' increasing estrangement from the world around them.[25] Bernhard's strategies of two, I would argue, have a pronounced similarity to the "double vision" that Vidler describes as the hallmark of a modernity increasingly concerned with the threatening aspects of space. This "double vision" emerges from the Enlightenment paradigm of light and transparency, which is coupled with a "spatial phenomenology of darkness" (Vidler, *Architectural Uncanny*, 169). For Vidler in *The Architectural Uncanny: Essays in the Modern Unhomely*, the pairing of transparency and obscurity is an essential precondition for the exercise of power within society:

> For it is in the intimate associations of the two [light and dark, clear and obscure], their uncanny ability to slip from one to the other, that the sublime as an instrument of fear retains its hold—in that ambiguity that stages the presence of death in life, dark space in bright space. In this sense, all the radiant spaces of modernism, from the first Panopticon to the Ville Radieuse, should be seen as calculated not on the final triumph of light over dark but precisely on the insistent presence of the one in the other. (*Architectural Uncanny*, 172)

Bernhard, too, is keen to subvert any stark opposition between life and death, light and darkness, learning and schooling, the architecture of power and that of powerlessness. But he has these tensions play out in more threatening spatial regimes that clearly show the "erosions of bourgeois bodily and social well being" (Vidler, *Architectural Uncanny*, 167). With his strategies of two, he undermines the separations we might initially have posited between the surveillant, phallic tower and the surrounding, splayed countryside, between life before a loved one's death and after it. Bernhard suggests the immediate subversion of order through a scintillating, oscillating double, and his intimations of the "modern unhomely" account for the novel's surreal tone.[26] The brothers, pressing their bodies against one another in bed and against the walls of the tower, become lovers, twins and hermaphroditic complements of one another.[27]

Their doubling in these various guises is echoed in the many allusions to twofold things. In light of the text's strategies of two and its focus on an occult, alternative order, it seems fair to speak of the number's magical incantation.[28] On the first page, for instance, readers find out that the brothers are sequestered for "two and a half months," a fact repeated in the first two sentences. Grammatical couplings structure the first page, where most participial adjectives used as nouns are paired ("handelnden und begreifenden Welt," "bewahrende und verbergende Zuflucht," "Zerrütteten und Zerschlagenen"). These semantic features lead to an unusual double ellipsis. The suicide that is discovered "two hours too early" leaves behind two living and two dead—double ellipsis—and the two brothers are brought to the tower wrapped in "two horse blankets."[29] This double ellipsis, emphatically indicated in Bernhard's final typescript of *Amras* and repeated in the print version of the novel, marks the inception of the tower text proper, when the brothers are in Amras's tower and its adjoining garden. Remembering the day of the attempted suicide, the brother K. relates how he saw "two sibling sisters, a brother pair, two professors" and their wives.[30] The authoritarian uncle responsible for bringing them to the tower functions as the father's uncanny double, inverting his downfall through the "doubling" of his fortune while the father loses everything.[31] The brothers are doubly connected with nature via their reason ("doppelt verstandesmäßig"), whose "doubled mirror image" ("doppeltes Spiegelbild") they become. The pictures of epileptics hang in vertical pairs in the Innsbruck doctor's office in a building from the time of the Secession (ca. 1900),[32] whose dark stairwell reveals it to be a double of the castle tower. These strategies of two do not end with Walter's suicide, when he jumps from the tower to his death below. At two o'clock in the morning, K. runs to the local tavern to inform others of Walter's suicide. Walter's corpse lies in the Medical Institute for two weeks, where two prosectors are supposed to examine it. The tower text itself doubles—the first part, which begins after the title "Amras," is mirrored in the second part with the alliterative title "In Aldrans." Instead of being radically different from the first half of the text, however, the montage of various genres continues, with letters, quotations, aphorisms, reflections. The supposed division occasioned by Walter's death is not a radical break or separation: "There is no first or last figure of the brother . . . no brother . . . Walter *is*. [. . .] death after all does not interrupt."[33]

Let me return for a moment to the passage about the "FLOORS AND WALLS," which I partially quoted. Bernhard shares Musil's fascination with topographical, prepositional, and *pre-positioning* presentation. In Musil's famous description of the "Other Condition," we find a clear architectonic, geographical, and topographical description of the utopian moment, when the brother Ulrich breaks open the closed space of the house and garden through the description of a mystical moment. In this instant, the otherworldly pull of the divine ends the experience of being incarcerated ("eingeschlossen"), and a sense of sinking downward into God ensues ("in Gott versenkt").[34] Ulrich describes an oceanic occurrence, where the contrasts between up and down, here and there, light and dark collapse in the temporal present. Superabundance and extinction characterize this fullness of time:

> The way I'd put it, [. . .] is that it's like looking out across a wide glimmering sheet of water: the eye seems almost to be seeing darkness, everything's so bright, and on the far bank things don't seem to be fixed on solid ground but floating in the air, in a delicate over-distinctness that's almost painful . . . bewildering. The impression one gets is both of intensification and of loss. One is linked with everything and at the same time can't get right *to* anything. There you are on the one side, and the world on the other, over-individuality and over-objectivity, but all almost agonizingly clear, and what at once separates and unites these generally fused elements is a dazzling darkness, an overbrimming and an extinction, a swinging in and out.

> Ich würde sagen, [. . .] es ist dem ähnlich, daß man auf eine große spiegelnde Wasserfläche hinausschaut: das Auge glaubt Dunkel zu erblicken, so hell ist alles, und jenseits am Ufer scheinen die Dinge

> nicht auf der Erde zu stehn, sondern schweben in der Luft mit einer zarten Überdeutlichkeit, die beinahe schmerzt und verwirrt. Es ist ebensowohl eine Steigerung wie ein Verlieren in diesem Eindruck. Man ist mit allem verbunden und kann an nichts heran. Du stehst hüben und die Welt drüben, überichhaft und übergegenständlich, aber beide fast schmerzhaft deutlich, und was die sonst Vermengten trennt und verbindet, ist ein dunkles Blinken, ein Überströmen und Auslöschen, ein Aus- und Einschwingen.[35]

The self melds with the universe, and the preposition "over" or "above" ("über") emphasizes the new emplacement in relation to what existed previously: "over-distinctness," "over-individuality," "over-objectivity," and "overbrimming" ("Überdeutlichkeit," "überichhaft," "übergegenständlich," "Überströmen"). A superior vantage point arises from this positioning on a threshold located above, a position not normally afforded a mortal human being.

In *Amras* we note a similar topographical anchoring of the brothers' "Other Conditions," which places them over and above their stultifying existence. As discussed in "Way Station 2," a plethora of composite nouns with the prefix "over" or "above" are noticeable in the first half of the novella, the tower text proper (e.g., "übergesund," "*Über*vorsicht," "Überdruck," "*Über*furcht").[36] The many composite words I mentioned containing the adjective "high" or "hoch" underline the raised perspective from the tower that seeps into every aspect of their lives (e.g., "höhern Geschwisterstumpfsinn," "Höhepunkt," "Hochgebirgslandschaft," "hoch aufgetürmte . . . Wellen," "hohe Wissenschaft," "Hochschulwesen," "Hochschulmartyrien," "hohe Kunst," "höhere Schulische," "hohe Erregung").[37] In this way, the text prepares the readers for the ecstatic climax, when the "highest moments" are spatialized. I return to a section of the text that I partly quoted earlier:

> [O]ften we truly rose to such heights in the contemplation of the constellations that the cold made us shiver, *ourselves* water, rock . . . in the privilege of mortality, when we listened and thus understood . . . we felt and we understood [. . .] no longer thrown back on speculation, we beheld the calculations of the lucid human mind . . . how fine, not mentally exhausting was the hush in which we could communicate, renew ourselves at such moments [. . .] The fantastical unveiled everything to us for seconds, only to plunge it back into darkness *for itself* . . . the most exalted moments, naturally, were always the shortest, indeed infinitesimal moments [. . .] (*A* 16)

> [O]ft waren wir wirklich so hoch in der Sternbildanschauung, daß uns fröstelte, *selbst* Wasser, Gestein . . . im Vorteil der Sterblichkeit, wenn wir horchten und dadurch begriffen . . . wir fühlten und wir begriffen . . . wir schauten, nicht mehr auf Vermutungen angewiesen,

> auf die Berechnungen klaren Menschenverstandes . . . in wie feiner, nicht kopfzerbrechender Schweigsamkeit konnten wir uns in solchen Augenblicken verständigen, uns erneuern [. . .] Das Phantastische enthüllte uns alles sekundenlang nur, um es wieder *für sich* zu verfinstern . . . die höchsten Augenblicke waren naturgemäß immer die kürzesten, überhaupt allerkürzeste Augenblicke [. . .] (*Am* 127–28)

Despite relatively little plot development, a high-pressure atmosphere and breathless pace is created on a grammatical and linguistic level with compound words, prepositions, and punctuation marks. In the way the ellipses puncture the narrative fabric, the brothers' mystical self-tutelage perforates their previous life. The pressure bursts open the tower's confining walls, affirming the possibility and potential of knowledge and perception beyond that which has been handed down to them—"Other Conditions" of the kind Musil describes. In this description, we have the clearest indication yet of a coming renewal that is also a restoration of an older, different way of learning.

As pointed out in the previous section, Bernhard's texts, with their elevated sites (tower structures, mountain peaks, tree lines, and balconies), display a multiplicity of prepositions denoting location and a plethora of compound words using these place markers. They are utilized not only to create the superlatives and hyperbole with which Bernhard is often associated, but also to bring movement into the texts, those "abject impulses from every point of the compass" referred to in *Amras* (*A* 4; "aus den Himmelsrichtungen bodenlos impulsiv zerstörten Gedanken," *Am* 112). After all, relatively little happens within each novel and relatively little changes from one novel to the next.[38] As if to offer a meta-commentary on this lack of plot development, the narrator K. claims that the brothers are the "sworn enemies of prose, we were sickened by that loquacious literature, by that stupid narrative vein, especially by the historical novel" (*A* 35; "*Feinde der Prosa*, uns ekelte vor der geschwätzigen Literatur, vor dem dummen Erzählerischen, vor allem vor dem Geschichtsroman," *Am* 152). A lot, however, happens on the formal level of sentence structure, where the ups, downs, and outward movements are charted minutely, offering many permutations on Bernhard's prevalent themes. The numerous nouns and names with "over," "under," "down," "up," and "higher" in particular create an oscillating narrative rhythm in German that destabilizes any fixed points. This rhythm eventually pulverizes the vertical towers and fortified buildings associated with higher education, the highest art, the heights of learning, and top rankings; it does away with readers' focus on plot development.[39] The editors of the new critical edition of Bernhard have remarked that the early typescripts show all sorts of crossings-out and over-writings, performing the dissolution of plot Bernhard claimed to have wanted from the outset of his writing career. In the process of eradicating the plot, Bernhard also dissolves the hermetic architecture, freeing his characters—and readers—for an entirely other experience.

Romantic Structuration and Potentiation: Novalis as Mentor

Although *Amras*'s alternative order is predicated on a kind of mystical communion, a rigorous structure underpins it. Indeed, the German term "structuration" or "structuredness" ("Strukturiertheit") is used in pedagogical-didactic circles to schematize the relationship between observer and observed during a lesson, when the observed is criticized in the hope of improving his or her performance. The term refers to the process of perception as well as the recording of the perception.[40] In Bernhard's learning environment in the tower, the brothers are constantly engaged in a process of mutual observation. Learning has to do with such structured perception within and around the mystical moments. The recording of the perception is as much a part of the brothers' development as any material they might be learning. The interaction of architectural reduction (their concentration within a space) and visual concatenation (interlinking chains that relate them to different spatial and temporal coordinates) shapes them, guiding their "structuration."

We have become so used to interpreting visuality as a pernicious thing that it seems retrograde to rehabilitate sight as a necessary precondition for learning—especially from a raised site. Forty years after the publication of *Discipline and Punish* (*Surveiller et punir*, 1975), we invariably think of the Foucauldian panopticon when we speak of such observation. In the common view, the observed is never the subject of communication but the object of information, and the existence of an unseen observer furthers the dispersion, decentering, and internalization of authority.[41] However, this association should not immediately lead to a denigration of Bernhard's propaedeutic project. His particular structuration is not overtly insidious, although there are problematic aspects, as I argue in the next chapter. In Bernhard, one person engages in watching another, often unbeknownst to the observed, from a raised window or an adjoining doorway. The inferences the viewer draws are recorded in the form of the text we read (occasionally, the observed's thoughts and written texts are cited as well, e.g., in *Amras*, *Correction*, or *The Lime Works*). The observations often reverse the hierarchy between teacher and student, with the student commenting on the mentor he is observing. The clandestine viewer's reflections on the person before him lead him to a point where personal boundaries become porous, and observer and observed meld. From the process of observation and recording, other thoughts emerge that move away from the actual situation at hand. The second-order observations often have a telescoping function, drawing together different temporal moments and relating them by analogy. These situations create the self-reflexivity of a feedback loop, where the protagonist emerges changed from the process of observation. He is decentered, as it were, and not necessarily in command of any information or greater control over the observed.[42] We do occasionally suspect, however, that he may have worked through an over-identification with his object of study.

Figure 12. Castle Ambras's cabinet of curiosities, or *Wunderkammer.* Image © Kunsthistorisches Museum, Vienna.

Drawing on the *genius loci* of Castle Ambras and its *Wunderkammer* (figure 12), Bernhard turns to the perambulating, decentering gaze in structured observation at numerous points in *Amras.* While the proto-museum of Ambras is not directly thematized in the novel, its presence is felt in the method that the narrator devises. K.'s "quick read" of a situation becomes possible when he transcends the particular coordinates of his own life to include his family members. Bernhard's characters perceive potentiated knowledge of a second order in such moments of synoptic-panoptic experience. The model for this quick read is the experience of the museum gallery rather than the isolated chamber discussed previously: the expansiveness of the museum visit leads outward à la Raimund Abraham, either problematizing or potentiating the prison cell experience that led inward à la Walter Pichler.[43] The narrator's experience of a mobile standpoint allows for a heightened sense of his own positioning within larger spatial coordinates. As the art historian Gabriele Beßler writes about early museums in her study of the *Wunderkammer*:

> The viewpoint becomes mobile: One can walk into the world represented in the chamber, and the individual (the gazing eye) stands in the center—the model for "Being-in-the-world" is born. The worldview has found a spatial equivalent and is immediately proportioned: It is only through the juxtaposition of one-point-perspective–vanishing point–virtual space that the real space can be recognized and defined

> through the movement of the eye/viewer. Only then can things be put into a spatial relationship with one another, through which correlations result. The great significance of this spatial equivalent is evident in the fact that the *Wunderkammer* also was understood to be an accessible miniature, a model. The world was mirrored in the spatial finitude of a chamber, which in turn referred to the relationship between man and the space around him and thus symbolized the relation to the outer (visible) border of corporeal being.
>
> Der Standpunkt wird beweglich: Die in der Kammer repräsentierte Welt ist begehbar geworden, und das Individuum (das schauende Auge) steht im Zentrum—das Modell für 'In-der-Welt-sein' ist geboren. Das Weltbild hat ein räumliches Äquivalent gefunden und wird sogleich proportioniert: Erst durch das Gegenüber von Zentralperspektive–Fluchtpunkt–virtuellem Raum wird der reale Raum durch Bewegung des Auges/Betrachters erkannt und definiert. Erst dann können Dinge miteinander in einen räumlichen Bezug gesetzt werden, wodurch Korrelationen entstehen. Welch große Bedeutung dieses räumliche Äquivalent hatte, zeigt sich besonders daran, dass die Wunderkammer auch als (begehbare) Miniatur, als Modell verstanden wurde: Die Welt spiegelte sich in der räumlichen Endlichkeit einer Kammer, die wiederum die Bezugnahme des Menschen zum Um-Raum und damit zur äußeren (sichtbaren) Grenze des körperlichen Seins versinnbildlichte.[44]

By linking this mobile gaze and self-perception with haptic-sensual experiences such as the tower's walls and floors, the touch of Philippine Welser's knife blade, or the staircase in the Innsbruck doctor's office, Bernhard addresses the central perspective that brings the subject into focus where the vanishing lines intersect. Viewing an object focalizes the spectator (and not the other way around), for whom relations and connections become visible and graspable.

Looking at an object, the next thing beside it already touches our peripheral vision; perhaps the object superimposes itself on other, similar objects in the mind's eye, drawing them together into one stereoscopic image. Our mental activity moves us from the spatial plane on which we are located with the object onto a temporal one, where the mind might play tricks by interlacing different historical moments. This method syncopates the experience, leading to a type of visual shorthand with visionary elements.

The *Wunderkammer* as a miniature model for learning to be in the world and beyond it represents an architecturally porous space fully coincident with human needs. In his aphorisms and disjointed musings, the brother Walter notes this possibility. He writes at a threshold between old and new as well as up and down, articulating a profoundly transformative vision of man as architecture. He *becomes* the architecturally formed space itself. While in "antique representation the *human element* disturbs" ("in der antiken Darstellung stört *das Menschliche*"), according to one of his jottings, a new reality emerges from humans *becoming* architecture or edifices of thought ("Denkgebäude"). Walter's very first proposition reads: "With me, entirely new surfaces, entirely new circles, entirely new rectangles, with me an entirely new architecture has *come into being*" ("Mit mir sind ganz neue Flächen, ganz neue Kreise, ganz neue Rechtecke, mit mir ist eine ganz neue Architektur *geworden*"). He articulates the hope that buildings could be transcended *tout court*; he could then enter into a symbiotic, structured relationship with his environment that would allow a *human*ist architecture to emerge. Architecture would no longer fulfill a mediating function—it would not be a mold shaping the person. Indeed, architecture in the generally understood sense would disappear, with the (decentered) subject becoming the "thought structures" or "edifices of thought" and these in turn becoming the environment. The effects of such a disappearance would be to rearticulate the human, not like in "antique representation" as a function of the landscape in which he moves (think of the "Vitruvian Man" as Leonardo da Vinci sketches him, with his perfect proportions taken as a measure for modern architects such as Le Corbusier), but as the living landscape itself. The thinking landscape is movement, rhythm, change: "Everything rhythm: thought-endowed mountains, thought-endowed rivers" (*A* 35–36; "Alles Rhythmus: denkende Berge, denkende Flüsse," *Am* 153). Walter's propositions correlate to Raimund Abraham's view of landscape as rhythm (Way Station 2); they anticipate the architect Hans Hollein's dictum that "everything is architecture" from 1967 (chapter 1).[45]

Novalis's Subterranean Pulse

In their fragmentary jottings, the brothers both imply that the tower schools them in the kind of perception that allows a fusion of man, landscape, and similar minds. It is an open-ended, infinite process, marked by its own impossibility—but nevertheless worth undertaking. Under Walter's heading, "A Book about *All the Observations that I Have Made in the Tower*," the following note can be found: "A book about all the observations that I made in the tower would of course have to be a book about *everything*, about the *totality of possibilities*. For that reason, it is impossible to compose a book about all the observations I made in the tower" (A 31; "Ein Buch über alle Wahrnehmungen, die ich im Turm gemacht habe, müßte natürlich ein Buch über *Alles* sein, über das *ganze Mögliche*. Aus diesem Grund ist es unmöglich, ein Buch über alle Wahrnehmungen, die ich im Turm gemacht habe, zu verfassen," *Am* 146–47). Walter's epistemological reflections echo not only the "sense of possibility" or "Möglichkeitssinn" we associate with Musil's "Other Condition," but also the fragments of the German romantic

Friedrich von Hardenberg (Novalis). Novalis, whom Bernhard calls upon over and over again as a kind of mentor for his writing and his characters' thoughts,[46] is invoked in *Amras* as a subterranean teacher. His ideas pulsate under the surface of the narrative.

In the 1,200 fragments comprising his 1798–99 work, *Notes for a Romantic Encyclopaedia* (*Das Allgemeine Brouillon: Materialien zur Enzyklopädistik*), Novalis attempts a classification of all scientific operations. Throughout the *Notes for a Romantic Encyclopaedia* and the *Miscellaneous Observations* (*Physikalische und medizinische Bemerkungen*, 1799–1800)—which are among the Novalis excerpts in a small edition in Bernhard's library[47]—the German romantic reflects on the conditions of possibility for his encyclopedic project, much as Walter does in the quotation from *Amras*. At times, Novalis seems confident of the project's realization. In fragments such as No. 527, Novalis utilizes the adjectival logic of high and low to map out his universalizing encyclopedism or "Encyclopaedistik": "Everything higher belongs together—everything lower."[48] The conceptualization of knowledge is far from static, as this quotation might imply. In Novalis, the coordinates are used to designate a ranking among the branches of science that is to be superseded. Novalis is more interested in the reconfiguration and reclassification of knowledge into new, interdisciplinary fields such as "poetical physiology," "pathological philosophy," or "logical pathology," going against then current disciplinary divisions.[49] As in the case of Bernhard, Novalis argues that only an interdisciplinary understanding allows people to recognize that the I is not a "fact" of nature, but instead something "constructed" ("Das Ich soll construirt werden"). And like Bernhard, Novalis subordinates the study of nature and art to the "higher science" of the moral sphere: "Nature and art will become united in a higher *science*—(the theory of moral development)—and be *reciprocally perfected*" ("Natur und Kunst werden in einer höhern *Wissenschaft*—[der *moralischen Bildungslehre*] vereinigt—und *wechselseitig vollendet*").[50]

Novalis turns our attention to the interplay between any totalizing thrust and the inability to represent such a totality, which we encounter in Walter's musings. In doing so, Novalis indirectly argues that the method of observation within the process of learning is as important as any insights to be gleaned—the structuration of the learner is paramount. In fragment 526, for instance, he challenges and critiques the scope of his own project ("*Kritik meines Unternehmens*"): "*Critique of my undertaking*—[. . .] If my undertaking becomes too large to execute—then I will only present my method of working—and examples from the *most general part*, and fragments from the specialized parts."[51] He acknowledges that such an all-inclusive illustration of knowledge is impossible. Rather, the method of the procedure has to take the place of the totality within representation. Examples and fragments should serve to illustrate the procedure and the belief in the unity of all science (in the same fragment we find the statement: "*All Science is One*").[52] In light of the encompassing project, the procedure becomes significant; the method of observation is as interesting as the particular observations themselves. In a spiraling process, the objective and subjective elements commingle. As observation itself becomes increasingly refined, it takes place on higher and higher levels ("höher grädig," "zum höhern Grade").[53]

Bernhard seems to have known specific Novalis texts only from the slim 1956 volume in his library. The Germanist Walter Rehm collates 208 pages of excerpts from *The Apprentices from Sais* (*Die Lehrlinge zu Sais*, 1802), *Pollen* (*Blüthenstaub*, 1798), *Christianity or Europe* (*Die Christenheit oder Europa*, 1799), "Faith and Love" ("Glaube und Liebe," 1798), and various fragments from the *Notes for a Romantic Encyclopaedia* and the *Miscellaneous Observations*, without designating the fragments' provenance. The flimsy, yellowed paperback in the Bernhard Archive in Gmunden, Upper Austria, contains a few passages annotated and underlined with ballpoint pen.[54] These marked sections are, to my mind, among the less noteworthy reflections in the compendium. Interesting for my purposes is the preface, in which Rehm stylizes Novalis into a spatial thinker with a synoptic goal. In Rehm's view, Novalis seeks the spatial reconciliation of the disparate arts and sciences into one whole, leading to a proto-paradisiacal state.[55] In his foreword, the editor does away with the distinction between Novalis's philosophical reflections and his poetic oeuvre. The second sentence of Rehm's introduction makes this clear: "But the poetic and the world of poetry are center and starting point of Novalis's inner life and determine and penetrate all spaces into which his thinking dares to venture" ("Aber das Dichterische und die Dichterwelt sind Mitte und Ausgangspunkt des inneren Lebens von Novalis und bestimmen und durchwirken alle Räume, in die sich sein Denken hineinwagt"). Rehm focuses on a central point, from which thinking moves outward into contiguous spaces—this parallels Bernhard's description of the brothers' thought spaces. If one cannot burrow down or move into the central core, one needs to rethink one's directionality: go from the middle ground outward, as the brothers attempt to do.

Moving into new thought spaces is an intellectual adventure and risk, broadening the categories of what was previously deemed possible. Echoing Musil's "Möglichkeitssinn," Rehm writes in his introduction to *Novalis*: "In his essays and especially in his fragments, Novalis advanced the category of the interesting to the limits of the possible: out of his always active and inspired delight in intellectual and poetic territorial extension and in mental play" ("In seinen Aufsätzen und vor allem in seinen Fragmenten hat Novalis die Kategorie des Interessanten bis an die Grenzen des Möglichen vorangetrieben: aus der immer regsamen und reizsamen Lust an der denkerischen und dichterischen Raumerweiterung und am geistigen Spiel"; Rehm, *Novalis*, 7–8). This spatial expansion and expansiveness may be present in Novalis's pseudonym, as someone who "settles or cultivates a new land or clearing in the woods" and "crosses boundaries of settled assumption to discover and possibly claim unknown, uncharted territories."[56] The expansiveness of play reconciles micro- and macrocosm, nature and man. The synthesis is a harmonious "Zusammenspiel"—meaning "interaction," but literally "play"—returning man to the universe like a child to its game: everything becomes a vast "play space," or "Spiel-Raum," with leeway.[57] Value accrues not to the finished work, but to the fragment that comes about in the play of thought. "In this sense," Rehm concludes, bringing the essay full circle, "and with this goal in mind one should read the essays and fragments of Novalis: as the foreplay of poetry."[58] The philosophical fragments have the task of creating a space of play and setting the stage for the philosophical poetry to come. The synthetic, synoptic impulse competes with an earlier, preliminary, dispersive one.

In this sense, we can read the conflicting impulses in Bernhard's text as an effort to potentiate Novalis, to tease out the possibilities of the encyclopedic undertaking for the present-day writer.[59] Bernhard one-ups Novalis's undertaking with the brothers' effort to transcend the status quo. The brothers' endeavor swells outward from the novelistic into a richly textured philosophical pre-space, where the letters, poetic aphorisms, parables, personal descriptions, and abstract reflections intermix. This pre-space adumbrates the many themes to which Bernhard returns in more cohesive fashion in his later works. If Novalis's fragmentary reflections expand the borders of possible "thought spaces" or "Denkräume," Bernhard's fragments in *Amras* do so, too. What comes into being is not a fixed system, but an infinitely malleable one. The space of intellectual foreplay ("Vor-Spiel")—with the erotic overtones and sensuous, haptic-optic knowledge I stressed—serves the preparatory function that Bernhard emphasizes in the brothers' case.

The subterranean, spatializing Novalis pulse may also be discerned in the novel's resolution, with the elimination of the hard boundaries between the natural sciences and the humanities. One of the detailed typescripts 15/2 to *Amras* makes explicit that the natural sciences and the humanities are ultimately not opposed to one another in the brothers' increasingly syncretic views. In fact, the natural sciences and the humanities are interchangeable and exchangeable, as are the possessive pronouns correlating the specific fields to one or the other young man. The brother K.'s quotation of Walter's speech illustrates this dissolution of hard borders:

> Each of us went, a hallmark of our childhood, by himself with the other. The sentence spoken by him on this afternoon in the waiting room, "Your (my) natural science is my music, my music, your natural science" is a good example for the great possibility of refinement for his research in what he recorded in the tower [. . .].
>
> Jeder von uns ging, ein Kennzeichen unserer Kindheit, für sich mit dem anderen. Der von ihm an diesem Nachmittag im Wartezimmer gesprochene Satz "Deine (meine) Naturwissenschaft ist meine Musik,

> meine Musik, Deine Naturwissenschaft" ist ein gutes Beispiel für die große Verfeinerungsmöglichkeit seines Forschens in dem von ihm im Turm Aufgeschriebenen [. . .].[60]

The union of brothers and fields of study is noticeable in the published text as well. In the course of *Amras*, the pronouns in the novel refer less and less to one or the other brother. After Walter's suicide, the indeterminacy of the pronouns "I" and "you" reaches its apogee. In fact, the surviving narrator increasingly speaks about Walter's thoughts as his own.[61] The symbiotic relationship between the two brothers is thus constructed according to the underlying principle of spatial dynamism motivating Novalis's encyclopedic undertaking. As their perception of the universe and learning changes through their structured observations, Walter and K. increasingly appear to be one person. The ever more refined descriptions of the method of observation, the complexly syncretic viewpoint that the narrator K. articulates in his observations of his brother, and the increasingly difficult interweaving of their thoughts all relate directly to this upward spiraling movement.

However, we witness the crumbling of an integrative, interdisciplinary kind of learning—in which botany, geology, and genetics mix freely in a melodic litany of specialized terms (*A* 57–58; *Am* 177)—and its architectonic dream of a *human*ist architecture set on new foundations. Significantly, *Amras* closes with a veritable pile-up of architectonic images: "soon, with the passage of time, we were afraid to open our books, our writings and letters, afraid to enter those gloomy, unventilated churches of the various philosophies, the monstrous dynalogies of cathedrals . . . fear of the trap doors in philosophical tunnels, the mills and lumberyards of the arts and sciences" ("bald hatten wir, mit der Zeit, Angst vor dem Aufschlagen unserer Bücher, unserer Schriften und Briefe, vor dem Hineingehen in die finsteren, ungelüfteten Kirchen der Philosophien, vor den ungeheuren Dynalogien von Kathedralen . . . Angst vor den Falltüren in philosophischen Gängen, wissenschaftlichen Mühlen und Sägewerken"). The opening of a window has the same consequences as the turning of a page. The view onto the world, which the page offers, disturbs the equilibrium and causes "an impaired sense of balance, headaches, and fainting spells."[62] The hermetic nature of the learning experiences in the tower is unable to lead into the "external environment" ("äußere Umwelt"). Darkness envelops their inner thought structures, and the influence of Alpine Tyrol's "*architectural nature*" on the brothers turns out to be deadly—a fact emphasized with italics in the original:

> Rejected by everything early on, seeking refuge, we had all our lives been locked within the hylozoism of all of us; that fact, with natural logic, overshadowed and darkened our relationship to our external environment, most devastatingly while we were at the university; it has darkened mine to this day . . . Walter and I had always been

> deceived; in a desolate composition of the air, in a patriarchal, fatal, antihuman galvanism caused by the perfidious heights and depths of its *architectural nature* . . . How many of our talents might we have been able to develop to amazing greatness in ourselves if we had not been born and raised in the Tyrol.
>
> Wir waren, schon früh von allem zurückgestoßen, Zuflucht suchend, zeitlebens immer nur eingeschlossen in unser aller Hylozoismus; das verdunkelte und verfinsterte naturgemäß folgerichtig, am verheerendsten in unseren Studienjahren, unser Verhältnis zur äußeren Umwelt; hat es mir bis heute verfinstert . . . Wir, Walter und ich, waren immer getäuscht worden; in trostloser Luftzusammensetzung, in einem patriarchalischen, tödlichen, von den perfiden Höhen und Tiefen seiner *Architekturnatur* hervorgerufenen menschenwidrigen Galvanismus . . . Wie viele unserer Talente hätten wir zu erstaunlicher Größe in uns entwickeln können, wären wir nicht in Tirol geboren worden und aufgewachsen.[63]

The German neologism "Architekturnatur" highlights the intimate connection between the "thought structures" introduced at the beginning of *Amras* and the failed edification at the end. A process of deception, more extensive than that in Bernhard's 1973 text "Plane/Plain," has kept the brothers incarcerated with no actual possibility of going up, down, and out of their confinement. The highs and lows of their "architectural nature" do not allow for the middle ground requisite for mystical communion, metamorphotic complementarity, or interdisciplinary poiesis and self-(re)generation.

Thus one might read *Amras* as the story of the unsuccessful individuation of a hermaphroditic creature, where Walter is the feminine, K. the masculine part, or as the failure to reach a utopian state via an incestuous relationship.[64] The short novel could also be interpreted as Bernhard's reckoning with the discourse of political rebirth and cultural continuity after 1945, or the stagnation of the brothers' educational journey in their inability to get beyond place names beginning with the letter "A" ("Amras," "Aldrans," "Ampaß").[65] Moreover, one might see the disintegrating of any *human*ist architecture based on new methods of cognition and perception in the architectural jumble I quoted. We could also see the text's ending as the abnegation of the strategies of two, when the novella segues from the oscillating doubles into a claustrophobic oneness. *Amras* concludes with another incarceration, K.'s complete withdrawal from society, and the termination of any *Bildung*. Although the remaining brother wants to continue his inquiries in the insane asylum, his is an entirely private vision of study. The architectonic constraints are presumably too great for any success. "My plan," K.'s final letter to his uncle states, alluding to the "shame" in the last line of Franz Kafka's *The Trial* (*Der Process*, 1925), "is not to abandon my studies, just to pursue them solely *within myself* in future . . . the conditions prevailing in our insane asylums [are] an *embarrassment* [*shameful*] to all of us" (*A* 60; "Mein Studium will ich nicht aufgeben, in Zukunft nur noch *in mir selbst* betreiben . . . herrschen in unseren Irrenhäusern uns alle *beschämende* Zustände," *Am* 179). I find these interpretations plausible; indeed, I have suggested some of them.

I would add one other possible reading. *Amras* reflects on what learning could achieve, when undertaken in the spirit of open-ended inquiry and interdisciplinary experimentation—precisely such failed individuation. If we read the text in this manner, the brother-pair is trapped in a world hostile to the synthesizing, synoptic views that they espouse, following Novalis, Musil, and the *Wunderkammer*. They literally move beyond disciplinary fragmentation, which an academia jealously guarding its demarcated terrain imposes on them, and transcend the floors and walls of the ivory tower. Indubitably, their efforts run counter to the process of becoming an individual through a particular course of *Bildung* that demands clear boundaries, but this may be just the goal. In Novalis's *Notes*, fragment 113 formulates a concept of individuation that is radically different from that of the society in which the brothers—and we—live: "The more diversely individualized something is—the more diverse its *contact* with other individuals—the more *variable its boundaries*—and *neighborhood*" ("Je mannichfacher Etwas individualisirt ist—desto mannichfacher ist *seine Berührung* mit andern Individuen—desto *veränderlicher seine Grenze*—und *Nachbarschaft*").[66] Becoming a diverse individual makes borders permeable and affirms "soft," negotiable differences over "hard," fixed ones; contiguity and overlap define this view of subjectivity. However, postwar society demands a fundamental separation of the brothers, from one another, other people and nature. It offers no hope of the kind of neighborly relationship envisioned in Novalis's fragment, where neighborliness leads to fluidity. Society demands a definitive cut with the curved knife that plays such a prominent role in the tower—Philippine Welser's fine Augsburg blade from the Ambras cabinet, to which Walter and K. are repeatedly drawn and at which Walter stares in horror and fascination. While the brothers' halting gait seems to make a mockery of the idea of intellectual progress, the anaphoric repetition of the letter "A" indicates the necessity of beginning over and over again, a rehearsal for the movement into and through hollow, porous, intermediary space.

Way Station 3

✦

The Schauraum and the Quick Read

Much ink has been expended resuscitating the early cabinet of curiosities as a proto-school of secular learning and institutionalized research.[1] Such cabinets of curiosities together with cabinets of art (*Kunstkammern*) come about in the sixteenth century and evince an interest in the far-flung places being discovered and explored. They evoke a sense of belonging to a marvelous earth that has suddenly become a much larger place but still is firmly within God's purview.

The cabinet of curiosities at Ambras Castle has something particularly spellbinding, luring visitors such as Michel de Montaigne and Johann Wolfgang von Goethe.[2] Since the early 1970s, this *Wunderkammer* is again situated in the tract of the Lower Castle that was originally devoted to it—its reinstallation marks a renewed fascination with this mode of display, juxtaposing unusual and grotesque objects in the service of activating the viewers' critical faculties. Visitors first approach through the garden to the Lower Castle. Then, the antechambers of armaments and armor lead to the cabinet proper, past Giovanni Batista Fontana's luminescent painted ceiling, which sets up the correspondence between man, myth, and nature. Eventually a plethora of vitrines with colored backgrounds appear, grouping objects according to a system of classification no longer apparent to the contemporary eye; portraits of excrescences of nature, exotica, *mirabilia*, *naturalia*, *artificialia* (monstrous and miraculous excrescences that defy any ascription to either art or nature); and, finally, busts of Julius Caesar, Caligula, Titus are artfully arranged in the Antiquarium.

The *Wunderkammer*, in turn, is a kind of antechamber or *Vor-Raum* to the High Castle of Ambras, now home to the Habsburg portrait gallery. As such, the cabinet of curiosities becomes a kind of pre-positioning, preparatory space, readying visitors for the collection of portraits by renowned painters ranging from Lucas Cranach the Elder to Hans Holbein the Younger. It serves a mediating function, as visitors move upward from the surrounding forest ("wild" nature) into the cultivated gardens ("tamed" nature) and then into the collection of man-made and natural objects—and upwards into a gallery space containing artistic products from the hand of man alone. This

Figure 13. The Antiquarium in Castle Ambras. Image © Kunsthistorisches Museum, Vienna.

distinction between artificial and natural, however, was highly permeable during the Renaissance, with natural objects that had been carved or edged in precious metals being counted among the artificial works.

In Ambras, eighteen wooden cases with backgrounds of various colors highlight both the relations among certain things as well as their differences from other items in neighboring displays. The formal properties of the materials such as gold, precious stones, wood, shells, corals, horn, and ivory were deemed so powerful, indeed magical, as to warrant their inclusion in precious handicrafts that allowed their essence to remain untouched—and so they suggest parallels to other, foreign things, which they only resemble in form (for instance, a coral is seen as a tree or a polished stone pattern as a landscape).[3] The art of display in these cabinets, as Gabriele Beßler has argued, is dependent on analogical thinking; because a cabinet reproduced the larger macrocosmic order on a smaller scale, it could be seen as mirroring a larger, perfect order of divine making.[4] In Ambras, views open through arches onto the eighty-five receding alcoves in the Antiquarium, lined largely with Renaissance copies of original works from classical antiquity (figure 13). The interconnected floor plan hints at an interrelated view of human history as well: the ideality of the past serves as a model, but also legitimates the present and its authorities.[5]

In the *Wunderkammer*, objects are brought together that would today be divided among various institutions (natural history, sculpture, rare books, etc.); some objects, such as the stuffed crocodile, blowfish, or antlers fused with wood would no longer be considered "worthy" of inclusion in a museum proper. The lack of hierarchy among natural and artificial objects is no longer possible with the emergence of the modern museum, in which the material and symbolic correspondences between objects in contiguous display cases are not self-evident anymore.[6] The *Wunderkammer*'s waning goes hand-in-hand with the increasing isolation of things once perceived as part of an interconnected cosmos. The exhibited objects and flowing spaces bear witness to the disenchantment of the world of learning with its increasing specialization and disciplinary fragmentation, which Bernhard once complains of as a cold "Wissenschaftswelt," or "world of science."[7]

As a "studiolo," the Ambraser cabinet of curiosities establishes a relation between knowledge acquisition and visual intake, between fluid floor plans and confined arenas.[8] Upon entering, we sense the underlying association between a penetrating gaze and an encompassing, if somewhat quirky knowledge acquired with the speed of a "quick read." This "quick read" was precisely the point: the princely ruler who viewed the systematized displays was supposed to synthesize the materials into a complex whole. In a moment of epiphanic, revelatory apperception, he makes inferences about the whole based on the part—thanks to the careful categorization and taxonomy of items. As Samuel Quiccheberg terms it in his *Inscriptiones vel tituli theatri amplissimi* (*Inscriptions or Titles of the Most Ample Theater*, 1565), the first treatise on the art of arranging such collections, the world, or better said the universe, engages in self-dramatization in this "Schauraum" or "space for looking."[9] For him, the cabinets are "sapientiae theatris," particular architectural forms facilitating a highly theatricalized viewing experience.[10] As "theaters of knowledge," the *Wunder-* and *Kunstkammern* serve as an encyclopedic compendium for the ruler who fashions himself a scholar: "It is recommended that these things be brought together here in the theater so that by their frequent viewing and handling one might quickly, easily, and confidently be able to acquire a unique knowledge and admirable understanding of things."[11] The sovereign, looking at his world-in-miniature, slips into the guise of a learned man and, with a roving gaze and caressing touch, he encompasses the entirety of human knowledge—all in the length of time needed to traverse the galleries and fondle some objects. Consequently, although the cabinet expresses the aristocrat's private interests, it attests to his self-transformative capacity in the service of the public. Indirectly hinting at the mnemotechnic arts that Quiccheberg's contemporary, Giulio Camillo, outlines in his *L'idea del teatro* (*Theater of Memory*), Thomas Brakensiek explains that the *Wunderkammer* becomes a way of outsourcing memory: all the correspondences between micro- and macrocosm no longer have to be located in the mind of one educated person.[12] What need for a mental cache, when the display cases function as such! Moreover, the *Kunst-* and *Wunderkammern*, in Quiccheberg's how-to manual on gathering, systematizing, and displaying, which was known to the Habsburgs, reconcile two competing imperatives: outward connection and inward concentration. On the one hand, the cabinet is linked to a whole system of workshops, studios, and exhibition spaces, suggesting the openness of the collection to the outside world and its pragmatic impulse. On the other hand, the cabinet is sequestered. Recognizing the need for inner focus, Quiccheberg refers to the proto-museum at times as a "conclavium"—a secure space that can be locked.[13]

In this manner, the *Wunderkammer* stages itself as a dramatic scene for an active, perambulating learner. This scenario is characteristic of Bernhard's later novels and plays with their separate spaces and enclosed subspaces, but with liberating views through apertures. In Bernhard's architectonic world, characters with an aristocratic sensibility for the "higher" things in life—above all *Bildung*—can emulate the nobility of a bygone era. They can become quick studies, capable of casting a penetrating gaze on many things at once, telescoping different epochs. They attempt to secure that knowledge in books written in a *refugium*.

Chapter 3

✦

The Museum and the Method in *Old Masters* (1985)

If we imagine *Amras* as forming the bottom stone of an archway, *Old Masters* may be its keystone.[1] In returning to the site of the museum, this time in its contemporary form, *Old Masters* revisits the original scenario from *Amras* to elucidate and refine the method of instruction and the process of observation. The Art History Museum is posited as a variation of Archduke Ferdinand II's cabinet of curiosities in *Amras*, an exhibition space for a collection of arms, armor, and paintings, as well as a panoply of exotic objects of unusual provenance and crafts attesting to profound manual skill.[2] The opening pages of *Amras* evoked, as we saw, a symbiotic, foundational, extensive, and synoptic learning that is at once embodied, momentary, penetrating, global, and haptic. The 1964 novella suggested an intellectual repatriation to paradise to which the cabinets of art and curiosities aspired: "The *Kunstkammer* became an analogue for the brain of humanity, which gradually reacquires the Edenic wisdom that has been extinguished."[3] The beginning of *Amras* also showed how the connection established between viewer and viewed radiates outward and perforates the walls of the tower, which can no longer be seen as a container that separates them from one another. However, as I have argued, the text charts the crumbling of the brothers' experiment in their counterspace, with their expulsion from the paradise-like garden and foray into "forbidden apple orchards."[4] As such, the disciplinary fragmentation they perceive and from which they suffer—where art and science are no longer reconcilable in any kind of romantic synthesis—is traceable to a kind of disintegration that sets in with the disciplinary divisions that make a cabinet of curiosities impossible as a coherent entity after the seventeenth century and hastens the rise of the specialized museum such as the Kunsthistorisches Museum.

In light of this background, *Old Masters* takes on the task of completion. The novel returns to the full-fledged modern museum to interrogate its potential as a site of learning. Has it continued the cabinet's academic function? Written near the end of Bernhard's life, this novel enriches his propaedeutic project through a triadic structure between a teacher, pupil, and work of art. A full-fledged method of teaching and learning comes into being. The museum carries on some of its predecessors' goals, but attempts an uneasy reconciliation. It encourages an extensive as well as a synoptic method; it prizes concentration and only occasionally completeness; it mixes emplacement with free-floating positioning, exactness with association; finally, it tries to valorize the "quick read" of the *Wunderkammer* over the comprehensive reading of modern academic study. In the 1980s, during an unprecedented boom in museum construction, with the increasing polemics against the museum's "white cube" function[5] and the birth of a discipline that comes to be known as museum studies,[6] Bernhard reflects on the importance of the museum's historic relation to learning and tutelage. In the twenty-first century, we may have moved beyond exhaustive reading, and our ever-connected Internet gaze permanently scans and roves through self-enfolding, topological spaces. In light of this change, we actually find in *Old Masters* an anticipation of our current state—which is simultaneously a return to an earlier kind of seeing and learning.

The Kunsthistorisches Museum

The novel's 82-year-old protagonist Reger expounds his theories on how to approach art seated on the cushioned bench of the Bordone Room in the Kunsthistorisches Museum. Contemplating Tintoretto's *Portrait of a White-Bearded Man* every second day for the last thirty-six years, he develops a theory of art appreciation in the presence of his students: his wife (recently deceased when the novel begins), Atzbacher (the meticulous scribe who records Reger's ideas), and Irrsigler (the provincial museum guard who parrots Reger's thoughts).[7] At the outset, a single statement does away with any aspirations to encyclopedic knowledge. Seated, Reger expounds on his theory of reading to Atzbacher:

> It is not necessary to read all of Goethe or all of Kant, it is not necessary to read all of Schopenhauer; a few pages of *Werther*, a few pages of *Elective Affinities* and we know more in the end about the two books than if we had read them from beginning to end, which would anyway deprive us of the purest enjoyment. But such drastic self-restraint requires so much courage and such strength of mind as can only rarely be mustered and as we ourselves muster only rarely; the reading person, just as the carnivorous, is gluttonous in the most revolting manner and, like the carnivorous person, upsets his stomach and his entire health, his head and his whole intellectual existence. (*OM* 18)

> Es ist nicht notwendig, den ganzen Goethe zu lesen, den ganzen Kant, auch nicht notwendig, den ganzen Schopenhauer; ein paar Seiten

> Werther, ein paar Seiten Wahlverwandschaften und wir wissen am Ende mehr über die beiden Bücher, als wenn wir sie von Anfang zum Ende gelesen hätten, was uns in jedem Fall um das reinste Vergnügen bringt. Aber zu dieser drastischen Selbstbeschränkung gehört so viel Mut und so viel Geisteskraft, daß sie nur sehr selten aufgebracht werden kann und daß wir selbst sie nur selten aufbringen; der lesende Mensch ist wie der fleischfressende auf die widerwärtigste Weise gefräßig und verdirbt sich wie der fleischfressende den Magen und die gesamte Gesundheit, den Kopf und die ganze geistige Existenz. (*AM* 27)

With great rhetorical flourish, the elderly music critic explains the pitfalls of what he considers academic thoroughness. Better to carefully read a few pages of Goethe's *Werther* or *Elective Affinities*, in his view, than to have worked one's way through the entire novel in haste. Reger boasts that he is a "highly talented page turner,"[8] who has mastered the art of penetrating a work by reading only a few lines with the greatest intensity. A revealing landscape metaphor enters Reger's description of his method, which returns us to the sites of learning and their importance in inducing a state of receptivity and openness:

> It is better to read twelve lines of a book with the utmost intensity and thus to penetrate into them to the full, as one might say, rather than read the whole book *as the normal reader does*, who in the end knows the book he has read no more than an air passenger knows the landscape he overflies. He does not even perceive the contours. Thus all people nowadays read everything by flying over, they read everything and know nothing. (*OM* 17–18)

> Es ist besser, zwölf Zeilen eines Buches mit höchster Intensität zu lesen und also zur Gänze zu durchdringen, wie gesagt werden kann, als wir lesen das ganze Buch *wie der normale Leser*, der am Ende das von ihm gelesene Buch genauso wenig kennt, wie ein Flugreisender die Landschaft, die er überfliegt. Er nimmt ja nicht einmal die Konturen wahr. So lesen heute die Leute alle alles im Flug, sie lesen alles und kennen nichts. (*AM* 26–27)

To penetrate a book (in the verb "durchdringen") means entering it in the way in which a tunneler digs into a mountainside and not the way in which an airplane traveler skims over the earth's surface, barely noticing the broad outlines.[9] Once again, the space below serves as an important counterpoint to the supposed heights of education. The point of impact and its intensity are important, not the amount covered with high speed and from a great distance.[10] Delving into a particular text slows progress in a way useful for thought. Reger stresses the concentration with which he reads and lessens the outlandishness of what seems to be a preposterous assertion. Twice he refers to how "gründlich," or "thorough" he is. In German, this exhaustive and thorough technique has a foundational function, as the references to "grounds" and "grounding" make clear. As Reger explains to Atzbacher, firming up the environmental metaphors with which he began:

> I enter into a book and settle in it, neck and crop, you should realize, in one or two pages of a philosophical essay as if I were entering a landscape, a piece of nature, a state organism, a detail of the earth, if you like, in order to penetrate into it entirely and not just with half my strength or half-heartedly, in order to explore it and then, having explored it with all the thoroughness at my disposal, drawing conclusions as to the whole. (*OM* 18)

> Ich betrete ein Buch und lasse mich darauf nieder, mit Haut und Haaren, müssen Sie denken, auf ein oder zwei Seiten einer philosophischen Arbeit, als wäre ich dabei eine Landschaft zu betreten, eine Natur, ein Staatsgebilde, ein Erddetail, wenn Sie wollen, um ganz und nicht nur mit halber Kraft und halbem Herzen, in dieses Erddetail einzudringen, es zu erforschen und um dann, ist es erforscht mit aller mir zur Verfügung stehenden Gründlichkeit, auf das Ganze zu schließen. (*AM* 27)

Such a reading technique lays claim; it involves a haptic element; it burrows into the details; it stakes out the perimeter to then assay a foundation; it allows the part to mediate the whole. It envisages the text as a landscape or formation ("Gebilde") that the human must enter with his intellectual, emotional, and sensual being. It privileges the fragment to establish a relation to the totality.

Reger's efforts at edification take place, as I mentioned, in Vienna's Kunsthistorisches Museum, built from 1871 to 1891 as part of the Ringstrassen development in the capital's center. In the Ringstrassen project, the ascendant liberal bourgeoisie constructed its important buildings—the parliament, city hall, university, and theater. As Carl Schorske explains in his unsurpassed description of the development of the ring that surrounds the inner imperial district and separates it from the suburbs, the upwardly striving middle class projected its values of constitutional government and high culture onto the buildings constructed around this boulevard. With its values expressed in stone and mortar, this class sought to counterbalance the dynastic neo-absolutism of the Habsburgs. The cultural buildings were to lift the "novi homines from their lowly origins" to a higher status.[11] In the architectural language Schorske uses to express this desire for cultural edification, one can discern the semantic history and social thrust behind Bernhard's architectonic undertaking, and his twentieth-century attraction to the idea of a middle ground or mezzanine:

> If entry into the old aristocracy of the genealogical table was difficult, the aristocracy of the spirit was theoretically open to everyone through the new cultural institutions. They helped forge the link with the older culture and the imperial tradition, to strengthen that "second society," sometimes called the "mezzanine," where the bourgeois on the way up met the aristocrats willing to accommodate to new forms of social and economic power, a new mezzanine where victory and defeat were transmuted into social compromise and cultural synthesis. (Schorske, *Fin-de-siècle Vienna*, 45)

The Art History Museum design was fraught with competition from the outset. It required a twenty-year balancing act to reconcile the demands for a prestigious building suited to separately housing large collections of naturalia and art with the various social and imperial exigencies. In the Neo-Renaissance building Gottfried Semper and Karl Freiherr von Hasenauer conceived, Reger prepares his students from all social classes for a state of receptivity. In this remarkable setting, with its faultless climate control, regulated lighting, and geometric arrangement, they learn to be receptive to beauty and mindful of taste. The perfect conditions for thought are not given elsewhere other than in the Art History Museum,[12] true to its origins in the *Kunst-* and *Wunderkammer*. The floor plan, lighting, and temperature provide the ideal coordinates for readerly intensity and extensiveness; the rooms in tandem with the artworks create an ideal space, both secluded and perforated, public and private.[13] In the novel's opening pages, much is made of the velvet-covered benches and their tasteful refurbishment, reminding readers that the immediate surroundings can be beneficial for thought.[14] The permeability of the room itself, with its four entryways and numerous standpoints for hidden observation, breaks open the seemingly constricting walls of the gallery. This porousness disqualifies the museum guard Irrsigler's comparison of the museum with a prison (*OM* 5; *AM* 9). From one of the doorways in the adjacent room, Atzbacher records his views of Reger, intermingling these observations and second-order observations with his own recollections.

The novel's unrelenting concentration on the minutiae of the spatial experience of the Bordone Room already shows that Reger emphasizes something other than the subject matter to be imparted. Instead, he attempts to teach an appreciation of art, which takes leave of disinterested contemplation while focusing on beauty. He resuscitates the dilettantish appreciation of art that has been so thoroughly discredited with the rise of academic study and schools his disciples in their mistrust of disciplinary divisions, artists, and institutions that collude with state power.[15] There are, in his view, two ways to look at art and its beauty. His thoughts leap back and forth between them, often passing from one to the other without clear transition.[16] In what follows, I attempt to disentangle the two strands of Reger's thought to show the internal coherence of what can only be termed a propaedeutics—a preparatory course of study and an initiation into the cultural sphere.

A Double Approach: Dilettantes and Men of Taste

In the first instance, there is the method of varied enjoyment. The appreciation of different artworks from an assortment of genres is most likely to bring about those effects the critic Elaine Scarry attributes to beauty in her book *On Beauty and Being Just* (1999). She contends that seeing one beautiful thing leads the beholder to extend care towards other things of the same type.[17] In other words, beauty is a force that impels us to distribute our concern—it furthers a kind of lateral regard with an ethical thrust.[18] It can be compared to the horizontal distribution of interest Raimund Abraham evoked in his essay on *Elementary Architecture* (Way Station 2). Scarry offers the example of a beautiful and fragile vase that garners our attention; it compels us to extend our concern to the general category of vases, all of which are fragile. For Reger, too, our experience of the beautiful in art engenders a care that moves beyond any particular instantiation of beauty. Simultaneously, it leads to a leveling of disciplinary boundaries. Listening to music, we are amenable to the visual beauty of paintings, and thoughts about paintings give rise to insights about music. Music criticism, Reger explicitly states, is impossible without an understanding of fine art and vice versa (*OM* 16; *AM* 24). He even tells Atzbacher that the cross-fertilization between his experience of fine art and music is what enables him to write masterful music reviews for the London *Times*.

This first approach, then, would be that of the dilettante, in the word's original sense. The dilettante is a "lover of the fine arts [. . .] who cultivates them for the love of them rather than professionally."[19] He ranges across the arts, alighting briefly on moments of beauty, continuing on to the next blue flower of poetry or visual masterpiece, all the while filled with a sense of love for that which makes such movement possible.[20] This dilettantism should be understood as a historical successor to that practiced by eighteenth-century English aristocrats, whose Society of Dilettanti (founded 1732) was meant to further an unprofessional mode of artistic enjoyment and edification. Reger's Anglophilia[21]—ranging from his employment with a prestigious London newspaper to his preference for Scottish tweed, and his praise of the novel's Welsh gentleman—gestures towards the ideal of the gentleman amateur. In Reger's view, the art lover who ranges freely can experience profoundly and without endangering himself. The avowed expert or specialist (who can also be an artist) is anathema to the true dilettante and is showered with the scornful, negative epithet of "dilettante" in the conventional, pejorative sense.[22] The so-called expert is actually the contemptible "dilettante," who must guard his careless, loveless approach to art like a dirty secret.

When the true dilettante speaks of his engagement with art, he sounds a sensual register. Reger's kind of dilettantism resuscitates the eroticism we saw in the brothers' approach in *Amras*: sensuous, non-professional, unacademic enjoyment can be found in this aspect of Reger's concept. Reger introduces both a sense of platonic love and physical involvement when speaking of his own dilettantish experience to his acolyte. This is the erotic approach of the earlier quotation, where Reger talks of complete physical contact and haptic exploration. Making love to beauty culminates in the "penetration" ("eindringen") of the text, an epiphanic moment when the soma melds with the psyche in the full force of the unguarded heart. No inexorable duality exists between nature and culture in the dilettante's love—the philosophical work is read as a landscape; the landscape as nature; nature as state formation. Reger's hermeneutic is certainly indebted to the idea of a totality: there is a correspondence, which love establishes, between the part and the whole.

Central to this method that moves slowly along surfaces, sometimes penetrating to another underlying meaning or aesthetic layer, is the synoptic look of the individual moving through the cabinet of curiosities (chapter 2). Contemplating Tintoretto's work, Reger moves from the immediate visual encounter to his own life experience. The telescoping moments from the early novels recur in *Alte Meister*, but a new name is given to the dilettante's constellations of past and present: the "Durchblick." This "looking through" is the X ray vision with which beholders of the beautiful find themselves endowed, but also the colloquial "savvy" to which German-speakers refer when they use the term "Durchblick."[23] The director of the Art History Museum in Vienna from 1973 to 1981, Friderike Klauner, lauds the loving approach of the dilettante or, better said, the amateur. In her view, the etymological resonances of "amor" should be strongly emphasized in the amateur's approach. Bernhard, who was familiar with her book *The Portrait Gallery of the Art History Museum in Vienna* (*Die Gemäldegalerie des Kunsthistorischen Museums in Wien*, 1978), mentions her as Reger's acquaintance in the opening pages of the novel and allusively incorporates her reflections on this kind of "Kunstliebhaberei" (*OM* 9; *AM* 16). Bernhard underlines certain passages in his copy of *Die Gemäldegalerie*, and he must have come across the following statement in the preface:

> But since a work of art can never be known in its innermost essence, different possibilities of cognition remain. [. . .] Art, however, is not only for art scholars, but also for art lovers. The love for art likes to develop—as, incidentally, is the case for all other things—exactly there where knowledge dissolves into prescience. And one needs patience and time to reach this border where the personal involvement with the work of art first begins.

> Da es aber so ist, daß ein Kunstwerk niemals bis ins Innerste erkannt werden kann, bleiben verschiedene Möglichkeiten der Erkenntnis. [. . .] Kunst ist aber nicht nur für den Kunstwissenschaftler da, sondern für alle ihre Liebhaber. Die Liebe zur Kunst—wie übrigens zu allem anderen auch—entsteht gerne gerade da, wo sich Wissen in Ahnung auflöst. Und es braucht Geduld und Zeit, um bis zu diesem Grenzpunkt, an dem erst die persönliche Auseinandersetzung mit dem Kunstwerk beginnt, zu gelangen.[24]

Klauner's concern lies not with the specialist perusing the work of art, but with the recipient in the widest sense. She (like Reger!) recommends slowness and patience in the approach to the artwork, in order to reach the border or threshold ("Grenzpunkt") where the dilettante's appreciation gives rise to something more than "mere" academic interpretation—to an intimation ("Ahnung") of other things.

The student Atzbacher has learned this amatory approach from his teacher. He claims to love the flashes of insight that occur during their museum discussions for the synthesizing view they present. When we, across from a beautiful object, reflect on our own past, Atzbacher suggests, an interest in our fellow man comes into being. Personal connections are created that transcend religious and class lines:

> I always love these perspectives into my long-past childhood and I surrender to them totally and I exploit them in whatever way I can, may this perspective of my childhood never end, I always reflect. What kind of childhood did Reger have? I reflected, I do not know much about it, Reger is not communicative about his childhood. And Irrsigler? (*OM* 21)

> Diese Durchblicke in die längst vergangene Kindheit liebe ich immer und ich gebe mich ganz und gar hin und ich nutze sie aus, wie ich nur kann, möge dieser Blick in die Kindheit nie aufhören, denke ich immer. Was hat Reger für eine Kindheit gehabt?, dachte ich, ich weiß nicht viel darüber, die Kindheit betreffend, ist Reger nicht gesprächig. Und Irrsigler? (*AM* 31)

Atzbacher moves from his individual history to that of Reger, the Viennese Jew presumably persecuted under National Socialism (we are led to believe his Anglophilia is related to the experience of exile),[25] and of Irrsigler, the blue-collar guard socially stigmatized because of his provenance from the provincial state of Burgenland. Atzbacher's comment about Reger's and Irrsigler's past intimates a further benefit of dilettantish contemplation: we never feel we know enough about the other person and desire to learn more about the other's commonality with ourselves. Although Atzbacher knows quite a lot about the other characters' personal histories, he wants to know more. As aesthetic reflection—understood as the reflection of and on beautiful art, before the eighteenth-century distinction between the beautiful and the sublime—engenders self-reflection, it gives rise to the "experience of virtual community."[26] This experience of community in difference lets the lover of art "feel at home in the world," without threatening him with dissolution or extinction, preserving what Elaine Scarry describes as his "irreducible solitude."[27]

However, the dilettante cannot always keep his love of the beautiful in check. When it overflows, it ruins the barriers between self and other. Scarry shows that this happens when we endow a beautiful thing with a sense of life and are ourselves in turn endowed with a "surfeit of aliveness."[28] Reger's erotic approach to art threatens to tilt into its obverse, violating the beautiful and its complement, the useful. Reger warns Atzbacher about the perils for the beautiful and the useful when a dilettante surpasses the limits of his usual enthusiasm and penetration:

> Beware of penetrating into a work of art, he said, you will ruin each and every one for yourself, even those you love most. Do not look at a picture for too long, do not read a book too intently, do not listen to a piece of music with the greatest intensity. You will ruin everything for yourself, and thus the most beautiful and the most useful things in the world. (*OM* 32)

> Hüten Sie sich vor dem Eindringen in Kunstwerke, sagte er, Sie verderben sich alles und jedes, selbst das Geliebteste. Schauen Sie ein Bild nicht lang an, lesen Sie ein Buch nicht zu eindringlich, hören Sie ein Musikstück nicht mit der größten Intensität, Sie ruinieren sich alles und damit das Schönste und das Nützlichste auf der Welt. (*AM* 44)

In this passage, temporal, analytical, and sensory intensity is inimical to the experience of beauty that Reger has encouraged. For intrepid art lovers, however, it is impossible to resist being drawn toward the danger to which beauty beckons. Eroticism threatens to become violation, a point to which Reger returns at the end of the novel, when he stresses how his use of art constitutes a "Mißbrauch"—a word connoting sexual abuse.[29]

When this point of overbearing closeness is reached, all is not lost, Reger's warnings and caveats notwithstanding: a different kind of appreciation begins. The critical acumen of the recipient, who has subjected the artwork to more than distracted-contemplative perusal, comes into play. The viewer now casts a critical, rather than an amatory eye on the object before him, freeing it from the accretions of tradition. He realizes that beauty does not allow for standstill and self-satisfied rest. No particular example of beauty can be made into a parameter for all time (the dilettante perhaps feels this, too, when he shifts his attention from object to object). Admiration relegates the beautiful object to a timeless void—to Foucault's heterotopian space of the museum[30]—when the beholder is blind to its particular, unavoidably momentary and fleeting beauty. For this reason, beautiful artworks must be continually submitted to a testing process. This is especially true for those contained within a museum, which endows them with an aura of ahistoricism and timelessness through the very act of inclusion. Reger elucidates the point while castigating the Austrian writer Adalbert Stifter (1805–1868) for his deficiencies: "Altogether we should never say this or that person is the thing, and will then remain the thing for all time, we should again and again put all artists to the test, because we keep developing our art scholarship and our artistic taste, that is unquestionable" (*OM* 39; "Wir dürfen überhaupt nicht sagen, dieser oder jener ist es und ist es dann für alle Zeit, wir müssen alle Künstler immer wieder auf die Probe stellen, denn wir entwickeln ja unsere Kunstwissenschaft und unseren Kunstgeschmack, das ist außer Zweifel," *AM* 52–53). The implications of this investigative process for a canon meant to constitute the beautiful (and useful) are clear. A fixed canon cannot withstand sustained, repeated probing.

"Kunstwissenschaft" and "Kunstgeschmack": Reger conflates, in his second approach, science and taste, aesthetics and art, the judgment of the beautiful according to intersubjective and subjective criteria. The purposeful melding of these categories is the second avenue along which Reger's pedagogy advances, when it cannot teach the appreciation befitting the dilettante. There is a specific reason why the concept of taste is inseparable from that of beauty in the age of aesthetics for Reger. Taste, the fickle faculty we have inherited from the eighteenth century, serves a mediating function between individual perception and more general truth claims. It calls into existence a second kind of "virtual community." In a discussion relevant to Reger's second approach, Michel Chaouli convincingly explains the relationship between taste and beauty:

> In its structure taste replicates precisely the philosophical gymnastics that the aesthetic subject is required to perform, namely reconciling and unifying the manifold particularity of experience with a standard assumed to be universal. Taste is intensely subjective, particular, and fused with bodily sensation, yet at the same time it makes claims to intersubjective validity, which is to say that it is socially motivated and abstract. The site at which the subjective and intersubjective claims of taste are yoked together with the greatest force is called beauty.[31]

Taste functions, then, as the hinge that connects the personal experience of beautiful art with that of a larger group. In discussions of the beautiful, taste serves as the ground on which the unique experience of the individual can be reconciled with the necessarily different experiences of other individuals.

It enables one person to break through to many people and offers a solution out of the solipsism sometimes ascribed to experiences of beauty.[32] For this reason taste enters on a literal and abstract level in the novel. Reger's multiple allusions to ingestion and digestion in the course of his perorations on art perform the reconciliation Chaouli ascribes to taste, when it progresses from the particularity of bodily experience to a universally assumed standard. Reger moves from an experience—such as the "indigestion" or "nausea" caused by certain readings of Heidegger—to generalizations such as "Heidegger is not a good philosopher."[33] However, his sweeping statements are always mindful of the historical moment: the general becomes linked to fashion, to the changing of styles over time. Heidegger isn't any good, in Reger's view, because the late 1980s obsession with nature led to an indiscriminate fusing of the philosopher and the flirtation with environmental issues.[34]

Reger couples the two seemingly irreconcilable quantities of taste and science in the spirit of intersubjective mediation. In doing so and in going beyond the aesthetic experience of the art lover, Reger develops the counterpart to—and the extension of—the dilettante: the man of taste. While the experience of beauty deeply affects this type of individual as well, the difference lies in the judgment that his taste will pronounce. The man of taste's judgment is of a decidedly moral nature. Reger's resuscitation of the *homme de goût*, who, as Giorgio Agamben shows in *The Man without Content* (*L'uomo senza contenuto*, 1970), comes into being concomitantly with the birth of aesthetics, understood as the philosophical discipline devoted to the experience of art. As Agamben explains, the man of taste is an early variant of today's professional art critic. His "sixth sense" enables the *homme de goût* to "grasp the *point de perfection* that is characteristic of every work of art."[35] Paradoxically, the ever more refined and rarefied sensibility of the man of taste increases, rather than decreases, the distance from the creative artist and the artwork itself. The French writer Jean de la Bruyère sums up this quandary in the following aphorism: "The pleasure of criticism robs us of being vividly touched by very beautiful things."[36] Beauty no longer profoundly affects the man of taste and does not transform him in mind and body—his critical consciousness lends him immunity against such experiences.[37]

When the beautiful no longer touches us, the good is also abrogated, as Agamben and Scarry both imply; this is the professional critic's miserable fate in the modern world. In the course of the nineteenth century, the man of taste gradually departs from the moral values that have accompanied his aesthetic judgment without perceiving this as liberating. Instead, he feels that his stance vis-à-vis the artwork has become uncanny. Validating himself through his taste, he is dependent on art. However, he is incapable of producing any art of his own. Moreover, he cannot discover in art a distinct truth that is in touch with his life and worldview.[38]

While Agamben does not dwell on the *homme de goût*, concerned as he is primarily with the artist's experience, his brief account does suggest certain things pertinent to my discussion. The man of taste, before he has passed beyond the morality inherent to aesthetic judgment, can presumably locate certain *points de perfection* in art that have a deeply moving and moral effect on the recipient. His ability to judge on these matters pertaining to beauty provides him with a privileged status. His taste is capable of reconciling the individual and the general, the subjective and the intersubjective via the beautiful. He is essentially a teacher, instilling a sense of the good life by way of the beauty in art.[39]

Let us return to the protagonist's second approach. The first one, as Reger has warned Atzbacher, does not always succeed. We cannot always love art as the dilettante does. At times the experience of beauty is overpowering. It threatens with its opposite, namely the destruction or dissolution of the beautiful. When we repeatedly subject a beautiful object to our gaze and ourselves to the experience of this seemingly animate beauty, we "ruin everything [. . .] and thus the most beautiful and the most useful things in the world." At such times, the beautiful object loses the "newly acquired, wretched immunity" it has come to possess in the course of the last centuries,[40] and a secular variant of the divine terror of aesthetic experience in ancient Greece makes itself felt. Reger's emotive outpourings, I would argue, arise from this source: his penchant to be touched to the quick exemplifies this salutary terror. If we cannot love art as the dilettante, then, we must love it as the man of taste—a new man of taste, that is, conceived of as a "creative critical artist," for whom the experience of ruination is beneficial: we "ruin everything" as a precondition of another kind of engagement with art.

Overcoming the perceived antinomy of critic and creator, between secondary and primary activities, between today's "wretched immunity" and yesterday's "divine terror," Reger thinks of criticism as a fundamentally artistic endeavor, which the italics in the text forcefully emphasize. Reger's boastful self-validation becomes comprehensible in light of this prototype he establishes:

> But of course I did not wish, nor was I able, to be a creative or even a performing artist, at least not a creative or performing musical artist, but only a critical one. *I am a critical artist*, he said, I have been a critical artist all my life. [. . .] I certainly regard myself as an artist, that is a critical artist, and as a critical artist I am of course also creative, that is obvious, hence a *performing and creative critical artist*, he said. [. . .] *I am a painter and a musician and a writer all in one.*
>
> Aber ich wollte und ich konnte natürlich nicht schöpferischer, aber auch nicht ausübender Künstler sein, sagte er, jedenfalls kein schöpferischer oder ausübender Musikkünstler, sondern nur ein *kritischer. Ich bin ein kritischer Künstler*, sagte er, ich bin zeitlebens ein kritischer Künstler gewesen. [. . .] Ich empfinde mich ja durchaus als

> Künstler, eben als kritischer Künstler und als kritischer Künstler bin ich naturgemäß auch ein schöpferischer, das ist klar, also *ausübender und schöpferischer kritischer Künstler*, sagte er. [. . .] *ich bin Maler und Musiker und Schriftsteller in einem.*

The art of criticism—which an education can call into being only if it is not primarily concerned with the transmission of information—represents the possible sublation of all sister arts in a higher one. "It is possible," Reger states, "that the critical artist is the one who practices his own art in all the arts" (*OM* 52; "Möglicherweise, sagte er, ist der kritische Künstler der, der in allen Künsten seine einzige betreibt," *AM* 67–68). The romantic potentiation of creativity and criticism advances the interdisciplinarity already present within dilettantism.[41]

The creative critical artist is drawn by a different kind of taste: he does not seek the mark of perfection in beauty, as Agamben's *homme de qualité* does, but rather the point of imperfection. Reger calls this the "grave flaw," or "gravierende Fehler."[42] The technique of singling out the grave flaw is an author-centered method that relies heavily on the concept of mimesis. For Reger, a flaw in beauty is a technical shortcoming, an artist's failure to represent life according to the dictates of proportion and measure we have inherited from antiquity via the Renaissance in painting or according to the standards of nineteenth-century realist fiction with its proliferation of lifelike effects through a superabundance of detail. These technical faults marring the work's beauty are not selected to discredit the artist's training, skill, or genius, but his moral failure. This is a remarkable (and counterintuitive) way of approaching the Habsburg collection in the Kunsthistorisches Musuem, which art historians tend to characterize as interested in "consummate perfection" rather than "ungainly development."[43] Because El Greco cannot paint a hand properly, that is, in an absolutely realistic manner,[44] Reger considers him morally lacking. And, as we know, for Reger a man's morality manifests itself in his taste. The artist himself has a deficient taste—as opposed to Reger's *homme de goût*. Reger explicitly yokes artistic taste and the artist's morality, denigrating his character on the basis of the grave flaw. In his words: "The painters altogether did not have a good character, in fact they always had a very bad character and therefore, basically, also always had very bad taste (*OM* 31; "Die Maler insgesamt haben keinen guten, sie haben sogar einen sehr schlechten Charakter, und deshalb im Grunde auch immer einen sehr schlechten Geschmack gehabt," *AM* 43).

To understand this seemingly absurd approach and the disparagement of renowned artists on questionable grounds, we could emphasize the personal history of the protagonist. The novel implies that Reger is a Viennese Jew driven into exile under the Nazis. As such, Reger would necessarily be wary of any collusion between artists and the powers that be. Seen from this perspective, those who work for oppressive regimes without criticism deserve to be unmasked for their opportunism and ideological obfuscation. For Reger, the National Socialist instrumentalization of art and beauty casts its sickly pall backwards through time, and all past methods of artistic patronage and systems of governance are discredited. This view turns artists before Nazism into corrupt and perfidious state ideologues. Atzbacher's statement, an indirect quotation of Reger, makes sense when seen against this backdrop: "Reger talks only of *state art* when he talks about art, *and when he talks about the so-called old masters he always only talks about the state old masters*" (*OM* 28; "Reger redet nur von *Staatskunst*, wenn er über die Kunst redet, *und wenn er über die sogenannten Alten Meister redet, redet er immer nur über die alten Staatsmeister*," *AM* 40). However, in this reading, Reger's method is sensible only in light of a personal history marked by catastrophe. Such an interpretation, for all its merits, disqualifies Reger's technique as illogical within logical biographical coordinates, or as logical only within an illogical brain. How could Reger attack mimetic flaws in general when the mimesis of power per se is the problem? The naturalness of El Greco's painted hands can hardly be the issue if it is the aura of naturalness with which El Greco endows power relations that is questionable.

Upon further reflection, the focus on the flawed detail also seems to cancel out Reger's entire pedagogy: it gives up on the mediating function of taste in the public sphere. As the elderly critic liberally breaks open the continuity of tradition, he privileges the fragment over the totality to which it belongs and remains true to the etymological meaning of "fragment" from the Latin *frangere*.[45] By disparaging the canon—around which a general discourse forms—in its entirety, Reger's second method would relinquish any claims to a wider significance. The subjective element of taste extinguishes any concern with the intersubjective dimension.

Yet this is not the case, since the grave flaw is not solely an indicator of technical imperfection, moral dissolution, or bad taste. It is, above all, the marker of a common humanity, connecting the artist and the creative critical artist. The flaw is the single most important reminder that another equally fragile human being produced the beautiful thing before us, perhaps under circumstances as painful and disharmonious as those in which we might find ourselves—like Reger, who is mourning his wife's passing. Realizing the artist's own helplessness vis-à-vis the totality of life he may be trying to represent, the new man of taste feels tied to the surrounding world. Experiencing the flaw in beauty, he recognizes the fallibility of every human endeavor.[46] Only the perusal of man-made artifacts of exceptional beauty can elicit this comforting sense of an intrinsically human imperfection. If the humanities go beyond the encouragement of the dilettante—who spreads his love and concern equitably between beautiful things and their relations—their task lies in embracing their own helplessness towards the world and life: "We only love philosophy and the humanities generally because they are absolutely helpless" (*OM* 19; "Wir lieben die Philosophie und die ganze Geisteswissenschaft insgesamt ja nur, weil sie absolut hilflos ist," *AM* 29). Our own frailty, paradoxically and disconcertingly enough, finds refuge in that of the humanities.

As such, the architecture in which Reger situates his pedagogical project befits his interest in the fragment and in fragility.[47] The museum building was meant, in Gottfried Semper's design, to be part of an imperial forum. Not only was it to mirror the Natural History Museum across the way, it was also to be symmetrically positioned along an axis connecting the imperial stables (today the Museumsquartier) with the imperial palace via the Heldenplatz. It had the goal of cutting through the Ringstrasse and opening the insular first district to the suburbs without the former fortifications.[48] Only the museum portion of Semper and Hasenauer's actual plan was completed, perhaps a sign of the fraught relationship between the two architects or the increasing weakness of the imperial sponsors.[49] As a remnant of an abrogated design, the Art History Museum acts like something of a fragment itself, a remainder of monumental plans that the vicissitudes of history cut short—a sign that even the greatest civic and imperial efforts of high culture are utterly delicate.

Mimesis and the Man without Content

Mimesis is given pride of place in Reger's pedagogy for a specific reason. For him, it is not the "ideologically suspect recirculation of the ready-made, a false belief in the fixity of meaning and the possibility of achieving full presence," as it would be for some post-structuralist theorists with whom Reger has been compared.[50] Rather, mimesis allows one person's distinctiveness from all others to emerge in representation. After all, the main feature of mimetic portraiture lies in its ability to depict the absolute particularity of any human being. Mimesis confers a sense of aliveness on an object in addition to that which beauty itself engenders. When we look at a portrait by a Venetian master, for example, time is transcended, as the individual from the past seems to live on in the present. Implicit in Reger's argument, then, is the idea that mimesis can also achieve the "looking through" of the dilettantish approach. Mimetic art suggests an affinity across time that does not become reified into a subject/object dichotomy. The location in which the looking-through of mimesis occurs is doubly important: the museum is, when used as a site of intimate dialogue, a variant of the perforated space from *Amras*. As an open site of learning, it permits the synoptic, synthesizing views discussed previously.

With this effect of aliveness in mind, namely the mimesis of life,[51] I turn to the painting that is central to Reger's project: Tintoretto's *The White-Bearded Man* (ca. 1570, figure 14). As a nonconformist and maverick in Venetian society, Jacopo Robusti or Tintoretto (1518–1594)—who associates himself with the tradition of the artisan-painter rather than the new individual artist-genius Giorgio Vasari champions in the sixteenth century—becomes

Figure 14. Tintoretto (Jacopo Robusti), *The White-Bearded Man.* Ca. 1570. © Kunsthistorisches Museum, Vienna.

an ally in Reger's anti-institutional, anti-establishment pedagogy. Tintoretto's decidedly democratic thrust, which is "seen as serving the visual appetites of the general populace,"[52] also connects the painter with Reger in his battle against the professional critic's orthodox relationship to high culture or the twentieth-century *homme de goût*'s suprasensibility to it.

Tintoretto's late Renaissance work presents an aged gentleman, dressed simply in black, who looks at the viewer. The portrait is an artistic milestone for Reger because it has long resisted his ability to find its grave flaw. This is a puzzling assertion, when we consider that the head in three-quarter profile is not drawn entirely correctly, that is, according to the rules of central perspective.[53] Furthermore, this painting is not one of the most renowned Tintoretto paintings in the Art History Museum, at least prior to the publication of Bernhard's novel (nowadays polite guards, when asked for the Bordone Room, knowingly smile: "You are looking for *the* portrait?").[54]

In their afterword to the critical edition of *Old Masters*, Wendelin Schmidt-Dengler and Martin Huber suggest that Bernhard chose this portrait because of his personal acquaintaince with the then director of the Art History Museum, Friderike Klauner. Her description of Tintoretto's *The White Bearded Man* in *The Portrait Gallery of the Art History Museum Vienna* highlights Tintoretto's formal innovation (which Bernhard marked in the book with a pen). Klauner comments on Tintoretto's willingness to dissolve the beautiful form and to let a "frightening darkness" break into the recipient's perusal. This darkness does not satisfy aesthetic contemplation, but engenders strong emotions and a visceral response.[55] Bernhard may perhaps also have been familiar with her views on the presentation of such singular works of art (divorced from the artist and patron's intentions) within the context of the museum and the artwork's role in *Bildung*, which she presented in 1983, making her voice on Tintoretto particularly important to him.[56]

There are, I would like to speculate, a number of other reasons why this specific painting plays such a seminal role. First, the aged critic identifies with the Tintoretto portrait.[57] Reger is, and always has been, in a precarious state. His frailty after his wife's death and his crumbling position as unsurpassed teacher, indicated subtly by Atzbacher's obstreperousness to Reger's teachings, augments his general lack of status within Austrian society—despite his international acclaim. He finds solace in a reflection that presents a self-assured and self-sufficient gentleman. This ideal mirror image returns us to the mimesis of life that the beautiful conjures into existence. Despite Reger's own fragility, his mimetic counterpart can offer an alter ego endowed with a "surfeit of aliveness," which in turn grants Reger a renewed sense of life. We can hear echoes of Scarry's idea—"beauty is for the beholder life-saving or life-restoring—a visionary fragment of sturdy ground"[58]—in Reger's words about the restorative properties of all art: "Music saves me time and again, the fact that music is still alive within me. [. . .] It is nothing else but just this cursed and damned [. . .] and embarrassing [disastrous] art that saves such as ourselves" (*OM* 121; "Die Musik rettet mich ja immer wieder, die Tatsache, daß die Musik in mir immer noch lebt [. . .] so rettet Unsereinen doch nichts anderes als eben diese verfluchte und verdammte und [. . .] fatale Kunst," *AM* 151). The idealized and idealizing image of the elderly dignitary becomes an affirmation rather than a denial of the uncanniness inherent in the position of the new *man of taste*. *The White-Bearded Man* makes possible the recognition of the model's alterity from the perceiving self; it creates a situation in which the self recognizes its own strangeness; it brings the viewer into focus where the perspectival lines intersect. The frank stare of the dignified Venetian, turned towards Reger and following him with his gaze from the darkened canvas,[59] signals to the beholder this enigma of difference in similarity and of commonality in alterity. In such instants, the self learns to cope with a world that is itself uncanny. Reger's admission to Atzbacher is testimony to the encompassing uncanniness with which we are daily confronted and from which the experience of art can rescue the man of taste: "*You are completely and totally at the mercy of this sinister world.* [. . .] The world is one big sinister [uncanny] place where no one can find shelter anymore" ("*Sie sind mit Haut und Haaren dieser unheimlichen Welt ausgeliefert.* [. . .] Die Welt ist eine einzige Unheimlichkeit, in welcher kein Mensch mehr Schutz findet").[60]

Figure 15. David Teniers the Younger, *The Archduke Leopold Wilhelm of Austria in His Gallery*. Ca. 1651. Image © Kunsthistorisches Museum, Vienna.

Second, precisely because it has been subjected to the classificatory impulse of the professional art critic, *The White-Bearded Man*'s uniqueness must be restored, its beauty resurrected. When I say that the portrait has suffered from its enshrinement in the museum, I am referring to its inclusion in the *Theatrum Pictorium* (1660) of David Teniers the Younger (1610–1690), a commissioned catalogue of Archduke Leopold Wilhelm's collection of Italian masters. This catalogue of the archduke's paintings marks a turning point in the collection of art and depicts what became the nucleus of the Art History Museum in Vienna.[61] Agamben uses the example of David Teniers the Younger's publication *Theatrum Pictorium* in *The Man without Content* to contrast the outward, radiating inclusiveness of the cabinet with the solipsistic, inward-turned sterility of the modern museum. For him, Teniers's catalogue marks the emergence of the museal practices that quell the involved experience of art. Agamben underscores the differences between the early cabinets and the later galleries into which they transmute.[62] On the surface, Ambras's cabinet of curiosities—with its suspended shark and blowfish, piled-up paintings, arrayed armaments, displayed shells and statuettes (Way Station 3)—may seem similar in underlying principle to the emergent Habsburg gallery of the seventeenth century as Teniers depicts the acquisitions of Leopold Wilhelm (see, for example, figure 15). In Teniers's paintings, we see masterwork stacked upon masterwork, hung on top of one another, leaning against the walls, set upon chairs or resting against their backs.[63]

The similarity, Agamben argues, between this gallery and the cabinet of curiosities preceding it is, however, deceptive. For him, Teniers's depiction marks a moment of scission: the work of art in Teniers's *Theatrum* no longer points beyond itself to a social and otherworldly realm that continues outside the walls in which it is displayed as the *Wunderkammer* did. The artwork is endowed with importance only through its inclusion in the "white cube," the four walls of the gallery:

> But while the microcosm of the *Wunderkammer* had its profound reason in its living and immediate unity with the great world of divine creation, it would be vain to seek an analogous foundation for the gallery: enclosed by the vivid colors of its walls, it rests in itself like a perfectly self-sufficient world where the canvases resemble the sleeping princess of the fairy tale.[64]

If we extend this line of argument to Bernhard, we can see how *Amras* as a proto-cabinet recalls a moment before the onset of the insidious division between the here and the hereafter, the world of art and of life, the degeneration into strict categorizations of things. It evokes the instant before the decline into the sealed structure of the modern museum that is marked in *Old Masters*, which confers "value" simply by containing the work and becoming its receptacle.[65]

Teniers's gallery pictures of the 1650s corroborate Agamben's dismal assessment. Tintoretto's portrait is among the copious canvases by Titian, Giorgione, Bassano, Palma il Vecchio, and Veronese adorning the walls.[66] *The White-Bearded Man* is included prominently in the bottom row, center, of *The Archduke Leopold Wilhelm in His Gallery in Brussels* (ca. 1651) and *Archduke Leopold Wilhelm in His Picture Gallery* (1653), behind the melancholy artist Teniers with the somber look.[67] As paintings have become objects of acquisition, their individual significance has been subordinated to the idea of a quantitative rather than qualitative experience of art—a gallery is only important if it has many famous works.

Reger picks up on this line of thinking, arguing that looking at one painting next to many others makes it difficult to appreciate a work's unique beauty.[68] Tintoretto must be saved from the "lateral disregard" that current museums advance,[69] since they do not expressly encourage the dilettante or the man of taste. In Reger's view, inclusion in today's museums is but one step on the capitalist road to iniquity and the degradation of a meaningful pedagogy. The museum's art historians further these negative trends as they guide groups past walls bedecked with masterpieces in a hasty trot. Such professional critics, whose regard is neither dilettantish nor creatively critical, must be banished from the art world, in Reger's sardonic view.[70] Only a return to the singular experience of the unitary canvas can counter the anonymity of cataloguing and exhibition in specially constructed spaces. Reger lauds the man from Tiflis, Georgia, who has come to Vienna's Kunsthistorisches Museum solely to look at Gainsborough's *Landscape in Suffolk*.[71] Reger's critical taste, by latching onto a work that is neither exemplary nor iconic, seeks to counter the instrumentalization of taste on multiple levels. With the rise of the museum, our taste has become commodified. With the rise of the institutionalized critic, our taste is prescribed. With the rise of fake art or kitsch—which Reger scathingly attacks—our taste is no longer secure in its judgment. Finally, with the rise of a state-sanctioned stake in art during and after the Habsburg reign, taste abets the aestheticization of politics.

Of course, Reger's humanist education cannot make a tabula rasa. After all, the museum, open to the larger public and with a carefully controlled environment of eighteen degrees centigrade and subdued lighting, facilitates the teaching of both dilettantish and tasteful appreciation—in the case of an old master like Reger.

The Forgery and the Qualification

A cryptic scene occurs toward the middle of the novel that initially casts doubt on Reger's pedagogy. I am speaking of the forgery episode with the Welsh visitor to the Art History Museum. He turns out not to be a reviled "Kunstfachmann," or "art expert," but instead a professed dilettante. "I am no art connoisseur," the Welshman confesses, no one knowledgeable in art ("Kunstkenner").[72] He has impeccable taste, however, as his fine clothing and choice of cologne demonstrate.[73] The gentleman in the plus fours owns a plethora of Italian masters ranging from Lotto to Bassano, but he has come to the Kunsthistorisches Museum only to examine the *White-Bearded Man* in detail. However, as Uwe Betz has shown, Reger's high esteem for this character is, upon further reflection, inappropriate.[74] The Welshman's taste stands in no beneficial relationship to his morality. He emphasizes his collection's financial worth, reintroducing the exchange values so anathema to Reger's pedagogy. Economic considerations automatically undermine the singularity of an artwork, with a collector's preference for many over one; they insist on quantifiable value as a necessary, indeed indispensable, supplement to the qualitative experience.

In an extended conversation with Reger, the Welshman explains that his reason for being in the Bordone Room is the existence of two versions of *The White-Bearded Man*. He negates Tintoretto's singularity, placing the painting within the context of his own larger collection and disqualifying it as a forgery: "The Englishman sat down once more on the Bordone Room settee [. . .] and said that it was in fact *one and the same painting*, the one hanging over his bed in his bedroom in Wales and the one here on the wall of the Bordone

Room at the Kunsthistorisches Museum" (*OM* 78; "Der Engländer setzte sich wieder auf die Bordone-Saal-Sitzbank [. . .] und sagte, daß es tatsächlich *ein und dasselbe Gemälde* sei, nämlich das, das in seinem Schlafzimmer in Wales über seinem Bett hängt, und das hier in der Wand im Kunsthistorischen Museum im Bordone-Saal," *AM* 98).

At first blush it appears that the Welsh visitor's words need not slight Reger's pedagogy. There may be historical circumstances to loosely corroborate the assertion that Tintoretto's work is not singular: David Teniers painted small copies after the originals in Leopold Wilhelm's collection, copies which varied in their dimensions. The sizes usually corresponded to those of the engravings that appeared in *Theatrum Pictorium*.[75] Many of these miniature copies entered the collection of Count Antoine Seilern (1901–1978), who came from an old Austrian family and settled in England in 1939.[76] The novel parodies this trajectory in the Welshman's description of the painting's relocation to and within England.[77] In alluding to the fate of much art in the period surrounding World War II, the Welshman's claim may merely support Reger's own, namely that art is easily appropriated and victimized for political purposes.

The accusation that, given the absolute likeness between the two Tintorettos, one of them must be fake, also seems to be a continuation of Reger's words in *Alte Meister*. There, the critic alludes to the Platonic conception of mimetic art as forgery, when he states that "every original is a forgery in itself (*OM* 57; "jedes Original ist ja eigentlich an sich schon eine Fälschung," *AM* 74). According to Socrates in section 597 of *The Republic*, artists must fail, since they cannot approach the realm of true forms and simply depict existent things. The philosopher compares an artist to a person with a mirror, reflecting things while lacking true knowledge of them. That Plato's Socrates defines the poet as an imitator of an imitator, three times removed from nature, is largely due to the artist's social function. As a servant of convention, the artist only gives the illusion of nature; this is very much in line with Reger's critique of the imbrication of art and politics.[78] From this perspective Reger's condemnatory words about all art being fake make sense. The production of forgeries indicates an artist's involvement in socio-politics—this is perforce the case for all art. It serves as the basis for the recognition of a common humanity in the grave flaw. If Reger were speaking literally about forgery, then the technique of the grave flaw would become impossible; the man of taste would be searching out a different kind of mistake vis-à-vis another artwork perceived as superior, like the Welshman does. Instead, Tintoretto's painting is, like all painting, per se a "forgery," and can be examined for the grave flaw, the point of imperfection where it diverges from verisimilitude.

However, the Welshman's argument introduces a disconcerting note into the novel's discourse on education and beauty; his stress on the distinction between the *one* and the *same* threatens to disintegrate Tintoretto's unique status and Reger's undertaking. Perusing the canvas at length, the Welsh gentleman argues that similarity has been displaced by sameness, since even the details coincide perfectly. From the recognition of difference in similarity—of "das gleiche," to use the German word that resurfaces multiple times in this episode—of the two portraits, the Welshman moves to an idea of absolute identity, expressed by the German "dasselbe." If identity trumps similarity, then Reger's pedagogy becomes moot, since the elderly man wants to instill a sense of the absolute singularity of a beautiful artwork and its singular relation to life. When the work can be replaced, the particular love or care for a work in its unique material existence is called into question.[79] From this interest in the materiality of the artwork stems Reger's focus on taste—with its visceral physical component—and his general concern with materiality. He is concerned with the inimitable work of art located in a very specific place. It should not be perused as a slide reproduction or a textbook photo, but in its singularity within a space devoted to originals. Indistinguishable copies would make any specific "Durchblick" a work engenders difficult, even impossible.[80]

Perhaps an anecdote that the literary scholar Rüdiger Görner relates about the late Bernhard makes the Welshman's approach understandable. Having met a despondent Bernhard in a Viennese café, Görner is told the source of Bernhard's consternation: the writer carries with him a broken window handle from his Viennese flat. He is searching for an exact replacement, Bernhard maintains, so that he can open his favorite window to the outside world. After artfully arranging the handle on some newspapers, topmost the *Neue Zürcher Zeitung* (an inside joke for readers familiar with other Bernhard texts such as *Wittgenstein's Nephew*, where the *NZZ* is praised), Bernhard closes with a rueful admission. He will never be able to find another handle just like this one, he informs Görner mournfully, since then it would necessarily be broken. Hence he will never be able to open his window with the beautiful view again.[81] This anecdote makes a mockery of the forgery episode in *Alte Meister*, unmasking any rhetoric of identity as ludicrous. Bernhard's disclosure destroys any illusions that sameness can trump difference, that identity takes precedence over similarity. Beautiful objects for which we care always exist alone in their materiality. When they disappear, the desire for their exact replacement may remain, but the knowledge that the desire can never be fulfilled does as well.

This story, however, calls into question Reger's ability as a teacher: he does not realize, apparently, the problematic aspects of the Welshman's views, holding him up as a role model for Atzbacher. His propaedeutic project is itself interested in identity over similarity, since it prepares students to become his mouthpieces, or "Sprachrohre."[82] This contradicts Reger's teachings, which seek to liberate students from accepted norms, canons, and, most significantly, teachers. What is required, in the end, is a paradoxical method of instruction, which enables the dilettante or the man of taste to emerge: a teacher must provide authoritative constraints—this explains the element of dominance implicit in Reger's *Bildungsmodell*—so that creative, spontaneous, or revolutionary innovation and independence become possible.

In the final instance, Atzbacher does rebel against the very constraints of Reger's alternative model. Because the story is focalized through the student-narrator, suspicion is cast on the elderly critic's authority and motives, and the shortcomings of his endeavors become manifest.[83] The younger writer, from the adjoining Sebastiano Room, must "submit" to Titian in order to observe Reger. Colloquially, he has to "buy" it ("in Kauf nehmen"), but he does not want to do so: "I was compelled therefore, entirely against my inclination, to submit to Titian in order to be able to observe Reger in front of Tintoretto's *White-Bearded Man*" (*OM* 1; "ich mußte also, ganz gegen meinen Geschmack, Tizian in Kauf nehmen, um Reger vor dem *Weißbärtigen Mann* von Tintoretto beobachten zu können," *AM* 7). This phrase suggests that a visual and gendered economy is established. The exchange relation Reger so vigorously condemns in the case of art historians is reintroduced into his own circulation of ideas. The concepts generated around images by famous male artists constitute a kind of "hom(m)o-sexual economy":[84] discussions concentrating on an exclusively male canon of the beautiful, based on insights between men about products by men portraying men, create a hermetically sealed system. Reger's testing process notwithstanding, a claustrophobic constellation comes into being—within a space that acts as a closed-off conclavium.[85]

The phrase "to submit to Titian" also suggests that Atzbacher is no longer willing to submit to Reger, to be his mouthpiece reproducing verbatim his opinions, for another, historical reason. To contextualize this comment we must imagine the fraught student-teacher relationship between Titian and Tintoretto in Cinquecento Italy. With Titian dominating Venetian painting until the 1560s, art historians have conjectured that the personal animosity of Tintoretto's master thwarted his early aspirations.[86] Reger's explication of *The White-Bearded Man* serves a dual function: on the one hand, it first encourages Atzbacher to take on Reger's preferences. On the other, it leads Atzbacher to identify with the defiant painter. *Alte Meister* is not only the chronicle of dialogues with Atzbacher's paternalistic teacher, but also of the younger man's œdipally inflected rebellion—as his appellation of Reger as the "father of his thoughts," or "Gedankenvater," underlines.[87] Under the domineering tutelage of Reger, Atzbacher has not published a single page of his own philosophical work.[88] In a similar vein, Tintoretto only emerges as an independent master after the waning of Titian's personal influence and his withdrawal from public commissions. Atzbacher's growing recalcitrance, his unwillingness to be an obedient pupil, can be surmised from his occasional negative epithets and evaluations of Reger. He may even be suppressing parts of the dialogues in the manuscript, making Reger appear overbearing. Atzbacher has identified with Tintoretto against the colossal Titian and produced a manuscript that is not entirely philosophical, but instead alternates between dilettantism and taste. His own text—as a transcription and reflection on Reger's project—can only come into existence with the surpassing of his elderly master. This resolution of the struggle between father/teacher and son/student answers the master's wish for an undisciplined disciple.

The closing lines of the novel intimate that this story has been one of increasing distance from Reger's *Bildung*, not simply a rehearsal of the method and the obligatory revolt. The elaborate mise-en-scène of the novel—with Atzbacher watching Reger from the adjoining Sebastiano Room before joining the critic in the Bordone Room—moves out of the space of the museum completely. In the end, we find ourselves in a nearby iconic site: the Imperial Court Theater. Atzbacher comments on a Kleist play, which tutor and tutee see together at Vienna's foremost stage, the Burgtheater: "Die Vorstellung war entsetzlich" (*AM* 193). Literally this can be read as it is also presented in the English translation, as "the performance was terrible" (*OM* 156). However, "Vorstellung" has numerous meanings in German, at once "performance," "conception," "imagination," "notion," "introduction," "perception," and "vision"—to name but some of the ideas the word transports. Thus we might interpret Atzbacher's words a bit more loosely, on a meta-level. We can understand them to mean that the concept behind Reger's teaching is terrible. Having come into his own and now able to form an independent opinion, Atzbacher indicts the "Vorstellung" guiding Reger's enterprise; his comment censures Reger's reliance on specific structures to speak directly, to call forth the genius loci or the accreted history of a place and its contents and mediate between part and whole. The spatial "Durchblicke" from the Sebastiano Room into the Bordone Room, which led the student outward through various temporal "Durchblicke," remain caught within the endless regress of the *mise-en-abîme* and the fragment space of the Art History Museum. In the end, this outward movement may not be enough to make good on the spatiotemporal promise of perforated space: the horizontal direction outward to the former Imperial Theater suggests that the contiguous spaces need a wider radius.

Atzbacher has, we can say, learned the paradox at the heart of Reger's *paedeia*: true educators must train students to liberate themselves from their very own teachings, painful as this may be for teacher and student alike. Only then can pupils become creative critical artists, "*schöpferische kritische Künstler*."

Way Station 4

✦

Dislodged

A graphic novel version of *Old Masters*, Nicolas Mahler's *Alte Meister* (2011), cleverly plays up the irreverence at the heart of Bernhard's text. Mahler potentiates Bernhard, emphasizing the despotic teacher's dethronement and the student's increasing independence within a cultural enclave. Mahler radically abbreviates the text, focusing on the art examples Reger cites in his reflections—Tintoretto, Dürer, Goya. Reger is shown as a stocky figure, dressed like a Franciscan friar and seated on a bench in front of Tintoretto's *White-Bearded Man*. Mahler caricatures the pomp and ceremony of the building, focusing on the marble inlaid floor, imperious central staircase, and heavy gilt picture frames. Reger's magisterial pronouncements on art float through these rooms, isolated in rectangular fields at the top of each panel, centered speech bubbles (and boxes), or prominent rectangles at the bottom of the frame. The critic's statements take on added weight when they partially occlude the sketched images underneath.

In Mahler's graphic novel, the Kunsthistorisches Museum is often a labyrinthine space inducing feelings of disorientation. At times, the perspective reveals numerous door- and picture frames that are hardly distinguishable from one another or infinitely multiplying museum barriers. In the drawings, the museum's hall is fanned out, open to different viewing angles. Mahler sketches the Bordone Room in which Reger is seated, varying the perspective; he jumps from Atzbacher's threshold location to Reger's central emplacement, and on to an omniscient narrator's (and our) viewpoint. We shift from observing Atzbacher observing Reger, to seeing Reger from behind—engaged in the process of observing—to close-ups of the paintings from either Atzbacher or (primarily) Reger's point of view. Occasionally, the paintings and objects come alive to illustrate a character's statements, hovering above, below, and in the middle of the black rectangle. For instance, the owls from Goya's 43rd *Capricho*, *El sueño de la razón produce monstruos* (*The Dream of Reason Produces Monsters*, 1797–99), fly out toward Reger when he complains that the Art History Museum does not own a single work by the Spanish painter. In another example, Reger imagines himself as one of the stooped figures portrayed walking with two canes when he talks about how much he hates strolling. Atzbacher's reflections on Reger's punctuality lead to the proliferation of clock faces, which migrate from the door to the wall and back to the door, until a clock face is shown in the middle of a gilt frame where Tintoretto was hanging in earlier panels. Temporality becomes all important for a brief moment, dwarfing the significance of space.[1] When Reger theorizes art's fallibility and the grave flaw, only fragments of famous paintings and themes are shown—a portion of what could be one of Titian's horses, a head of the Madonna without child, a glimpse of the Christ child and turban in what seems to be an *Adoration of the Magi*, a partial outline of van Dyck's 1626 *Susanna in the Bath*.[2]

In one prominent image, the surrounding environment is replaced with cascading lines to show the darkness of Reger's musings—the pen marks suggest a black vortex. He has just mentioned his wife's death and the necessity of habits such as visiting the museum and reflecting on the Old Masters, despite his aversion to them. The lines form a circle around one of his assertions, which is now located in the very picture frame that surrounded Tintoretto's portrait of the *White-Bearded Man* on the preceding page. Here, Mahler cites one of Reger's statements: "I have to go to the Old Masters in order to be able to continue to exist, exactly to these so-called Old Masters" ("Zu den Alten Meistern muß ich gehen, um weiterexistieren zu können, genau zu diesen sogenannten Alten Meistern," *Alte*, 36–37). At this stage, the white, blank canvas with Reger's words stands at the center of the black vortex, taking on an existential dimension in the confrontation with death. The museum, we infer, is the "vanishing point" ("Fluchtpunkt") that remains for Reger, and all his thoughts are literally centered on it and in it—they take over and fill the picture frames and the panel frames. When the black vortex recurs nearly a hundred pages further on, the words in the vortex's center now read: "having arrived at the decisive point of our existence" ("an dem entscheidenden Punkte unserer Existenz"); the sentence trails off and is only completed in the rectangle at the bottom of the same page with the words "nothing more," "nichts mehr." The decisive point in life, like the grave flaw, leads Reger—and readers—to question art's "rescuing" function: death becomes the vanishing point. It pulls art into its maelstrom, leaving "nothing more."[3] Gone is the artwork, vanished is the frame that both draws out and contains Reger's thoughts.

The vortex is the circular counterpoint to the lone black square on an earlier page, which represented the death of Reger's wife and his mourning for her (Mahler, *Alte* 111). Efforts to fill the bigger "box" of life through particular artworks fail. In a self-reflexive gesture, Mahler calls attention to his own craft and the *Grundriss* his art can—and cannot—provide (especially since his drawn Atzbacher resembles the real-life artist). How do you represent death in a serious graphic novel that reflects on art's potential to reground the self and on art's collusion with the powers that be? Where does the voluptuousness of the drawn line fail, requiring a return to the comic strip's most basic element, its single black box? In the interplay between the various boxes outlined in black, Mahler sets up a complex jostling for argumentative advantage. The declarations in certain rectangles can be set against others; larger rectangles "frame" the figures; disembodied statements in other boxes are displaced when characters appear in their place; characters can be made to disappear after being introduced, dissolving into minimalist black squares; they can reappear as well (as in the case of Reger's wife, who is shown in a small yellow box, *Alte*, 123); their disappearance can haunt the following panels, with the black square cropping up as a faint dotted outline, literally casting a shadow on the events. In Mahler's interpretation, art cannot provide a new *Grundriss* or floor plan for a more fulfilled, more utopian life. Had the circular floor mosaics found their architectural counterpart in the black vortex with the white emptiness at its center, the museum's rectangular floor plan finds its complement in the black box signifying death.

After his wife's passing, only the pedagogical enterprise itself affirms life for the despondent teacher. Reger gradually returns Tintoretto's *White-Bearded Man* to the heart of the vortex's blackness—he refills the spiraling blackness with Tintoretto's portrait five pages after his statement of existential angst, near the graphic novel's end (Mahler, *Alte* 135). This effort at restitution comes across as his last-ditch attempt to escape death's maws via elaborate disquisitions. Around him, however, the black box has left its ominous dotted outlines, marking Reger as a man of the same fragility and ephemerality as his wife and the artworks whose frailty and imperfection he so loudly proclaims.[4]

Mahler also shows how the rooms inspire defiance. The submission that the imposing edifice demands of the student becomes unbearable: Reger's disembodied words, which hover in the single panels of the pages as well as in the gilt frames of the artworks themselves, become an intrinsic part of the museal space, whose meaning they seek to control (figure 16). The pronouncements' source disappears, and they emanate from everywhere and nowhere, as if from a god. They have the power to extinguish the contents of the things on which they pass judgment, as the empty picture frames beneath them reveal; the word "nothing" or "nichts" pulverizes the frames' content, rendering them empty. Precisely for this reason, the declarations call forth rebelliousness. Indeed, their enshrinement in a temple of high culture demands disobedience.

The museum's sketched interiors come to life, moreover, and give the book a narrative drive all its own. The mise-en-scène in the Art History Museum stresses the whirring, round mosaic floors, replicating queues, and floating picture frames—lending the whole museum a mobility that conflicts with the temporal stasis we associate with museums (see Way Station 1). The décor propels Reger's obsessive thoughts and confers an insistent, overbearing energy on them. The museum's own vitality conflicts with Reger's efforts at control. Any teacher, no matter how seemingly in command of a situation,

Figure 16. Nicolas Mahler, *Alte Meister*, p. 79. © 2011 Suhrkamp Verlag.

can be dislodged from the very space his words perforate, illustrate, and attempt to dominate.

The museum itself, shown from the outside numerous times in the course of the graphic novel, also insists in its material presence. The sketches emphasize the building's outer substantiality. The closing pages of the book display the pencil-thin Atzbacher following the bulbous Reger out of the gallery, into the square in front of the Kunsthistorisches Museum, where the elderly man puts forward the idea of going to the theater with Atzbacher. For teacher and student alike, the departure is a comic and wordless scene of flight from *The White-Bearded Man*, the Bordone Room, and the Art History Museum in toto. In front of the Maria Theresa Monument the last scene of submission occurs, where Atzbacher acquiesces to his master's request to visit the State Theater, the Burgtheater: "Yes, if it is your express wish" ("Ja, wenn es Ihr ausdrücklicher Wunsch ist").[5] The book ends with a frame within the frame, the curtains surrounding two hilariously drawn actors on a stage, heads bent toward the cracked pitcher from Kleist's play *The Broken Jug* (*Der zerbrochene Krug*, 1806). The closing image returns us to the weight of the inherited past that the museum signifies and evokes the static tableaux characterizing typical Bernhard productions in the German-speaking world, especially those of Bernhard's premier director Claus Peymann. Mahler's sparse theater with its hermetic containment of Kleist's anarchic drama is thus not without its own delicious irony, literally arresting the vertiginous movement (a play within a graphic novel based on a spatial novel about paintings) in a stationary frame.

As in the Bernhard novel, we sense the student's increasing detachment from his mentor—but the architectonic implications are more explicit in Mahler. The distance is first intimated through the visual repetition of a nearly empty white wall and stanchion. Replicated in narrow, juxtaposed rectangles across four pages, the whiteness illustrates the laughable aspect of the self-professed "page turner's" surface reading. The snippets of the room approximate the quick turning of pages—which thereby become nearly blank (we see less and less of Tintoretto's portrait; Mahler, *Alte*, 40–43). Also, toward the end of the graphic novel, the fourfold replication of the empty bench in the Bordone Room visually demonstrates the repetitiveness of Reger's speeches, which he has already stated hundreds of times according to Atzbacher's commentary.[6] In the closing frame, the comment "The performance [concept] was terrible," borders the bottom of the image, giving Atzbacher the last word and the power of closure—as in Bernhard's book. The frame-within-the frame bottles up Kleist's power to subvert established hierarchies and conceptions of justice; it also limits art's role in Reger's *paideia*. Perhaps the caption "The performance/concept was terrible" ("Die Vorstellung war entsetzlich") rails against this doubled containment. Readers already witnessed the same reterritorializing move in Reger's effort to restitute Tintoretto's portrait to the center of the black vortex, restraining its centrifugal, dispersive, outward energies.

Mahler zeroes in on Atzbacher's difficulties with Reger's theory. On the one hand, Reger advocates a kind of deep interpretative strategy that relies on what Paul Ricoeur in 1970 calls a "hermeneutics of suspicion": the reader, aware of the ideological underpinnings of artworks, looks for another, hidden truth, a latent meaning that is not apparent when perusing the manifest content. For the suspicious reader, the fragments of well-known artworks still gesture toward the whole (history) of which they are a part. We recognize Tintoretto's *White-Bearded Man*, Correggio's *Jupiter and Io*, or Dürer's *Madonna and Child at the Breast* without too much difficulty, despite Mahler's alienating bubbly lines, and we infer something about the historical, ideological context to which these singular works belong. On the other hand, Reger's conception also relies on what Susan Sontag, only four years prior to Ricoeur, advocates as an "erotics of art"—a rejection of the hermeneutics of depth, with its heroic mode of reading that excavates a repressed history. In Reger's erotics, defiant short shrift is given to scholarly argumentation in favor of attention to the surface topography of the painted image, which is entered like a wanderer entering a landscape. For him, the viewer responds to the aesthetic "come-on" via a psychosexual engagement with art.[7] Clearly, surface and depth cannot be contrasted in any facile manner, especially since the surface fulfills a quasi-religious, near-mystical desire: looking at the surface means seeing through it, recognizing instantly the various social, political, and religious networks to which the part is linked. This surface reading looks for webs of power relations apparent in gestures, clothing, and architectures; it attends to the artists' relationship to the state and to institutionalized religion.

A tension between deep and surface reading results from this method.[8] Perhaps the back-and-forth between these two conflicting modes calls forth the viewer's *Erregbarkeit*—his ability to be aroused, in both senses of the German and English terms. This ability, in turn, must be translated into Bernhard's famous *Erregung*: the arousal must be lived in every fiber of one's body and verbalized or otherwise expressed. In a sense, we can read the Art History Museum inVienna in Bernhard's novel and Mahler's work as the center of what Elaine Scarry calls "the felt experience of cognition."[9] Strange, wondrous, funny, and disturbing objects glide into and out of the perceptual field, touching us cognitively and haptically. They simultaneously dematerialize the place where this engagement occurs and make its experience more visceral.[10]

Bernhard's final pedagogical endeavor engages in the vertiginous *mise-en-abîme* with which Mahler plays in this "felt experience of cognition." It is a bit like standing at the farthest end of the Bordone Room, which affords a view along the entire axis of large exhibition hallways leading to the main staircase. The infinite regress of space, when beheld through black marble arch upon arch upon arch, leads to a kind of dematerialization in the process. The awe-inspiring museum suddenly loses its solidity; it becomes porous for all kinds of aesthetic and ethical reflections and for a "quick read" that reconciles surface and depth.

This is, as I intimated in my discussion of Mahler's graphic novel, a lot for which to ask: there is a certain too-much-ness to a reading strategy that requires an ongoing hijacking of our emplacement and the oscillation between depth and surface, actual place and virtual space. Only a special kind of student can withstand its conflicting imperatives and thrive.

Conclusion

✦

Demolition and Restoration in *Correction* (1975)

Let me backtrack to Bernhard's elementary geometries and perforated spaces of 1972, a halfway mark between his early and late writings. In that year, a series of prizes solidifies his preeminence in the German-speaking world, which his compatriot, the Nobel Prize winner Elfriede Jelinek, calls Bernhard's "towering" stature.[1] Moreover, 1972 is an important year for another reason: the Wittgenstein House, which the philosopher Ludwig Wittgenstein designed and constructed for his sister Margarethe Stonborough-Wittgenstein between 1926 and 1928, has just narrowly been saved from demolition after a protracted battle between so-called preservationists and concerned architects and artists (it achieves landmark status in 1971). The debate marks the renewed interest in the Austrian expatriate philosopher—his *Tractatus Logico-Philosophicus* (1918) as well as his *Philosophical Investigations* (*Philosophische Untersuchungen*, 1953)—at the juncture when Bernhard moves from the utopian-syncretic education we found in his early works toward the articulation of a complete propaedeutics in his last novel, *Old Masters*. These events call attention to Bernhard's development of an ethics of care about architecture, at a point when the writer has proceeded from the status of an apprentice beholden to older, more experienced writers to a master in his own right.

The novel entitled *Correction* (*Korrektur*), which Bernhard publishes in 1975, skillfully interweaves the themes and stylistic characteristics we encountered in the preceding chapters with the architectonic emphases of the Wittgenstein debate. It responds to the issues of extinguishing, refashioning, and restoring, which the contentious discussion surrounding Wittgenstein's building raises. *Correction* "corrects" the mystical educational emphasis of *Amras*, while again articulating the anti-establishment mantra of "Plane/ Plain" ("Ebene"); the novel develops a complex view of elementary architecture in all its forms, which both the visionary architects and their modernist predecessors propound. I focus on the moment of transition as it is concretized in the Wittgenstein House; it suggests a model for the spaces *connecting* up-and-down, in-and-out that Bernhard's pedagogical method eventually espouses.

Correcting and Connecting

Roithamer, the dominant teacher-figure in the novel's triad of characters, is dead by his own hand when the narrative of *Correction* begins. The anonymous first-person narrator, who has to deal with Roithamer's intellectual bequest, functions as a kind of acolyte; while he is of the same age, he seems beholden to Roithamer's ideas and ideals. As in the case of *Old Masters*, however, we can read him as an increasingly doubtful and obstreperous pupil. He is entrusted with his mentor's myriad architectural and personal notations regarding the construction of a building in the shape of a cone in the Kobernausserwald (forested hills in Upper Austria).[2] Roithamer designs and executes the structure for his beloved sister, the only family member to whom he is close. In attempting to emancipate himself from his teacher, the narrator damages the bequest. He inverts Roithamer's written "tower," a heap of notations entitled "*About Altensam and everything connected with Altensam, with special attention to the Cone*,"[3] which accompany the various permutations of the manuscript. After hemming and hawing about what to do with the stack of papers he has inherited, the narrator spontaneously grabs the knapsack containing the notes—a "Hochgebirgsrucksack," a special kind of knapsack for treks in the highest alpine regions. He dumps out the contents to free himself from Roithamer's domineering tutelage and posthumous control.[4] The tower of notes cascades downward. Lacking numerical notations, Roithamer's papers regarding the Cone and the parental estate are thereafter in even greater disarray than they were at the outset of the novel. Readers are left unsure whether the reflections they read in the following section, entitled "SIFTING AND SORTING" ("SICHTEN UND ORDNEN"), have been reordered, although the novel implies that they could not be reorganized in an entirely coherent manner. There are many jumps in this section, with shifts from Roithamer's first-person account to his reported speech in the subjunctive to the narrator's first-person musings, articulating plans to scrutinize the papers.[5]

The reversal of the trajectory from up to down and the forcible upending of the bequest render visible the student's internal rearrangement. There are notable parallels between the end of Roithamer's architectural project and the narrator's actions. After the death of Roithamer's sister, who passes away as soon as the Cone is completed, the tower is left to decay in the forest. Similarly, the spontaneous action of the first-person narrator leads to the literal "downfall" of Roithamer's observations. As a result, however, the hollow spaces and openings necessary for the pupil's development come into view. "I [. . .] watched from the window," the narrator recounts, "with my back to the window, that is, how some of the pages slid down from the top of that heap of papers, which was still in motion as I watched from the window, where there were still some air spaces left in the heap of papers, these air spaces caved in and more papers slid to the floor" (C 132–33; "Ich [. . .] beobachtete vom

Fenster aus, mit dem Rücken also am Fenster, den Papierhaufen, der sich jetzt, wie ich ihn vom Fenster aus beobachtete, noch bewegte, nach und nach rutschten noch ein paar Blätter des Nachlasses Roithamers von oben nach unten, wo Hohlräume in dem Papierhaufen waren, gaben diese Hohlräume nach, sah ich, und wieder gingen Blätter zu Boden," *K* 160). As he stands between the outer and inner world, positioned at the window ledge with the glass panes at his back (through which he had first observed the taxidermist Höller at work), the narrator is willing to reevaluate the most formidable intellectual influence of his life. While the beginning of *Correction* was still written from the perspective of a bereaved disciple, the end of the first section increasingly reveals the necessity and usefulness of reordering the "hollow space"—translated too loosely as "air spaces" in English—separating the narrator from Roithamer and from the world beyond. The chaos that the narrator unleashes is the destructive impulse toward the overarching schema his teacher put into practice, even if remorse accompanies it. His paradoxical gesture is, as I argued in earlier chapters, constructive and necessary for Bernhard's *Bildung*.

While the narrator responds to the conflicting imperatives of his mentor's teachings in this manner, Roithamer is never able to muster the energy and will required for his own emancipation. According to Roithamer's own estimation, he himself has foundered at his lifelong project of intellectual and emotional separation from those who helped mold him and his environs. In *Correction*, the parental realm acts as the negative foil for Roithamer's utopian building project, giving rise to the originally beneficial but ultimately damaging Cone. As we read in the second section of the selected papers, Roithamer has not become fully independent through a proper act of edification. He has not freed himself from his parents' pernicious influence and indoctrination despite building a tower for his sister. Roithamer offers an extended variation on the ideas expressed in "Plain/Plane" ("Ebene"), the 1973 essay accompanying Walter Pichler's sketches (Chapter 1). The parents have neglected their role as teachers; their primary concern has been rearing and shaping their progeny into mirror images of themselves. They trapped Roithamer in a "childhood dungeon" or "Kindheitskerker" in their estate named Altensam, located in what seems to be an incongruous location high up—the higher location stands in direct contrast with the family's minimal intellectual aspirations and only accords with their social pretensions and pretentiousness.[6] The hilltop redoubt separates the well-to-do family from the common folk below, from what Roithamer perceives as the locals' greater authenticity and stronger community. In the constrictive space of Altensam,[7] his parents did not fulfill their function as guides. They are authorized educators without any real authority: "Our parents were not the right teachers for us, our rightful educators as it's called, but they had no right to educate us" ("In unseren Eltern haben wir keine Lehrer gehabt, Erziehungsberechtigte, wie es heißt, die aber kein Recht auf unsere Erziehung gehabt haben"). Their authority is delegated to the authors with whom Roithamer spends his time in intellectual comity (discussed below). The parents, in particular his mother, confine Roithamer in a small southeasterly "turret room," an "Erkerzimmer" like a "Kerker" ("jail cell") where the "highest punishment" ("Höchststrafe") is meted out; they thereby hope to make him submissive.[8] This room is imagined as an enclosed space within a larger constrictive space, similar to the spaces within spaces that Walter Pichler designs in the 1960s and 1970s (chapter 1). Significantly, the windows in the sunny turret room—the openings to the outside world—are so dirty that they do not provide views. Furthermore, the window bolts are so rusty that they cannot be unfastened to release him from the doubled confinement.[9]

As was the case in *Amras*, *Correction* shows how architectonic constraints further a creative impulse and sharpen the senses and mind for different avenues of inquiry and fields of exploration. The environment of Altensam, despite all its oppressive aspects, is also "artistic" ("kunstvoll") and "cultivated" ("kultiviert"). Altensam allows those first views into another world and state of being that Ernst Bloch describes as utopian vistas or liberating perspectives (see the Introduction). In some of the notes he leaves behind, Roithamer admits that the "Anblick," the look *at* the landscape around the estate, is equivalent to the "Durchblick," the view *through* or X-ray vision we encountered in chapter 3.[10] From the perception of the beautiful things close at hand, care should be extended outward in concentric circles to the surrounding landscape. This is only marginally the case in Altensam. Despite the high altitude, Roithamer suffers from others' demeaning behavior and his own lowered ("erniedrigt") self-esteem; despite the open views from the estate, the others close their eyes to the splendor. The son perceives his humiliation and society's willed blindness to the children's maltreatment in Altensam's architectonically rich environment:

> I felt more and more intimidated and humiliated, they could easily bully us, our parents, we were so naive. Such a beautiful house, so artistic, so cultivated, our visitors always said, what could anyone say to the contrary? Such delightful surroundings, every piece of furniture a work of art, all the interiors they ever got to see the most splendid anywhere, all the vistas from Altensam opening on the loveliest, most far-flung landscapes. How, I often asked myself, how is it possible to see oneself going to ruin in so, to quote my mother's constant phrase, luxurious an atmosphere? To be dying by inches, for no reason any outsider could see.

> Ich [bin] mehr und mehr eingeschüchtert und erniedrigt gewesen, sie konnten uns gut mißhandeln, die Eltern, weil wir nicht aufgeklärt gewesen waren. Ein so schönes, ein so kunstvolles, ein so kultiviertes Haus, sagten unsere Besucher immer und sie fragten sich, was es

> daran zu zweifeln gab. Eine solche kostbare Umgebung, alle Möbelstücke, Kunststücke, alle Räumlichkeiten, die sie zu sehen bekommen haben, die herrlichsten, alle Ausblicke von Altensam in die Landschaft die schönsten, weitesten. Wie, fragte ich mich oft selbst, ist es möglich, sich zugrunde gehen zu sehen in einer solchen, so meine Mutter andauernd, luxuriösen Atmosphäre? Absterben, wo für den Außenstehenden kein Grund zu sehen gewesen war.

The view is turned first in- and then outward. The interior is described like a cabinet of art, filled with precious items ("Möbelstücke, Kunststücke"). While the rooms ("Räumlichkeiten") themselves contain these objects, they also mediate between inside and outside; from the inside, vistas open onto the surrounding expanses. These views surprise, delight, and excite because of their breadth. Roithamer realizes that Altensam does not leave him untouched and that he, too, perceives the beauty of the countryside from this particular perspective. He continues:

> Of course I wasn't wholly a stranger to such concepts of joy, beauty, even the love-of-life, the beauty-of-nature andsoforth, so Roithamer. My eyes were as open in that direction as in the other. A man like me, who finds his greatest happiness in thought, most of all when engaged in thought out in the open, in the free (philosophical) world of nature, is saved by the fact in itself, by such an observation as this in itself, so Roithamer.

> Aber naturgemäß war ich nicht gänzlich ausgeschlossen gewesen von den Begriffen Freude, Schönheit, Lebensfreude selbst, Naturschönheit undsofort, so Roithamer. Meine Augen waren auch in dieser Richtung, genauso wie für die andere, offen gewesen. Ein Mensch wie ich, dessen höchstes Glück Denken, und vor allem Denken in der freien (philosophischen) Natur ist, war allein in dieser Tatsache, ist allein in einer solchen Bemerkung gerettet, so Roithammer.

A dialectic between enclosure ("ausgeschlossen") and openness ("offen," "frei"), between isolated concentration and aesthetic expansiveness results from the experience of Altensam. The openings toward the outside condition Roithamer's "persistent, relentless brooding," colorfully expressed in German as "bohrende[s] Denken" or "probing thinking."[11] In German, we generally refer to "bohrende Fragen" or nagging questions, but Bernhard changes the idiomatic phrase, turning the nagging questions into a type of piercing thought more generally. This thinking that maneuvers inward and down enables the young person to delve deeper and concentrate on developing a counter-strategy to the status quo, to restore the ground or "Grund" that is nowhere to be seen ("kein Grund zu sehen"). After carefully examining the given conditions, Roithamer penetrates below the surface: he argues that people must explore the "whole surface of our world and its subsurface, and keep probing it deeper and deeper" (*C* 175; "diese ganze Ober- dann auch Unterfläche und schließlich immer tiefer und tiefer hinunter und hinein zu sondieren," *K* 209). The slew of adjectives in German, "always down and deeper down and inward" ("immer tiefer und tiefer hinunter und hinein"), draws the reader inward with a drill's spiraling motion. The neologism "Unterfläche" (instead of "Oberfläche") is created as an equivalent for the subsurface, stressing the need to think about the underside as much as the upper area.

The confinement within an already confining space—the turret room within the building complex—does not have the intended effect of concentrating Roithamer on his purposes as inheritor of Altensam: instead, he becomes an "eccentric" character in his family's opinion.[12] The word, derived from the Greek "ekkentros" meaning "out of the center," describes Roithamer's behavior; ex-centrism works against the exclusive focus on the estate, moving him outward at the same time as his thought burrows downward. The landscape's reconnoitering and probing thought give birth to Roithamer's architectural project: he wants to create the perfect counterspace to Altensam, one which would extinguish his parents' malevolent influence and lack of guidance. His architectonic gesture marks a total break with inherited tradition: "we must turn it into a world to suit our own ideas, acting first behind the scenes, inconspicuously, but then with all our might and quite openly, so that we can say after a while that *we're living in our own world, not in some previous world*, [. . .] not in the given world of our parents."[13]

In his increasing distance from Altensam, Roithamer literally progresses outward as if through larger and larger concentric circles; the vertical drilling motion is turned outward and the spiraling motion spread horizontally. A whole discussion of "radiuses" permeates this section in the novel. This countermovement is as necessary as the drilling down for thought to develop. Roithamer states: "To think a subject through, one has to assume a position at the farthest possible remove from this subject [. . .]" (*C* 168; "Um eine Sache durchdenken zu können, muß die größtmögliche Entfernung von dieser Sache, also die größtmöglich entfernte Position zu dieser Sache eingenommen sein," *K* 200). Roithamer distances himself from the prison-fortress of Altensam in Upper Austria, relocating to the nearby garret belonging to his friend Höller and then on to Cambridge University, retracing with slight modification the philosopher Ludwig Wittgenstein's movement from Vienna to Lower Austria and then to Cambridge, England. Höller's garret or "Dachkammer" becomes Roithamer's "thought chamber" or "Denkkammer"—a nice alliterative wordplay in German that again underlines the relationship between the spaces in which we are and the architectonics of our thought.[14] The proximity to both Wittgenstein and Bloch is explicitly mentioned when the narrator reflects on Roithamer's proclivities and intellectual affinities in this anti-Altensam garret, so conducive for his own thoughts about his mentor. Roithamer finds himself drawn to the works of "Montaigne, Novalis, Hegel, Schopenhauer, Ernst Bloch." The affinity to Wittgenstein is particularly strong, since Roithamer and Wittgenstein share a thoughtscape that arises from the actual experience of the land. These books, which had shared their owner's nomadic existence, now come to rest on a bookshelf in the "Denkkammer." The narrator explains:

> I knew them from his constantly reiterated remarks in which he established a connection with these books, they were always basically the same: Montaigne, Novalis, Hegel, Schopenhauer, Ernst Bloch, and, because he thought that he recognized himself in them, the writings of Wittgenstein, a native of the same region as Roithamer and always a keen observer of Roithamer's regional landscape, they were always just the same few books of philosophy and poetry which, with his name inscribed on the flyleaf, he always carried about with him. (*C* 45)

> [I]ch kannte sie durch immer wiederkehrende Bemerkungen Roithamers, in welchen er einen Zusammenhang zu diesen Büchern hergestellt hatte, im Grunde waren es die immer gleichen Montaigne, Novalis, Hegel, Schopenhauer, Ernst Bloch und weil er in ihnen sich selbst zu erkennen glaubte, die Schriften von Wittgenstein, welcher aus der gleichen Landschaft wie Roithamer gekommen und immer ein aufmerksamer Beobachter der roithamerschen Landschaft gewesen war, immer nur einige wenige philosophische und dichterische Werke, die er mit seinem Namenszug versehen, immer bei sich hatte. (*K* 57)

The reader's repeated engagement with specific authors within a specific landscape and architecture gives form and contour to thought. Words indicating this iterative activity within a temporal continuum permeate this description. Note the German adverbs "immer" ("always") and "immer gleich" ("same"/"similar"), which recur five times—the same authors in the same or similar landscape, always and ever present, despite Roithamer's mobility. Roithamer's thought spaces are also sites of inner and outer vision, "scenes of thought" or "Schauplätze unseres Denkens," where thinking becomes theatrical and self-dramatizing ("in Szene setzen").[15] That is, by placing themselves within particular coordinates and rooms, the characters open themselves to a new frame of mind; this enables the quick read of the "Schauraum" and creates the vivid mise-en-scène facilitating innovative thought that I examined in Way Station 3.

The Cone, unlike the garret, evidently fails to institute a new preparatory course of study leading from the structured observation of a person to the creation of an essentially perfect architecture befitting another's needs. So what goes wrong? Why does Roithamer, as a kind of Wittgensteinian avatar, commit suicide and end his project, leaving behind his friend and tutee? Why does his tower, at the exact center of the Kobernausser Forest, not recenter and reterritorialize his *ex*centric personality? Why is the sequestered space in the Höller attic, a midpoint and threshold location, unsuccessful as a "thought chamber" or "Denkkammer" (Roithamer is located geographically "between" Cambridge and Altensam as well as in the uppermost space of a house in a gorge)? Why is the Cone not a properly humanist architecture through which Roithamer realizes his goal, namely to construct an architectonic form that is in perfect accordance with a person's being? Is the Cone or "Kegel" less a liberating elementary architecture than a vanishing funerary monument, marking the death of the sister for whom it was built according to exacting specifications and left to decay in nature?

Some of these questions can be answered with recourse to the history of architecture summoned up in the middle of the novel, where Roithamer articulates his rationale for building the Cone and his aversion to the supposed specialists who threaten to destroy it. In lambasting the architects who are interested in Roithamer's undertaking as "professional riffraff" or "Fachgesindel," he uses their purported lack of familiarity with architectural history to disparage them. The disqualification—like that of the parents as intellectual and moral authorities—opens a historical bracket that allows Roithamer to posit an acceptable, self-chosen "lineage" of teacher-models (even if his own work does not adhere to their precepts). The narrator quotes from Roithamer's papers, telling us exactly whom and what Roithamer emulates:

> Professional riffraff, so-called architects, intellectual charlatans, so Roithamer, exploiters of their clients, knuckleheads, brains of cement. Never answered a single inquiry, its origin suspect, some architect or building professional might be behind it. They never heard of James Gandon, for example, Sir John Soane, John Nash etcetera. When we act, we know the source of our action, when we think, the source of our thinking. Boulle, Hamilton, Vignon, conceptual change etcetera, so Roithamer, we mention in vain. I'd merely make a suggestion, and they go to pieces. Nothing from Neutra's publications, everything from Mies van der Rohe's, "nothing" and "everything" underlined. No dealings with the professionals because they destroy our ideas [sic], they are single-mindedly intent upon undermining our idea, upon destroying it. (C 155, no italics)

> Fachgesindel, sogenannte Architekten, Geistesscharlatane, so Roithamer, Bauherrenausnützer, Dummköpfe, Betonstumpfsinn. Keine einzige Zuschrift wegen Verdacht auf Architekten- oder Baufachherkunft beantwortet. James Gandon zum Beispiel, Sir John Soane,

> John Nash etcetera haben sie niemals gehört. Wenn wir handeln, kennen wir den Ursprung unseres Handelns, wenn wir denken, den Ursprung unseres Denkens. Boulle, Hamilton, Vignon, Konzeptionswechsel etcetera, so Roithamer, wir reden vergeblich. Wenn wir nur andeuten, zerfallen sie schon. *Nichts* aus den Schriften von Neutra, *alles* von Mies van der Rohe, nichts und alles unterstrichen. Der Grund, sich mit Fachleuten nicht einzulassen, weil diese unsere Idee vernichten, nichts im Sinn haben, als unsere Idee schwankend zu machen, sie zu vernichten. (*K* 186, emphasis in original)

This passage, envisioning a "proper" architecture based on "proper" foundational models, evokes an entire neoclassical architectural history. Its measure befits man and is proportioned according to his body; its substance is the plane or wall rather than the ornamental, dramatic feature such as a column or the interplay of light and dark. Roithamer lists James Gandon (1743–1823), an English architect of Palladian buildings in Ireland; John Nash (1752–1835), architect of the East Wing of Buckingham Palace; Sir John Soane (1753–1837), neoclassical English architect of the Bank of England and the Soane Museum in London housing Greek and Roman antiquities, Chinese ceramics, and Peruvian pottery; Scottish architect David Hamilton (1768–1843), designer of the Royal Exchange in Edinburgh; Pierre Alexandre Barthélémy Vignon (1763–1828), architect of the Madeleine Church in Paris and student of the famed architect Nicholas Ledoux, and, finally, Étienne-Louis Boullée (1728–1799), the neoclassical visionary and promoter of an emotionally engaged "speaking architecture" with an edifying purpose.[16]

With this list, an intimation of the Cone's death drive—its impulsion toward extinction and self-extinction—enters the novel's discourse on architecture and the architectonics of thought. Boullée provides the jarring note suggesting death rather than development (all the more irritating because his name is misspelled as "Boulle"). The architect and theorist Boullée became known for his *architecture parlante* during the French Revolution. As a teacher at the École Nationale des Ponts et Chaussées from 1778 to 1788, he designed fantastically monumental buildings of stark, three-dimensional forms, never to be executed.[17] Boullée is best known for his funerary cenotaphs, such as his spherical *Cenotaphe à Newton* (1784) or the *Cénotaphe conique* (1780), inspired by Egyptian archaeological finds of the time. With their simple symmetry, Boullée speculated that they easily could be grasped on a sensory level; their tremendous scale refocuses man on his small proportions in relation to a dominant nature.[18] Boullée appeals to what Anthony Vidler describes as "death forms," describing them at length in his *Essai sur l'art* from 1796–97.[19] Rather than working with the standing figure as a guiding proportion, Boullée uses the reclining figure as his measure for a "buried" or "sunken" architecture ("architecture ensevelie") of "low and compressed proportions, sinking into the earth, forming [. . .] by means of materials absorbent to the light, the black picture of an architecture of shadows," as Boullée himself explains his undertaking.[20] If the naming of the other eighteenth-century architects in *Correction* had implicitly condoned Roithamer's idea of an architecture built to man's (or better said: woman's) measure, Bernhard's reference to Boullée ambiguates the humanist associations the other architects evoke. Indeed, the allusion to Boullée's humic conception of architecture brings to mind the semi-submerged figures in Walter Pichler's drawings from the early 1970s (chapter 1), adding to the lugubrious overtones.

The historical bracket is closed with the mention of two prominent figures of more recent vintage: the Austrian émigré Richard Neutra (1892–1970) and the German émigré Mies van der Rohe (1886–1969). The novel cites them, I would argue, in order to further highlight the shortcomings underlying the Cone's conception. In aligning Roithamer solely with Mies van der Rohe rather than Neutra, Bernhard reveals the fallibility of Roithamer's architectural dogmatism, which does not integrate humans into their environment and prizes an overt functionality reliant on technical considerations. The disqualification of Neutra serves to call into question Roithamer's own architectural expertise and shows his inability to give credit where it is due.

Neutra propagates a "biological realism" in many books of the 1960s and 1970s,[21] according to which pure functionalism should be overcome in favor of an integrative view of man within nature. He bases his model on the kind of viewing I earlier described as structured observation (chapter 2), but Neutra complements it with a scientific focus on biology and, specifically, neurology and physiology. In his much publicized autobiographical book from 1962, *Mission for Tomorrow* (*Auftrag für morgen*), Neutra impugns contemporary life in "empty space" ("leeren Raum"), in which technology overwhelms organic life to create a vacuum (393). The architect describes the need for careful observation in the superlative terms characteristic of Bernhard: "Before we can do anything fitting for man, we have to know him—as well as human nature in general—to examine him through keen observation in the smallest detail and every context" ("Bevor wir irgend etwas Passendes für den Menschen tun können, müssen wir ihn—wie das allgemein Menschliche—kennen, ihn durch scharfsichtige Beobachtung bis ins kleinste und in allen Zusammenhängen erforschen").[22] In books such as *Building with Nature* from 1971, originally published as *Naturnahes Bauen* (1962), Neutra emphatically argues that the process of observation modifies the observed, influencing the architectural design: "It is also clear, however, that the observer modifies the observed!" (9; "Nun ist es aber auch klar, daß der Beobachter das Beobachtete modifiziert!", 9).

Like Neutra, Roithamer claims that those who build need to be schooled in looking. Roithamer generalizes from his own experience with his sister's Cone to mandate structured observation for all who build. Proper observation requires painstaking research and hence becomes a duty: "Those who build should investigate those for whom they are building, they must investigate them, the investigation of the man for whom a building is being put up should be the duty of the man who is doing the building, the builder should be forbidden to build for someone he has not thoroughly investigated" ("So sollten die, die bauen, die, für die sie bauen, erforschen, erforschen müssen, die Erforschung des Menschen, für den gebaut wird, sollte dem, der für diesen Menschen baut, immer zur Pflicht gemacht werden und es solle ihm verwehrt sein, für einen Menschen zu bauen, den der, der für ihn baut, nicht durchforscht hat").[23] In *Correction*, mental interpenetration and empathic identification are linked to such exacting observation, to what is called both an "art" and "science of observation" ("Beobachtungskunst" and "Beobachtungswissenschaft"), which conforms to the standards of *Wissenschaftlichkeit*: "Knowing that I must never relax this observation of my sister, must never relinquish this observation, mustn't allow my judgment to be swayed, to become imprecise" (*C* 158; "Das Bewußtsein, daß ich in der Beobachtung meiner Schwester niemals nachlassen, diese Beobachtung niemals aufgeben und daß ich in dieser Beobachtung niemals bestechlich sein darf, ungenau," *K* 189). However, Roithamer disregards the imbrications of built space and natural environment, human physiology and nature's properties, and he discounts the possibility that the observed person may influence the observer or vice versa. In denigrating Neutra *tout court*, Roithamer reacts less to the content of the architect's texts than their conversational tone, esoteric style, and logical drift when they attempt to integrate physiological, neurological, and biological development in the design process. Neutra advocates an integrative thinking that is perhaps too enmeshed for Roithamer, with the latter's increasingly desperate attempts to distinguish man from environment: "Outer and inner world, environment and you are fully meshed, not separable, not truly different from each other," Neutra writes in *Survival through Design* from 1954, an idea that recurs throughout all his later works.[24] The Austrian émigré's argument that the "biological balance" has vanished due to the hypertrophic Euclidean geometry of the modern city goes against the grain of Roithamer's stereometric site in the Kobernausser Forest.[25]

Turning his back on Neutra, the protagonist espouses Mies van der Rohe. Roithamer embraces the master builder of the modern era and his affirmation of technological innovation, shunning the Austrian compatriot who speaks more about the relational nature of buildings and the people who dwell in them. In this regard, Roithamer perhaps partakes of the vogue surrounding Mies van der Rohe in the late 1960s and the general deprecation of Neutra.[26] Shortly before Mies van der Rohe's death, major exhibitions and publications such as *The Master Builders* (1961, translated into German in 1962 as *Drei Meisterarchitekten*) mark the pinnacle of his international career and renown.[27] The superlatives present in the essays about the "master builder" correspond to the superlative statements in Roithamer's architectonics with the emphasis on all or nothing; hence "*everything* from Mies van der Rohe [. . .] 'everything' underlined" (my emphasis added to restore that of the original). In the novel's hyperbolic stress on the superlative nature of the tower and its elementary architectural form made of basic materials we can make out correspondences between Roithamer's project and contemporary laudatory descriptions of Mies van der Rohe's formal originality.

Indeed, how deeply indebted Roithamer is to the architectural rhetoric of his day! In the catalog accompanying a traveling exhibition in the United States and Germany of Mies van der Rohe's works in 1968, for instance, he is hyperbolically described as the "greatest living architect" producing the "most extraordinary buildings." Mies van der Rohe builds structures that can easily be classified according to basic type ("High Buildings, Low Buildings, Groups of Buildings") and material (steel or concrete)—the taxonomic impulse appeals to those ascetics interested in elementary architectures. For contemporary observers, Mies van der Rohe's implementation of such elementary forms and strong materials heralds a new kind of space. The lack of difference between the standards van der Rohe sets for "structural bones and finished surfaces" evidences an immediate architecture that does away with the distinctions between outer surface beauty and inner structure. Roithamer similarly tries to de-differentiate space: he leaves the Cone's rooms undesignated, paints white inner and outer walls, and only uses basic materials such as stone, brick, glass, and iron.[28] The curator A. James Speyer's description of Mies van der Rohe's architecture equally befits Roithamer's project: Mies van der Rohe, Speyer claims, is "called a purist for obvious reasons: his building lines are straight and sharp, his surfaces sheer, and his spatial relationships precise. More significantly, he is a purist in the sense that he wishes to reduce his architecture to its essential and eliminate every irrelevant feature."[29] Thus the novel, with its stress on purity, precision, reduction, and the essential, shares the vocabulary of art and architecture scholars of the late 1960s. (The hymns to the master builder belie Mies van der Rohe's own aversion to architecture as an individualistic experience and undertaking.)

As I have argued, Roithamer's building is ultimately an anti-humanist architecture, following neither Neutra's nor Mies van der Rohe's tenets in toto. In the overemphasis on the pure, reduced, private, and essential, the Cone is a miscalculation on the draftsman's part, demonstrating his inability to think productively about humans and their buildings, which his parents' home Altensam still managed to do, at least to some extent.[30] While he pronounces the architectonic form and the person living in it mutually dependent and adaptable, the rigidity of his counterspace belies any openness and changeability. There is no correspondence between inner and outer, between person and space; the design's hermeticism does not allow for permeability and interpenetration. For Roithamer, the problem is not just maintaining the balance between outer and inner, ground and height, but also guaranteeing the absolutely static nature of the tower—and thereby of the sister sequestered in the tower. As such the tower progressively closes down the vistas and opportunities for *Aus-* and *Durchblicke*: "First, the Cone offers views in all directions, then, the Cone offers views only southward and northward, then, only to the west and to the east, finally, only to the north."[31] Nine of the seventeen interior spaces do not have windows, but sealed "look-outs" or "Ausblicke," which cannot be opened or closed. In a cryptic passage, this aspect is underlined: "No windows but look-outs that are neither to be opened nor shut, natural airing of the inner-spaces always without having to open or shut the look-outs" (*C* 163–64; "Die Ausblicke sind keine Fenster, es sind Ausblicke, die nicht zu öffnen und also auch nicht zu schließen sind, die Lüftung ist, ohne daß die Ausblicke geöffnet oder geschlossen werden müssen, immer naturgemäß," *K* 195). Since the Cone is built to match the heights of the surrounding trees, the northerly windows at the top furthermore do not actually offer views onto anything. Like the tower in "Two Young People," the view turns out not to exist at all (Way Station 1).

The Cone disregards the criticism of functionalism, which the philosopher Ernst Bloch voices in *The Principle of Hope* at around the same time the Mies van der Rohe vogue sweeps the Western world. For Bloch, functionalism is directly related to capitalism and mirrors its inhumane demands. Bernhard's debt to Bloch—"everything from Ernst Bloch!", he writes in a letter to his publisher, echoing his character's words about Mies van der Rohe[32]—is evident in the implicit critique of functionalism to be found in *Correction*: "Functionalist architecture reflects and doubles the ice-cold automatic world of the commercial society anyway, of its alienation, of its human beings subject to the division of labour, of its abstract technology" ("Die funktionalistische Architektur reflektiert und verdoppelt ja ohnehin die eiskalte Automatenwelt der Warengesellschaft, ihrer Entfremdung, ihrer arbeitsgeteilten Menschen, ihrer abstrakten Technik").[33] In Bloch's section on modern architecture entitled "Building on Hollow Space"—or, more accurately translated, "Building *in* the Hollow Space" ("Bauen im Hohlraum")—the hollow space is a function of the "de-internalization" of buildings, their self-proclaimed but fallacious "adjustment" to the forbidding outside world and existence in a kind of bourgeois vacuum.[34] Modern functionalist architecture, in Bloch's view, has not fulfilled its promise to create an interchange between in- and outside, between public and private. The puristic constructs are shams, hiding the surveillant nature of the state or glossing over their capitalist irreconcilability with lived, corporeal existence.In Roithamer's hyperfunctionalist, self-referential construct, the singular trumps the universal and the particular the general. The Cone signals the ultimate isolation of the person for whom it is intended, and it warns of the dangers that any merely individualistic architectonics may hold: his sister dies, Roithamer maintains, when confronted with the completed Cone. The Cone's purported modernism is monotonous, hostile, at odds with the "messy vitality" of life.[35] *Bildung* via edification requires a flexibility that Roithamer's model cannot muster, an overlap with the society of which it is a part, an entanglement with the surrounding landscape, and a mutability that the Cone denies.

Wittgensteinian Openings

I would like to turn to the relationality between man and environment in the case of the Wittgenstein House. Margarethe Stonborough-Wittgenstein commissions the architect Paul Engelmann to design a house in the Kundmanngasse in the early 1920s, but her brother Ludwig takes over and builds it, finishing in 1928. In the stacked structure in the Third District of Vienna, the visionary architects' call for pure architecture finds a perfect, if much earlier, realization. In the newspaper discussions surrounding the mansion's proposed sale to a developer (who planned to replace the low cubic structure with a high-rise tower) in the 1970s, journalists stress the elementary character of Ludwig Wittgenstein's house. One writer lauds the building's "constructed body [. . .] of unprecedented severity," its "fanatical striving for order," and "Spartan asceticism."[36] In another article, the same writer remarks on the "fanatical obsession" and "logical severity" of the project.[37] The image of a precision maniac, bringing to bear his formidable technical skills in the design and supervision, also arises in the journalistic description by the Austrian writer Hilde Spiel, a friend of Thomas Bernhard's. Spiel, drawing on Hermine Wittgenstein's family chronicle, makes the following remark about Ludwig Wittgenstein in a newspaper article praising the structure:

> He drew, according to a family chronicle, every window, every door, every window handle, every radiator with an exactness as if they were precision instruments, and with the noblest measurements, and then, with his uncompromising energy, he saw to it that the things were also made with the same exact precision.
>
> Er zeichnete, so eine Familienchronik, jedes Fenster, jede Tür, jeden Riegel der Fenster, jeden Heizkörper mit einer Genauigkeit, als wären es Präzisionsinstrumente, und in den edelsten Maßen, und er setzte dann mit seiner kompromißlosen Energie durch, daß die Dinge auch mit der gleichen Genauigkeit ausgeführt wurden.[38]

The stress on the categorical design and fastidious implementation serves an ulterior motive: it suggests a correlation between Wittgenstein's language philosophy and his architectural composition. Arguments like Spiel's are meant to counteract the image of the dilettantish Wittgenstein, which the head of the preservation commission publicly propagates in order to have the house demolished.[39] By labeling Wittgenstein a philosopher and denigrating his

Figure 17. Exterior of Wittgenstein House on the Kundmanngasse, Vienna. Image © Moritz Nähr, Wittgenstein Archive, Cambridge.

architectural bona fides, Peter Pötschner of the Federal Monuments Office maintains that the Kundmanngasse mansion is not worth saving.[40]

The three-story structure in the Third District is, needless to say, an architectural marvel. As Nana Last has argued in her book on the interrelationship between Wittgenstein's architecture and his philosophy, *Wittgenstein's House: Language, Space, and Architecture* (2008), the exterior view of massed white cubes and rectangles of varying size and asymmetrical grouping has dominated the building's reception (see figure 17.)

The austerity of Wittgenstein's early language philosophy is correlated to the building's emphatic rectangularity (its overall *Grundriss* is nearly square). The Wittgenstein House's minimalism is seen as part and parcel of the *Tractatus*'s "mysteriously" sparse prose,[41] occasioning the kinds of descriptions I mentioned. However, Nana Last concentrates on the inside, taking her cue from one of the architects instrumental in saving the house, Bernhard Leitner. She calls the inside the "scene of inhabitation" to argue that it more accurately attests to Wittgenstein's philosophical conceptions and evolution. For her, the house becomes a site of conflict between the "idealized pictorial view dreamed of by the *Tractatus*" and the "spatial practices of architecture subsequently developed in the *Investigations*"—a conflict that leads Wittgenstein from a formalistic, abstracted view of the logic of language to a more flexible, encompassing view of language's (and language philosophy's) imbrications in everyday life. Wittgenstein's practical experience of architecture forms the hinge between the two seminal works, as it were. Readers familiar with the scene of inhabitation can broaden their understanding of Wittgenstein's conceptualization of resemblances, boundaries, praxis, and visualizing. They can recognize his movement outward from the concentrated focus of the early work. In her introduction, Last summarizes this development:

> The *Tractatus* had attempted to define the limits of "what cannot be thought by working outwards through what can be thought." Beyond the bounds of the thinkable or sayable was that which could only be shown. Effectively, this thinking subdivided philosophy's traditional territory, casting aesthetics and ethics out beyond language into the realm of showing and practice. Logic in the *Tractatus* held the privileged, if tenuous, position of connecting saying and showing and thereby allowing language to represent the world. The *Investigations* removed the limits that the *Tractatus* had imposed on language and philosophy by rejecting the *Tractatus*'s view that language represents the world in accordance with the rules of logic. Instead, Wittgenstein's late philosophy saw that the proper task of philosophy was to reconnect the philosophical study of language with language's everyday practices. (Last, *Wittgenstein's House*, 3)

In Last's view, Wittgenstein's involvement with both the design and execution of the house allows him to radically reconceive language as something we inhabit and cannot view, describe, or apprehend from the outside, because we are already within it.[42] The way one lives—more specifically, the way his sister lives—and the way one builds become the necessary spatial experiences permitting Wittgenstein's movement away from the "(nonmaterial) order of logic." Wittgenstein then renegotiates the border between private and public language, between the sayable and the showable.[43] In his architectural plans, he carefully links interior and exterior, makes porous boundaries between public and private spaces, creates multiple foci of interest (the entry hall, the salon), and produces an interplay between the larger structural asymmetry of the house and smaller symmetries specific to certain rooms. In doing so, Wittgenstein rethinks his philosophy of language, which tries to locate speaking man in relation to others and the realms of ethics and aesthetics.

The mansion in the Kundmanngasse has various means of emphasizing passage and transition—it achieves the adaptability that Raimund Abraham implicitly espouses, Konrad Wachsmann extols, Richard Neutra embraces, and Thomas Bernhard upholds as the ne plus ultra of a lived *Bildung*. This assertion may be illustrated using the entry and main hallway, with its 1:1 relationship of length and width, from which rooms, terrace, passages, and so on radiate outward.[44] The entrance to the building gradually leads inward

Figure 18. Paul Engelmann and Ludwig Wittgenstein, Ludwig Wittgenstein House, Vienna. © Margherita Spiluttini.

by degrees: first, one passes through glass doors into a small, nearly square projecting antechamber (273 cm × 255 cm); then, through glass doors into a perfectly square vestibule or *Vorraum* (322 cm × 322 cm) with another set of high glass doors. From the vestibule, ten stairs bordered by a short wall on either side lead upward into an elevated larger hall area, also nearly square (650 × 685 cm). From this elevated plateau, all the adjoining rooms, private and public, spread into the interior (salon, breakfast room, music room) and exterior (terrace). These areas are separated from the hall via high glass doors with metal partitions.[45]

In this manner, the constricted vestibule opens onto increasingly expansive areas, transitioning the visitor from street to house, from the outer domain into the private realm (and vice versa, as the case may be) with the help of smoothly flowing squares in the *Grundriss*. The interior, too, is not homogeneous, as the slight shifts and imperfect squares foreshadow, but concretizes the changing configurations between more and less public areas through a complex set of doors and door casings.[46] There is no harsh break between public and private sphere or outer and inner realm, just an implied axis of movement upward, reiterated in the two beams running along the ceiling as extensions of the vestibule walls.

The linear symmetries establish a visual and tactile rhythm upon entering. The metal partitions of the entry door parallel the square columns flanking the stairs at the top. They create a staggered pattern of vertical lines with the door partitions on both sides of the elevated entry hall and the pilasters at the base of the staircase. The strong sequence of vertical lines subtly structures the field of vision, setting up a cross-rhythm to the horizontal lines of the stairs. Within the house, too, there is no severe cut between more sequestered personal spaces and general rooms for entertaining. With the use of special doubled glass doors that mimic the double-paned windows used in façades,[47] Wittgenstein creates a flow between the various rooms and carries elements of the exterior over into the interior.

While I cannot go into a complete analysis of Wittgenstein's house—indeed, I refer readers to Leitner's and Last's detailed analyses—I would like to briefly mention the importance of glass in Wittgenstein's emphasis on transitions, passageways, and openness. High doors open between rooms on the first floor, with glass of varying transparency (some milky, others clear) and thin metal partitions between the double glazed panes. The use of glass produces different axes of vision in the case of transparent glass or increased depth in the case of translucent glass. Leitner's description is worth quoting, since it resonates with the kind of Bernhardian "Durchblicke" I have been emphasizing: "Curiously, the hall—which is narrow in terms of scale—is opened up by the doors and the glass wall to the terrace, even when all the doors are closed. The transparent glass doors allow a view through; the translucent glass intimates that the space extends further" ("Merkwürdigerweise ist die maßstäblich enge Halle durch die Türen wie durch die Glaswand zur Terrasse—auch wenn alle Türen sich im geschlossenen Zustand befinden—geöffnet: bei transparentem Glas dem Durchblick, bei transluzentem Glas dem Ahnen einer Raum-Vertiefung").[48] Even when the doors are closed, they suggest porousness and the existence of vistas beyond. The architecture never becomes hermetically self-referential or self-contained. The influx of light and possibility of views suggest the open nature of the rooms grouped around the central entryway. The metal subdivisions between the panes and polished concrete floor pleasantly lend some heft and solidity to the airy interior.

Wittgenstein calibrates the size of the rooms and the changing perspectives to lengthen the experience of arrival or departure. In certain doorframes between rooms on the first floor, doubled glass doors open in opposite directions. This emphatic architectural signal prolongs the moment of arrival and extends the period of transition. Bernhard Leitner even speaks of a "ceremonial" gesture in his analysis of Wittgenstein's house.[49] He notes that this feature highlights the act of passage, creating an elongated transitional space. Opening the double doors has a highly theatrical effect:

> Thus, Wittgenstein emphasizes, or indeed almost celebrates the short route, in which the temporal sequence of leaving and entering is

> abolished. The connection, the "joint" becomes an architectural symbol depicting the time of transition and extending the line separating two spaces in the direction of both. When the two pairs of doors are closed, this transitional space is folded back into the wall.
>
> Das Betonen, fast Zelebrieren einer kurzen Wegstrecke, in der das Nacheinander von Verlassen und Betreten aufgehoben wird. Die Verbindung, das Gelenk, wird zum architektonischen Zeichen. Ein dynamischer, gerichteter Raum, der die Zeit des Übergangs abbildet—die Trennlinie zwischen zwei Räumen in beide Richtungen dehnt.

In Leitner's attentive documentation and interpretation of the Wittgenstein House, he includes floor plans that show the perspectives for the visitor standing in certain rooms or looking out from particular vantage points.[50] Nowhere do we find the rooms lacking "look-outs" as in Roithamer's Cone; perforations, porousness, and permeability are everywhere in evidence in Wittgenstein's house. The perforations have their place in the structure—the openings (doors, windows, entryways) have as much staying power as the erected walls and anchored foundations.

As I mentioned, Wittgenstein's house was known primarily from photos of its exterior at the time Bernhard conceived and wrote his novel. So it may seem speculative to infer that there is a correlation between Wittgenstein's interiors and Bernhard's thoughts on the relation between *Bildung* and building in *Correction*. Indeed, the Bulgarian Cultural Forum purchased the Wittgenstein House in 1975, four years after its rescue, and I am not aware that it was open to the public before the novel's publication. I would argue, however, that this does not matter too much. Bernhard, with his careful restoration of the old farmhouse in Obernathal, the miner's home in Ottnang, and the old farmhouse named "Krucka" near the Traunsee, picks up on certain features that Wittgenstein borrows from Austrian architectural history. For Wittgenstein appropriates from the archaic and elementary architectures in which he resides in the province of Lower Austria, where he is an elementary schoolteacher from 1920 to 1922 (and puts together a dictionary for his lower school students).[51] A staircase in his simple home in Trattenbach leads from a side entry upward to a small hallway that opens onto what was probably his room, containing his self-designed wooden bedstead from Cambridge (figures 19 and 20). Above the side entry we find a tripartite glass window, with a split structure like that of the doors in the Kundmanngasse.

However, when we leave the second-floor room Wittgenstein rented to go toward the street and the school where he worked, we sense a difference. On walking downward, the moment of elongated transition we experienced ascending feels abbreviated: the steep stairs seem to throw us directly onto the street. We now experience a shortened passage, which Wittgenstein reconfigures and stretches in his sister's Viennese home.

Figure 19 (*above*). Side entrance to house where Wittgenstein boarded in Trattenbach.
Figure 20 (*below*). Wittgenstein's self-designed bedstead. Photos © author.

The Hidden Cone

Let me come to a conclusion. As a crumbling structure, the tower in the Kobernausser Forest in *Correction* is a monument to the broken compact between the environment and human beings; it stands as a reminder of their careless attitude toward their surroundings. Because of humans' hubris, they cannot conceive of an architectural form embodying humanistic development in line with their and nature's needs. The tower's outrageousness contrasts with the care Martin Heidegger outlines in his talk "Building Dwelling Thinking" ("Bauen Wohnen Denken," 1951),[52] where he explores what it is to be human and to live on this earth. To dwell means to live in the "vicinity of shared things that are manifest to all," to preserve and to spare—although it also means to recognize a permanent homelessness.[53] It may be hard to take Heidegger's etymological reflections on the word "building" ("bauen"), "living" or "dwelling" ("wohnen"), and "space" ("Raum") too seriously—especially in light of the hilarious and vicious drubbing he and his Todtnauberg chalet get in *Old Masters* (indeed, I have not been able to read him with a straight face since encountering him in Bernhard's late novel). Heidegger's unease with radical architectonic novelty is of course stronger than Bernhard's and Wittgenstein's—hence Heidegger's use of the Heidelberg Bridge and Black Forest farm as examples in his 1951 talk, rather than any new construction taking place in Germany at the time of the Darmstädter Symposia (Darmstädter Gespräche). But there is a moment of overlap with Wittgenstein and Bernhard. All three reflect on the attraction of traditional structures. Heidegger, too, seems to return to an elementary shape: he uses the obsolete word for square in conceptualizing his "Geviert" or "fourfold," in which mortal men live carefully on earth with a view toward heaven and the gods.[54] Since building is inseparable from dwelling—and building means to spare ("schonen")—the Cone becomes a travesty of Heidegger's ideal of living in a neighborly relation with the world. As it does in Bernhard.

In closing, I would like to posit another intertext for Bernhard's Cone. Its implicit vanishing point may be the one painting not mentioned in *Old Masters*, for which the Art History Museum is, after all, most famous: Pieter Bruegel's 1563 work *The Tower of Babel* (figure 21). As in *Correction*, the enormous construction site stands in no relation to man's measure. Men are small ants in the tower's shadow; the conical structure dwarfs the city of Ghent, shown below and behind it. Its solidity seems like a pretense, with masons covering brickwork haphazardly. Excrescences—barracks or sheds—sprout from the tower, undermining its symmetry. Primeval rocks jut out like recalcitrant formations, seeming to defy workers' efforts at subjugation; ultimately, nature cannot be dominated. Heavy machinery for lifting boulders along the tower's terraces is reminiscent of cannons and gallows, adding a belligerent note. As if a premonition of coming doom had guided the masons' hands, the tower tilts to one side. The rebirth of classical antiquity is already

Figure 21. Pieter Bruegel the Elder, *The Tower of Babel*. 1563. Image © Kunsthistorisches Museum Vienna.

a decline: one empire's monument hints at another's colossal failure, with the allusions to Rome's Coliseum in Bruegel's arches. At the same time that the tower beckons the seafarer or traveler as a safe haven, the proximity of the harbor points to the possibility of escape and flight.

Bruegel's tower is hardly a good vantage point for observation: two indistinct figures at the top are not privy to the political drama playing out below. There, the king, at a remove from the site, is heavy of mien, while groveling laborers look to placate him. Stern and unhappy expressions dominate on all sides. Finally, the capstone (or is it the foundation stone?) is missing from the finished structure—Bruegel's engraved name on the block in the painting's immediate foreground is far, far away from the tower itself. Hardly visible, too, is the small farm at the tower's base, which is a counterpoint to the looming structure destined for decay. Sheltered from wind and storm, this farmhouse with its slanting, thatched roof is a place where the various ages of life can be imagined running their course from cradle to grave, as in Heidegger's farmyard at the foot of the mountain in his essay "Building Dwelling Thinking."[55]

We generally interpret Bruegel's cone as reflecting a negative trajectory along the lines I have sketched here, much as we tend to see Bernhard's novels as having a pessimistic teleology. We neglect the fact that Bruegel lends the tower its own dignity, portraying it *before* its collapse into Babelian pandemonium. It is also a testament to other, more positively connoted things: humans' striving for the "higher," abstract things in this life and the next; their attraction to elementary architectural forms, even as these depart from any strict typology; their yearning for edifices that afford them new vistas; their need for secure foundations that provide a grounding in specific landscapes; and the honest, if futile longing to produce structures that outlast time's vicissitudes. In Bernhard's novels, students struggle for such higher things and look to their mentors to provide the thought structures that are analogous to certain elementary edifices, both boxes and cones, within which their instruction takes place. They search for someone who might guide them out of the disorienting and debilitating hollow space between the commercial and familial realm. They seek out alternative ivory towers and the architectonic promise they hold. Once there, they need elongated spaces of transition and extended periods of initiation; they profit from the give-and-take with the dynamic landscape and from unrestricted views. Only then can the peripatetic nature of thought, with its digressions, bifurcations, haphazard stackings, and fits and starts combine with other haptic-optic sensations. Only then can mobile thought reconcile the horizontal space of outward extension with the upward direction of utopian aspiration and the downward burrowing of studied concentration.

In our historical moment, an ivory tower of this sort is coming to seem as fanciful and perhaps doomed as Bruegel's tower—but I think it is necessary to uphold such an image as an ideal without devolving into sentimental kitsch or cultural pessimism. Bernhard's *Bildung* rightfully envisions such a space.

NOTES

Preface

1. Images of the houses and surrounding grounds can be found in Wieland and Erika Schmied's coffee table book, *Thomas Bernhards Häuser* (Salzburg: Residenz, 1995). An entire chapter is devoted to his furniture designs from 1976, the year he purchased his apartment in Gmunden (147–57).

2. Ibid., 103–33.

3. The Castle already crops up in the fragment "The Italian" ("Der Italiener" 1964), which antedates the purchase of Ottnang by nearly a decade (see Schmied, *Häuser*, 105). In 1970, Bernhard reworks the material into a film script of the same title; Ferry Radax directs the film in 1971. See the brochure accompanying the Suhrkamp DVD of *Der Italiener*, especially the essay by Hans Höller and Georg Schmied (16–45, esp. 23–25).

4. One is reminded of the distinction Christian Norberg-Schulz, drawing on Heidegger, makes between the vertical and the horizontal in *Architecture: Presence, Language, Place* (Milan: Skira, 2000): "While the built form rises vertically and incarnates the character of the situation, 'spatial organization' illustrates the way in which place extends horizontally admitting human use. 'To admit' in general means making room for the opinions of others, but in this case the original significance of giving space to an action comes back into play" (189).

5. The legacy of modern architecture in relation to Bernhard's project will be dealt with in the conclusion devoted to *Correction*. On the topic of modernist architectural aesthetics and its imbrications with culture, I have found the writing of Edward Dimendberg particularly useful. See his book *Film Noir and the Spaces of Modernity* (Cambridge, Mass.: Harvard University Press, 2004); his essay on "The Limits to Emplacement" in *Rethinking History* 11, no. 4 (December 2007), 513–16, or his book on *Diller Scofidio + Renfro: Architecture after Images* (Chicago: University of Chicago Press, 2013). On the ethics of this architecture, see Norberg-Schulz's *Genius Loci: Towards a Phenomenology of Architecture* (London: Rizzoli, 1980), who writes about Frank Lloyd Wright and the modern movement: "The traditional order of building tasks is [. . .] reversed. This means that architecture is no longer based on dogma and authority, but ought to grow out of daily life, as an expression of man's understanding of nature, of other men and of himself. The 'higher' building tasks thus become a result rather than a condition, and they represent something man must conquer in his own life. The *esprit nouveau* therefore should free man from the 'systems,' and conquer the split between thought and feeling which was a characteristic product of bourgeois society." In *Genius Loci*, Norberg-Schulz goes on to explain that the modernist "loss of place" is related to problematic "confusions of scales," that is, the open floor plans work well for suburban or rural dwellings but not for urban buildings (194–95).

6. For a very different, but highly interesting approach to the sense of space in Bernhard, see Thorsten Carstensen's essay "Keine Spuren hinterlassen: Bauen, Wohnen und Erben bei Thomas Bernhard," in *Gegenwartsliteratur* 13 (2014): 111–35. Carstensen argues for the non-representational, non-specific nature of Bernhard's places/spaces.

7. For some of the voluminous scholarship and more esoteric writing on the genius loci, see also Christopher Day, *Places of the Soul: Architecture and Design as a Healing Art* (London: Harper Collins, 1993) and his *Spirit and Place: Healing Our Environment* (London: Architectural, 2002); James and Roberta Swan, *Dialogues with the Living Earth: New Ideas on the Spirit of Place from Designers, Architects, and Innovators* (Wheaton, Ill.: Theosophical Publishing House, 1996).

8. The volume of theoretical writing on space and place has taken on vast dimensions, and I will be referring only to select texts in the course of this book. For a useful overview of important writings, see K. Michael Hays, ed., *Architecture Theory since 1968* (Cambridge, Mass.: MIT Press, 1998); as well as Jörg Dünne and Stephan Günzel, eds., *Raumtheorie: Grundlagentexte aus Philosophie und Kulturwissenschaften* (Frankfurt am Main: Suhrkamp, 2006); see also Oliver Simons, *Raumgeschichten: Topographien der Moderne in Philosophie, Wissenschaft und Literatur* (Munich: Fink, 2007); and John David Rhodes and Elena Garfinkel, eds., *Taking Place: Location and the Moving Image* (Minneapolis: University of Minnesota, 2011). Underpinning my thinking is Michel Foucault's seminal essay "Of Other Spaces" (1967, first pub. 1984); Henri Lefebvre's *The Production of Space*, trans. Donald Nicholson-Smith (Cambridge, Mass.: Blackwell, 1991; orig. pub. 1974); and Michel de Certeau, *The Practice of Everyday Life*, trans. Steven Rendall (Berkeley: University of California Press, 1984), referred to in the section entitled Way Station 1.

9. In her introduction in *Theorizing a New Agenda for Architecture*, Kate Nesbitt notes that some post-industrial architectural theorists distance themselves from Christian Norberg-Schulz's focus on the phenomenological aspects of place. They see it as a nostalgic concept in a time of increasing dematerialization and simulation. See Nesbitt's *Theorizing a New Agenda for Architecture: An Anthology of Architectural Theory 1965–1995*, 2nd ed. (Princeton, N.J.: Princeton Architectural, 1996), esp. 50–51.

10. See Wilhelm von Humboldt's famous organizational plan for the founding of the University in Berlin, "Über die innere und äußere Organisation der höheren wissenschaftlichen Anstalten in Berlin" (1810): "Wissenschaft ist als etwas noch nicht ganz Gefundenes und nie ganz Aufzufindendes zu betrachten und unablässig als solche zu suchen" (*Gesammelte Schriften* X, 253). In contradistinction to the ideas Bernhard puts forward, Humboldt is against seeing scholarship and research as dependent on any kind of philosophical propaedeutics. See also Gutschmidt's essay, "Von der 'Idee einer Universität' zur 'Zukunft unserer Bildungsanstalten'—Bildungsbegriff und Universitätsgedanke in der deutschen Philosophie von Schiller bis Nietzsche," in *Bildung als Kunst: Fichte, Schiller, Humboldt, Nietzsche*, ed. Jürgen Stolzenberg and Lars-Thade Ulrichs (New York: De Gruyter, 2010), 160–62; and Tilman Borsche, *Wilhelm von Humboldt* (Munich: C.H. Beck, 1990), esp. 63.

11. This is a point Henri Lefebvre amply makes in *The Production of Space* (1974).

Introduction

1. Friedrich Kluge, *Etymologisches Wörterbuch der deutschen Sprache* (Strassburg: K. J. Trübner, 1883), 115.

2. Achleitner studied with the renowned architect Clemens Holzmeister at Vienna's Academy of Fine Art from 1950 to 1953; he became a member of the experimental Wiener Gruppe (Vienna Group) in 1955. After a short period as a practicing architect, he turned to architectural criticism and poetry. See Thomas Eder's short entry on Achleitner, where he embeds Achleitner's poetic experiments in the socio-historical context, in Konstanze Fliedl, Marina Rauchenbauer, and Joanna Wolf, *Handbuch der Kunstzitate: Malerei, Skulptur, Fotografie in der deutschsprachigen Literatur der Moderne* (Berlin: De Gruyter, 2011), 1–2.

3. See Friedrich Achleitner, *quadratroman* (Salzburg: Residenz, 1972), 168–69.

4. Ibid., n.p.

5. On the relationship between images and models, of "Bilder" and "Vorbilder" in *Bildung*, see Eric Downing's *After Images: Photography, Archaeology, and Psychoanalysis and the Tradition of Bildung* (Detroit: Wayne State University Press, 2006).

6. Important scholarship has been done on the relationship between buildings and *Bildung*: Susan Bernstein's *Housing Problems: Writing and Architecture in Goethe, Walpole, Freud, and Heidegger* (Stanford, Calif.: Stanford University Press, 2008); Claudia Brodsky's *In the Place of Language: Literature and the Architecture of the Referent* (New York: Fordham University Press, 2009); and Daniel Purdy's *On the Ruins of Babel: Architectural Metaphor in German Thought* (Ithaca, N.Y: Cornell University Press, 2011) deserve particular mention.

7. Ernst Cassirer, *Philosophie der symbolischen Formen: Mythisches Denken*, vol. 2 (Darmstadt: Wissenschaftliche Buchgesellschaft, 1977), 98–99; Ernst Cassirer, *The Philosophy of Symbolic Forms: Mythical Thought*, vol. 2, trans. Ralph Manheim (New Haven, Conn.: Yale University Press, 1955), 84.

8. See Achleitner's quotation of Cassirer, *quadratroman*, 32–33.

9. In words strikingly reminiscent of Bernhard's sudden turns of direction ("Kehrtwendungen"), Cassirer writes: "we require a peculiar reversal of perspective, a *negation* of what seems immediately given in sensory perception, before we can arrive at the 'logical space' of pure mathematics" (*Philosophy of Symbolic Forms*, 83; "es bedarf vielmehr einer eigentümlichen Umkehr der Blickrichtung, einer Aufhebung dessen, was in der sinnlichen Anschauung unmittelbar gegeben erscheint, um zu dem ‚Gedankenraum' der reinen Mathematik vorzudringen," *Philosophie*, 98).

10. Achleitner quotes Cassirer: "If we start from this standard of comparison, there would seem to be [no] doubt that *mythical* space is closely related to the space of perception and strictly opposed to the logical space of geometry. Both mythical space and perceptive space are thoroughly concrete products of consciousness" (*Philosophy*, 84; "Geht man von diesem Maßstab der Vergleichung aus, so scheint es nicht den mindesten Zweifel zu leiden, daß der mythische Raum dem Wahrnehmungsraum ebenso nahe verwandt ist, wie er auf der anderen Seite dem Denkraum der Geometrie strikt entgegengesetzt ist. Beide: der mythische Raum wie der Wahrnehmungsraum sind durchaus konkrete Bewußtseinsgebilde," *Philosophie*, 99, qtd. in *quadratroman*, 33).

11. See Achleitner, *quadratroman*, 33, where he quotes Cassirer's statement: "Es haftet an ihm [jedem Element] ein besonderer auszeichnender Charakter, der sich nicht mehr allgemein begrifflich beschreiben läßt, der aber als solcher unmittelbar erlebt wird" (99); the English quotation is from Cassirer, *Philosophy*, 84.

12. Cassirer, *Philosophy*, 84.

13. Achleitner, *quadratroman*, from *Meyers Enzyklopädisches Lexikon*, 168.

14. His site-specificity is noticeable in the orthography of many of the texts, with their distinct Austrian dialect, but also comes to the fore in the definition of "Quadrat . . ." I cited; Achleitner singles out the German abbreviation (*quadratroman*, 89).

15. Here Achleitner alludes to German exactitude ("deutsche [. . .] genauigkeit") as opposed to the stereotypical Viennese lassitude and sloppiness ("wiener sc/hlamperei," *quadratroman*, 176).

16. On the relationship between Bernhard and the Viennese avant-garde, see Matthias Konzett, *The Rhetoric of National Dissent in Thomas Bernhard, Peter Handke, and Elfriede Jelinek* (Rochester, N.Y.: Camden, 2000), particularly ch. 2 (25–56).

17. To be found in his library are the complete nine-volume works of Ernst Bloch in the *Gesamtausgabe* from 1962 (Frankfurt am Main: Suhrkamp).

18. With the exception of Adorno's text in the eponymous *Erziehung zur Mündigkeit* (Frankfurt am Main: Suhrkamp, 1970, 133–47), which has been translated by Robert French, Jem Thomas, and Dorothee Weymann as "Education for Maturity and Responsibility" in the journal *History and the Human Sciences* 12, no. 3 (1999): 21–34, the other titles are available only in German (see the list of Works Cited). Further Suhrkamp texts are Gisela Stütz, *Berufspädagogik unter ideologiekritischem Aspekt*, 1970; Manuela du Boys-Remonds *Strategien kompensatorischer Erziehung*, 1971; Wolfgang Lempert's *Leistungsprinzip und Emanzipation*, 1971; and Konrad Wünsche, *Der Volksschullehrer Ludwig Wittgenstein*, 1985. Many architectural volumes such as Reinhard Bentmann and Michael Müller's *Die Villa als Herrschaftsarchitektur* (Frankfurt am Main: Syndikat, 1970), Wolfgang Döring's *Perspektiven einer Architektur* (Frankfurt am Main: Suhrkamp, 1973), Friedrich Achleitner's *Österreichische Architektur im 20. Jahrhundert* (Salzburg: Residenz, 1980), and Eduard Sekler's *Josef Hoffmann: Das architektonische Werk* (Salzburg: Residenz, 1982) are also part of his library.

19. In regard to Bernhard and his conception of the public sphere, see Konzett's chapter, "Publikumsbeschimpfung: Thomas Bernhard's Provocations of the Austrian Public Sphere" (*Rhetoric*, 25–56).

20. Rüdiger Görner, in an essay on Bernhard's mediating constructions between one's personal life and the larger public, briefly mentions education as a form of "Weltbezug," or connection with the world. In his essay "The Broken Window Handle: Thomas Bernhard's Notion of *Weltbezug*," he writes: "The very instrument that should provide meaningful access to the world, mediating between the small world of the province and tout le monde [. . .] is education." Görner cites Bernhard's autobiographical text *An Indication of the Cause* (*Die Ursache*, 1975) as evidence that "this instrument called education fails completely to accomplish this aim" (in Matthias Konzett, *A Companion to the Works of Thomas Bernhard* [Rochester, N.Y.: Camden House, 2010], 89–104, esp. 95). However, while the scholar may be correct that the novels demonstrate the breakdown of old

institutional forms of instruction, Görner's denigration of education per se is overhasty.

21. The speech, in which Bernhard claims "die Märchen sind vorbei," is now a part of the compendium *My Prizes* (*MP*, 117–20). About the German educational debates, see Katharina Rutschky's polemical edited volume, *Schwarze Pädagogik: Quellen zur Naturgeschichte der bürgerlichen Erziehung* (Berlin: Ullstein, 1977); and Alice Miller, *Am Anfang war Erziehung* (Frankfurt am Main: Suhrkamp, 1980). I provide a summary of the debates in the chapter on Michael Haneke's 2009 film *The White Ribbon* in *Trügerische Vertrautheit: Filme von Michael Haneke* (Vienna: Synema, 2010), 129–45.

22. See Theodor W. Adorno, *Dissonanzen: Musik in der verwalteten Welt*, in *Gesammelte Schriften*, vol. 14 (Frankfurt am Main: Suhrkamp, 1990), 7–167.

23. Adorno's 1959 speech "Education after Auschwitz" ("Erziehung nach Auschwitz") takes aim at this overt "becoming science," "Verwissenschaftlichung," linking it to technology in particular. In a world dominated by technology, it becomes an end rather than a means; the irrational, fetishistic relationship people entertain to machines makes them lose sight of the human, in whose service technology is supposed to be employed. Adorno locates one of the reasons underlying the general emotional glaciation in this fetishization ("Erziehung nach Auschwitz" in *Gesammelte Schriften*, vol. 10.2, Frankfurt am Main: Suhrkamp, 1977, 674–90).

24. See Heinz-Joachim Heydorn's untranslated *Zu einer Neufassung des Bildungsbegriffs* (Frankfurt am Main: Suhrkamp, 1972).

25. "Die Vernunft kennt keine Grenzen," qtd. in Heydorn, *Zu einer Neufassung*, 121. Heydorn alludes to another kind of *Riss* or tear in this section, when he quotes Hegel's *Phenomenology* with its section on pedagogy, where consciousness comes to know about itself and its torn nature ("Zerrissenheit," ibid., 122).

26. Ibid., 7–36.

27. Bernhard uses these terms in *Correction* (*C* 143; *K* 172).

28. On the controversy surrounding Bernhard's date of writing *Auslöschung*, see J. J. Long, *The Novels of Thomas Bernhard: Form and Its Function* (Rochester, N.Y.: Camden House, 2001), 162–63; also Manfred Mittermayer, *Thomas Bernhard* (Frankfurt am Main: Suhrkamp, 2006), 110.

29. Heydorn writes: "Only via living persons can elements of *Bildung* be translated into altering action; established specifications cannot be jumped over historically. The teacher will have to endure this task, which contradicts the institution whose servant he is" ("Erst über lebende Personen werden die Bildungselemente übersetzbar in veränderndes Handeln; man kann nicht gegebene Fixierungen geschichtlich überspringen. Der Lehrer wird diese Aufgabe im Widerspruch zur Institution aushalten müssen, deren Diener er zugleich ist," *Neufassung*, 126).

30. Ibid., 148.

31. *Ext* 309; *Aus* 481. While an extensive discussion of this novel goes beyond the scope of this book, I would like to point readers in the direction of important scholarly work. See Joachim Hoell, *Der literarische Realitätenvermittler: Die Liegenschaften in Thomas Bernhards Roman Auslöschung* (Berlin: Van-Bremen, 1995); Georg Jansen, *Prinzip und Prozess Auslöschung: Intertextuelle Destruktion und Konstitution des Romans bei Thomas Bernhard* (Würzburg:

Königshausen & Neumann, 2005); and the essays in Hans Höller and Irene Heidelberger-Leonard, eds. *Antiautobiografie: Zu Thomas Bernhards Auslöschung* (Frankfurt am Main: Suhrkamp, 1995).

32. See Jarzombek's fascinating interpretation of the rise of the corridor as an element of architectural design. For him, the corridor comes to signify a host of sociocultural changes, which a single-minded insistence on the corridor's failure hides. The corridor for him is less a symptom of the rise of individualism than of the powerful forces of change in modernity (the rise of empire and its need for administrative bureaucracies; the spread of national armies and their desire for a particular kind of masculinity; the development of parliamentary democracy and its demand for new forms of publicness; the expansion of German universities and the wish for social integration; the spread of corporations and their initial desire to manifest their civic stature). See Mark Jarzombek, "Corridor Spaces," *Critical Inquiry* 36 (2010): 728–70.

33. Before Bernhard publishes novels that make explicit the connection to the exterior and interior spaces that simultaneously shape a person and express certain innermost thoughts (such as *The Lime Works* [*Das Kalkwerk*, 1970]; *Correction* [*Korrektur* 1975]; *Concrete* [*Beton*, 1982]), he himself trades in his condition of financial and intellectual unhousedness for the security of two "houses." On January 15, 1965, he writes to Siegfried Unseld, the man who would become his lifelong publisher, that he has no plans of leaving Unseld's prestigious publishing house: Bernhard envisions his "future in your house, which I won't dream of leaving" ("meine Zukunft in Ihrem Hause, das zu verlassen mir nicht einfällt"). Bernhard's relationship with the Suhrkamp Verlag makes possible the acquisition of his own home, the ruined farmhouse in Obernathal, Upper Austria, which he has been moved to buy with his lucrative contract in mind. He resides there, he continues in the same letter, as in the "belly of an Upper Austrian giant" ("ab Anfang Februar [hause ich] in der Wirklichkeit im Bauch eines oberösterreichischen Riesen"). In his reply, the publisher Unseld refers to the newly purchased farm more neutrally, as an "ideal work domicile" ("ein ideales Arbeitsdomizil," in *Der Briefwechsel*, with Siegfried Unseld, eds. Raimund Fellinger, Martin Huber and Julia Ketterer [Frankfurt am Main: Suhrkamp Verlag, 2009], 16).

34. In German, Bernhard writes: "Mein Hof, von dem ich glaube, daß er mich nicht umbringen, sondern züchtigen für die Zukunft, auf mein Ziel konzentrieren und so wenig als möglich konfus machen wird" ("Meine eigene Einsamkeit," *Die Presse* [December 24, 1965], rpt. in Schmied, *Bernhards Häuser*, 5–6).

35. Bernhard uses a loaded term for this imagined companionship. "Genossenschaft" is also the Marxist term for "cooperative": "meine Genossenschaft sind die wirklichen und die erfundenen Bibliotheken von Tausenden und Hunderttausenden und von Millionen erfundenen und wirklichen, geschriebenen und ungeschriebenen Büchern" ("Einsamkeit," 5).

36. Compare Ed Dimendberg's description of the "The Spatiality of Film Noir." In the movement between textual metaphor and concrete historical and spatial allusion, between cinema art and the physically existent city, late modernist culture reveals itself (Dimendberg, *Film Noir*, 139).

37. Bernhard lauds the salutary concentration: "The walls are white, the doors green, the floors from larch boards. Alone with these white walls, green doors,

larch boards, I now succeed in concentrating in the best possible manner" ("Die Wände sind weiß, die Türen grün, die Böden aus Lärchenbrettern. Allein mit den weißen Wänden, den grünen Türen, den Lärchenbrettern, gelingt es mir jetzt, mich auf die beste Weise zu konzentrieren," "Einsamkeit," 5). See, by comparison, the "Dachkammer" in *Correction*, a "four-by-five-meter garret Roithammer was always so fond of, which was so ideal, especially in his last years, for his purposes" (*C* 3; "viermalfünf Meter große, von Roithammer immer geliebte und vor allem in seiner letzten Lebenszeit ihm für seine Zwecke ideale höllersche Dachkammer," *Ko* 8). Here Roithammer can discover Hegel, Schopenhauer, Goethe's *Elective Affinities* and Sterne's *Sentimental Journey*.

38. Bernhard, "Einsamkeit," 5–6. Bernhard plays with the many meanings of "Hof" as both "farm," "courtyard," and "court," to evoke many spatial associations simultaneously, from grand to humble.

39. Many of these sites such as the lime works, the animal preparer's home, and the Castle Wolfsegg have been identified in the scholarship on Bernhard. See, for instance, Manfred Mittermayer's *Thomas Bernhard* (Stuttgart: Metzler, 1995) and his *Thomas Bernhard* (Frankfurt am Main: Suhrkamp, 2006), as well as Hans Höller's *Thomas Bernhard* (Reinbek: Rowohlt, 2000).

40. See Bernhard and Unseld, *Briefwechsel*, 185–86. In a book that came to my attention after the completion of this manuscript, Hans Höller draws attention to the affinity Bernhard felt for Bloch; Höller links Bernhard's view of society to Bloch's critical theory in various works. See Höller's chapter "'Darf ich Sie um ein Geschenk bitten: alles von Ernst Bloch!': Literarische Elemente einer kritischen Theorie der Gesellschaft im Werk Thomas Bernhards," in his *Der unbekannte Thomas Bernhard* (Mattighofen: Korrektur Verlag, 2014), 61–76.

41. Ernst Bloch, *The Principle of Hope*, vol. 2, trans. Neville Plaice, Stephen Plaice, and Paul Knight (Cambridge, Mass.: MIT Press, 1986), 699–700; *Das Prinzip Hoffnung*, vol. 2 (Frankfurt am Main: Suhrkamp, 1959), 819–20.

42. The metaphor recurs at the end of the section "Festive Decorations and Baroque Stage Sets" ("Festschmuck und barocke Bühnenbauten"), where Bloch remarks on the *mise-en-abîme* designs of Giuseppe Galli-Bibiena: "The buildings stand there in a sensory-supersensory way, and the beautiful which here celebrates consummation with the sacred does not rest itself, but sweeps and soars" (ibid., 706; "Die Bauten stehen sinnlich-übersinnlich da, wobei das Schöne, das mit dem Heiligen hier Beilager feiert, selber nicht ruht, sondern schwingt und schwebt," ibid., 826).

43. Ibid., *Principle*, 703; *Prinzip*, 823.

44. Bloch writes: "A world beneath the magic wand arose in the stage and backstage area: angels and demons stretched their wings, magicians produced seas of flame and floods through which innocence strode all the more touchingly or all the more victoriously, Elijah ascended into heaven in a fiery chariot, and in the end the practice of hell and the radiance of heaven were constructed as strikingly as if people really were transported to another place. But the architect had to shape the space in which the incredible appeared credible and the spectacular fairy-play an attainable condition" (*Principle*, 704; "Eine Welt unterm Zauberstab ging im Bühnenraum auf: Engel und Dämonen spannten den Flügel, Magier bewirkten Flammenmeere und Überschwemmungen, durch welche die Unschuld desto rührender oder desto siegreicher schritt, Elias fuhr auf feurigem Wagen

gen Himmel, am Ende wurden Höllenpraxis und Himmelsglanz so täuschend aufgebaut, als ginge es wirklich an einen anderen Ort. Der Architekt aber hatte den Raum zu gestalten, worin das Unglaubwürdige glaubwürdig erschien und die Feerie als erreichbarer Zustand," *Prinzip*, 824).

45. Bloch, *Principle*, 705–6; "Dergleichen verkörpert, auf meisterhaft-unsolide Weise, wieder nichts Geringeres als das Wunschbild, in einem anderen als dem vorhandenen, ja in einem gewollt unmöglichen Raum zu leben. Es ist ein waghalsiger Architekturzirkus aus Perspektive, es ist gleichzeitig ein Kunstwerk aus hinübertreibender Illusion, aus Baufahrt," *Prinzip*, 825–26.

46. Bloch, *Principle*, 721–26; *Prinzip*, 844–50.

47. Bloch, *Principle*, 733–36, 742; *Prinzip*, 858–62, 869.

48. Bloch writes: "And the thus erected Humanum, transposed to strictly significant spatial form, is as a task both migration from the organic and humane into crystal, and above all permeation of the crystalline with the buoyancy developed within it, Humanum and profusion. When the conditions for the order of freedom are no longer partial, the path finally becomes open again towards the unity of physical construction and organic ornamentation, towards the gift of ornamentation. It becomes open in reality for the first time, without Egypt on the one hand, Gothic on the other, i.e., that which is thus described as crystal or tree of life, having to be alternated over and over again, mixed or envied in isolation" (*Principle*, 744–45; "Und das so aufgerichtete, zu streng-bedeutender Raumform transponierte Humanum ist als Aufgabe ebenso Hineinwandern von Organischem, Humanem in den Kristall, wie vor allem Durchdrungensein von Kristallhaftem mit darin ausgebautem Auftrieb, Humanum und Fülle. Wenn die Bedingungen zur Ordnung der Freiheit nicht mehr partial sind, wird der Weg endlich wieder offen zur Einheit von physischer Konstruktion und organischem Ornament, zum Geschenk des Ornaments. Er wird zum erstenmal realiter offen, ohne daß Ägypten hier, Gotik dort, das heißt, das damit als Kristall oder Lebensbaum Bezeichnete, immer wieder zu alternieren, zu mischen oder isoliert zu beneiden wäre," *Prinzip*, 872).

49. Nietzsche couches his concern with the institutions of higher education in the form of a personal narrative, in which he recounts a number of educational dialogues he witnessed as a young, enthusiastic student. In line with the skepticism toward existent political and educational structures in *Gargoyles*, Nietzsche discerns problems in the inherited structures of education. In the lectures, a carefully scripted mise-en-scène places two young students, the young Nietzsche and a close friend, on higher ground on the banks of the Rhine—they are on a mountain plateau, where they are separated from the mass of students below them. On this plateau, an older philosopher and his accompanying disciple instruct the two bright, but cheeky youths in the vital importance of philosophical thought and the decrepit state of public schools. The older philosopher despairs of current efforts to bring education to the many: the democratizing impulse robs the people, in his estimation, of their rootedness in culture. The downward thrust of the argument, which is conveyed in landscape metaphors, is clear: "[T]he individual lower levels where, generally speaking, the masses come into contact with culture, where the people nourishes its religious instinct, where it poeticizes its mythological images, where it keeps up its faith in its customs, privileges, native soil, and language—all these levels can scarcely be reached by direct means, and

in any case only by violent demolition" ("Die eigentlichen, tieferen Regionen, in denen sich überhaupt die große Masse mit der Bildung berührt, dort wo das Volk seine religiösen Instinkte hegt, wo es an seinen mythischen Bildern weiterdichtet, wo es seiner Sitte, seinem Recht, seinem Heimatsboden, seiner Sprache Treue bewahrt, alle diese Regionen sind auf direktem Wege kaum und jedenfalls nur durch zerstörende Gewaltsamkeiten zu erreichen"). Inadvertently, *Bildung* destroys the up-down coordinates that are necessary for the individual and society, where the solitary thinker resides above the "grounded" and "rooted" masses (Nietzsche, *On the Future of Our Educational Institutions*, 3rd lecture; http://www.gutenberg.org/files/28146/28146-h/28146-h.htm; *Die Zukunft unserer Bildungsanstalten*, in *Sämtliche Werke: Kritische Studienausgabe*, vol. 1 [Munich: Deutscher Taschenbuch Verlag, 1988], 641–752, esp. 699).

50. *G* 41–42; *V* 44. The Winston translation is not quite felicitous, translating the "hollow space" as a "no man's land."

51. See Walter Schweidler, who writes: "Das Paradox, dass der Schüler zu dem erzogen werden muss, zu dem er sich nur selbst erziehen kann, bestimmt die Ambivalenz von Nietzsches Verhältnis zur Tradition ebenso wie die Bedeutung seines Denkens für die Pädagogik." See his "Friedrich Nietzsche: Über die Zukunft unserer Bildungsanstalten," in *Hauptwerke der Pädagogik*, eds. Winfried Böhm, Birgitta Fuchs and Sabine Seichter (Paderborn: Schöningh, 2009), 317–19, esp. 317.

52. Nietzsche's original reads: "Aufgebaut auf dem thönernen Grunde der jetzigen Gymnasialkultur, auf zerbröckelndem Fundamente, steht ihr Gebäude schief gerichtet und unsicher bei dem Anhauche der Wirbelwinde. [. . .] Es erschreckt ihn, in enger kleinlicher Fachmäßigkeit so frühe zu versinken; und nun greift er nach Stützen und Pfeilern, um nicht in jene Bahn gerissen zu werden. Umsonst! diese Stützen weichen; denn er hatte fehlgegriffen und an zerbrechlichem Rohre sich festgehalten" (*Zukunft*, 741–45).

53. The passage continues with the fall from heights: "Dann wieder stürzt er aus der Höhe der erträumten Selbsterkenntniß in eine ironische Skepsis" (*Zukunft*, 745).

54. See Chapter 1. The burrowing action should not be confused with the creation of a Kafkaesque rhizome as philosophers such as Deleuze and Guattari conceive it: Bernhard's tunnel inward does not lead on myriad, deterritorializing, subterranean pathways (even though there are similarities to the French philosophers' idea of the machine).

55. The following passage makes the centrality of "looking through" explicit, as well as Bloch's teaching: "'Bloch has the art of seeing his life as an easily understood mechanism that he can keep regulated, speed up or slow down, according to his needs,' my father said. 'However he uses his powers, the result is always practically useful, which makes the whole thing bearable. He finds pleasure in this art and is always trying to teach it to his family" (*G* 22–23; "Bloch beherrsche die Kunst, das Leben als einen in seinen wichtigsten Funktionen leicht zu durchschauenden Mechanismus je nach seinem persönlichen Bedürfnis auf eine schnellere oder langsamere, aber immer wieder von neuem brauchbare und also erträgliche Gangart einzustellen, und er sei ständig bemüht, seine Familie in diese Kunst, die ihm Vergnügen mache, einzuweihen," *V* 26).

56. The characters themselves both encourage and discourage such a reading, referring to other figures' alleged madness (e.g., *AM* 18, 20). On the role of

madness, see Samuel Frederick's chapter on Bernhard in *Narratives Unsettled: Digression in Robert Walser, Thomas Bernhard, and Adalbert Stifter* (Evanston, Ill.: Northwestern University Press, 2012), 101–28.

57. W. G. Sebald, *Die Beschreibung des Unglücks: Zur österreichischen Literatur von Stifter bis Handke* (Frankfurt am Main: Fischer, 2003), 103–14.

58. Alfred Pfabigan discusses Reger's wife in *Alte Meister* as an "object of pedagogy" (*Thomas Bernhard: Ein österreichisches Weltexperiment* [Vienna: Zsolnay, 1999], 414). Konzett describes the tutee Atzbacher in *Alte Meister* as a "disciple" (Konzett, *The Rhetoric of National Dissent in Thomas Bernhard, Peter Handke, and Elfriede Jelinek* [Rochester, N.Y.: Camden House, 2000], 44). Bernhard Sorg mentions the autobiographical volumes as "Momente [der] Erziehung" (*Thomas Bernhard* [Munich: C.H. Beck, 1992], 133).

59. Mark M. Anderson speaks of Bernhard's stream of prose beginning in the late 1960s as "deluge fragments," with their unbroken paragraphs and lack of conclusive ends. See his "Fragments of a Deluge: The Theater of Bernhard's Prose," in Matthias Konzett, *A Companion to the Works of Thomas Bernhard* (Rochester, N.Y.: Camden House, 2010), 119–35, esp. 120–21.

60. These are the books mentioned in the boys' home in *Amras* (*A* 9; *Am* 118).

61. Certainly, Bernhard's focus on unusual, elderly teachers has its basis in certain biographical coordinates: he always acknowledged his debt to his grandfather, the writer Johannes Freumbichler (1881–1949). In this regard, see Höller's chapter, "Die Großväter sind die Lehrer: Leben als Nachfolge," in *Thomas Bernhard* (Reinbek bei Hamburg: Rowohlt, 1993), 34–48; see also Gitta Honegger's chapter "In Search of Family," in *Thomas Bernhard: The Making of an Austrian* (New Haven, Conn.: Yale University Press, 2001), 17–41, esp. 18–22.

62. This comment is the one most closely associated with Hollein (although there is no dearth of other, equally pithy statements in his writing). See, e.g., the article "Alles ist Architektur: Der Wiener Baukünstler Hans Hollein im Gespräch," in *Neue Zürcher Zeitung*, May 10, 2012, http://www.nzz.ch/nachrichten/kultur/aktuell/alles_ist_architektur_1.2284434.html. The full German text for "Alles ist Architektur" can also be found on Hollein's website http://www.hollein.com/ger/Schriften/Texte/Alles-ist-Architektur. It is reproduced together with the entire issue of the journal *Bau: Schrift für Architektur und Städtebau* from which it is taken (23, no. 1/2) in Johannes Porsch, ed., *The Austrian Phenomenon: Architektur Avantgarde Österreich 1956–1973 I* (Basel: Birkhäuser, 2009), 1048–49.

63. In "Alles ist Architektur," he writes: "The consequences that the new communication means (such as telephone, radio, television, etc.) bring with them are even greater; the concept of a building (school) in which one learns or is educated will completely disappear and be substituted by these other means" ("Viel weitergehend jedoch sind die Konsequenzen, die etwa die neuen Medien der Kommunikation (sei es Telephon, Radio, Fernsehen u.a.) mit sich bringen, und es wird so ein Begriff wie der des Lehr- und Lerngebäudes (Schule) unter Umständen ganz verschwinden und durch diese Mittel ersetzt werden," in Porsch, *The Austrian Phenomenon I,* 1049). He plays with the double meaning of "Lehrgebäude" as a building where one is instructed and a philosophical, dogmatic schema.

64. Bernstein, in a different context in *Housing Problems*, also discusses the *Grundriss* and the possibility of translating any design into an actual construction (Stanford, Calif.: Stanford University Press, 2008), 4, 22.

65. Bernstein is interested in showing that the "architectonic of selfhood" never coincides with its material expression: "The wall, the architectural boundary between the two, marks the blind spot or gap that divides the subjectivity that *Bildung* ought to render whole" (ibid., 22).

66. On the role of atmosphere in architecture, see Gernot Böhme's *Architektur und Atmosphäre* (Munich: Fink, 2006).

Way Station 1

1. I am referring here to Gaston Bachelard, *The Poetics of Space*, trans. Maria Jolas (Boston: Beacon, 1994; orig. publ. as *La Poétique de l'éspace*, 1958); Hannah Arendt, *The Human Condition* (Chicago: University of Chicago, 1958); Henri Lefebvre, *The Production of Space*, trans. Donald Nicholson-Smith (Malden, Mass.: Blackwell, 1991; orig. publ. as *La Production de l'espace*, 1974); Michel de Certeau, *The Practice of Everyday Life*, trans. Steven Rendall (Berkeley: University of California, 1984; orig. publ. as *L'Invention du quotidian*, 1980). See the excellent compilation by Jörg Dünne and Stephan Günzel, *Raumtheorie* (Frankfurt am Main: Suhrkamp, 2006).

2. Michel Foucault, "Of Other Spaces," trans. Jay Miskowiec, *Diacritics* 16, no. 1 (Spring 1986): 22–27, esp. 24; Foucault, "Des espaces autres," *Architecture, Mouvement, Continuité* 5 (October 1984): 46–49; here http://foucault.info/documents/heterotopia/foucault.heterotopia.en.html.

3. Foucault, "Other Spaces," 26; "Espaces autres," n.p. On the mathematical underpinnings of Foucault's spatial concepts and their development in his work, see Oliver Simons's chapter "Foucaults Geometrie" in *Raumgeschichten: Topographien der Moderne in Philosophie, Wissenschaft und Literatur* (Munich: Fink, 2007), 25–49.

4. Peter Handke elaborates on this intervention in his essay "Zur Tagung der Gruppe 47 in den USA," in *Ich bin ein Bewohner des Elfenbeinturms* (Frankfurt am Main: Suhrkamp, 1972), 29–34.

5. Handke, "Ich bin ein Bewohner des Elfenbeinturms," 26.

6. See Peter Handke's emphatic self-definition: "Eine normative Literaturauffassung freilich bezeichnet mit einem schönen Ausdruck jene, die sich weigern, noch Geschichten zu erzählen, die nach neuen Methoden der Weltdarstellung suchen und diese an der Welt ausprobieren, als 'Bewohner des Elfenbeinturms', als 'Formalisten', als 'Ästheten'. So will ich mich gern als Bewohner des Elfenbeinturmes bezeichnen lassen, weil ich meine, daß ich nach Methoden, nach Modellen für eine Literatur suche, die schon morgen (oder übermorgen) als realistisch bezeichnet werden wird, und zwar dann, wenn auch diese Methoden schon nicht mehr anwendbar sein werden, weil sie dann eine Manier sind, die nur scheinbar natürlich ist, wie jetzt die Fiktion als Mittel der Wirklichkeitsdarstellung in der Literatur noch immer scheinbar natürlich ist" ("Ich bin ein Bewohner," 26).

7. Note Handke's double stress on the word "Erziehung" ("Ich bin ein Bewohner," 26, emphasis in original).

8. *E* 195. "Two Young People" was first published in the *Almanach auf das Jahr 1964* (Fischer Verlag), but included in the complete collection of *Ereignisse*-texts in a publication from the Literarisches Colloquium Berlin in 1969. See the editors' discussion of the publication history in vol. 14 of Bernhard's *Werke* (esp. 556–63).

9. In *Ereignisse*, see "The Large Landowner" ("Der Grossgrundbesitzer") (200), "The President" ("Der Präsident") (204), "A Few People" ("Ein paar Menschen") (227), "The Dictator" ("Der Diktator") (223), "An Unknown Person" ("Ein Unbekannter") (232).

10. Their journey upward is as futile as the journey downward in "Plain/Plane" (see Chapter 1).

Chapter 1

1. Peter Cook was a member of the utopian group Archigram. Both Peter Bode and Gustav Peichl comment on the importance of the Archigram architects (Peter Cook, Warren Chalk, Dennis Crompton, David Greene, Ron Herron, and Michael Webb) for Austrian practitioners. The Archigram group presented images of a thoroughly technologized, science fiction world in their utopian designs. Their innovations rendered fluid traditional concepts of the city. See Peter Bode's introduction "Österreichische Architektur seit 1960," 9–31, esp. 12, and Gustav Peichl's "Zeichnungen—Projekte—Utopien," in their jointly edited book *Architektur aus Österreich seit 1960* (Salzburg: Residenz, 1980), 153–72, esp. 153.

2. See not only Peter Cook's chapter on "National Context and International Pressure" in *Experimental Architecture* (New York: Universe Books, 1970), 68–76, esp. 71–73, but also Friedrich Achleitner's articles "Der 'Aufbau' und die Aufbrüche" in *Architektur im 20. Jahrhundert* and "Aufforderung zum Vertrauen: Architektur seit 1945," in *The Austrian Phenomenon I: Architektur Avantgarde Österreich 1956–1973,* ed. Johannes Porsch (Basel: Birkhäuser, 2009), esp. 833–35 and 846–54 resp., as well as Günther Feuerstein's "Visionäre Architektur im Österreich der sechziger und siebziger Jahre," in Porsch, *The Austrian Phenomenon I*, 866–69, esp. 866.

3. Peichl, "Zeichnungen," *Architektur*, 168.

4. "Synthetic spaces" ("synthetische Räume") is the term the Graz-based architect Friedrich St. Florian uses to describe the "imaginary architecture" of the near future in an essay from 1970. His particularly prescient piece—foreseeing the advent of Internet communication, telecommuting, and the movement from localized places to what Marc Augé has termed the "non-places" of supermodernity—envisions an active role for the user. In transmuting physical place into disembodied space and back into place again, a person's movement and usage ultimately defines the architecture of the future. See his "Imaginäre Architektur," in the *Austrian Phenomenon I*, 814–15, as well as Feuerstein, "Visionäre," *Austrian Phenomenon I*, 867–68, and Bode, where he discusses the influence on nearly simultaneous interventionist groupings such as Haus-Rucker-Co., Missing Link, and Coop Himmelblau, "Österreichische Architektur," 12.

5. See Dietmar Steiner's preface to *The Austrian Phenomenon I*, 6–7.

6. See the essays collected in Arno Ritter, ed., *Reprint: Ein Lesebuch zu Architektur und Tirol* (Innsbruck: Studienverlag, 2005), esp. Josef Lackner's unpublished essay "The Eight Naïve Giants" ("Die acht naiven Giganten," 152–53) and Friedrich Achleitner, "But No Olympics for the Art of Building: Architecture in Austria Is No Longer Representative" ("Aber keine Olympiade der Baukunst: Die Architektur in Österreich ist kein Repräsentant mehr," 149–50), both from 1963. See also Feuerstein, "Visionäre," in *The Austrian Phenomenon I*, 866–69, esp. 866.

7. Bernhard meets Holzmeister in Innsbruck in 1955. Also see note 8.

8. See Gitta Honegger, *Thomas Bernhard: The Making of an Austrian* (New Haven: Yale University Press, 2001), 77–79, and, more pertinently, "Viktor Hufnagl" in *Die Architektur und ich: Eine Bilanz der österreichischen Architektur seit 1945,* ed. Maria Welzig and Gerhard Steixner (Vienna: Böhlau, 2004), 66–79. A number of elements connect Bernhard to Hufnagl, who was also an illegitimate child raised near Salzburg by his artistic grandfather. Hufnagl comments on the twenty-year relationship to Bernhard as follows: "My self first crystallized in opposition to him. Because he was an egocentric. [. . .] He once said that one of the first or second tasks he set for himself was to destroy Hufnagl's buildings" ("Es hat sich erst mein Ich herauskristallisiert in der Polarisierung zu ihm. Denn er war ein Egozentriker. [. . .] Er hat einmal gesagt, als Erstes oder als Zweites hat er sich zur Aufgabe gestellt, die Bauten von Hufnagl zu vernichten." Hufnagl was also important in revitalizing the discussion of urban planning with his exhibition "Neue städtische Wohnformen" (Welzig, *Architektur*, 68, 70). On Bernhard's contact to Holzmeister, see Christina Riccabona, "Begegnungen—Die Österreichischen Jugendkulturwochen in Innsbruck (1949–1969)," in *Ex.Position: Avantgarde Tirol 1960/75*, ed. Günther Dankl (Innsbruck: Tiroler Landesmuseum, 2004), 77–86.

9. Hundertwasser's influential "Moldering Manifesto" or "Verschimmelungsmanifest" is somewhat of an outlier in its democratic impulse and romantic thrust. He decries the utilitarian component of overly "rationalist" architecture in no uncertain terms. I quote his colorful hyperbole in full: "The material uninhabitability of the slums is preferable to the moral uninhabitability of functional, utilitarian architecture. In the so-called slums only the human body can perish, but in the architecture purported to have been planned for humans his soul decays. For that reason the principle of the slums, i.e. wildly sprawling architecture, should be improved and is to be taken as the starting point, and not functional architecture" ("Die materielle Unbewohnbarkeit der Elendsviertel ist der moralischen Unbewohnbarkeit der funktionellen, nützlichen Architektur vorzuziehen. In den sogenannten Elendsvierteln kann nur der Körper des Menschen zugrunde gehen, doch in der angeblich für den Menschen geplanten Architektur geht seine Seele zugrunde. Daher ist das Prinzip der Elendsviertel, das heißt der wild wuchernden Architektur, zu verbessern und als Ausgangsbasis zu nehmen, und nicht die funktionelle Architektur," my own translation). See Friedensreich Hundertwasser, "Verschimmelungsmanifest gegen den Rationalismus in der Architektur," *Schöne Wege: Gedanken über Kunst und Leben* (Munich: Langen Müller, 2004), 216; rpt. in Porsch, *Austrian Phenomenon I*, 780–83, esp. 780, 782.

10. Hundertwasser's talk, together with its addenda from 1959 and 1964, tends to mix serious argumentation with outlandish claims, e.g., every man should have the right to lean out of his window and scratch off the plasterwork or paint the exterior pink around his window to express his originality; the ruler is a sign of a new illiteracy (Porsch, *Austrian Phenomenon I*, 781–83). A similar argumentative technique characterizes Bernhard's teachers—the sudden swerve from high seriousness to what seem to be laughable assertions.

11. Hundertwasser, in Porsch, *Austrian Phenomenon I*, 782.

12. Günther Feuerstein, "Thesen zur 'Inzidenten Architektur'," in Porsch, *Austrian Phenomenon I*, 275.

13. Hans Hollein and Walter Pichler, *Architektur* (Vienna: Galerie nächst St. Stephan, 1963), n.p.; rpt. in Porsch, *Austrian Phenomenon I*, 15–37.

14. See Wendelin Schmidt-Dengler's important monograph, *Der Übertreibungskünstler: Studien zu Thomas Bernhard*, 2nd ed. (Vienna: Sonderzahl, 1989).

15. These are the terms Peter Bürger uses to describe the historical avant-garde's ambivalent undertaking in his *Theorie der Avantgarde* (Frankfurt am Main: Suhrkamp, 1974), 67–68.

16. Under point nine, Feuerstein lists his preferences for, among other things, "poverty" ("die Armut"), "raw material" ("das rohe Material"), and "rough" ("rauh") hewn wood, stone, and brick. See his "Thesen zur 'Inzidenten Architektur'," in Porsch, *Austrian Phenomenon I*, 275.

17. On the importance of the journal *Bau*, see Craig Buckley, "From Absolute to Everything: Taking Possession in 'Alles ist Architektur,'" *Grey Room* 28 (2007): 108–22.

18. The entire brochure is reprinted in Porsch, *Austrian Phenomenon I*, 15–33. The text itself can also be found on Hollein's web page, with a complete list of his other writings: http://www.hollein.com/ger/Schriften/Texte/.

19. In "Back to Architecture," Hollein criticizes the philosophy behind modernism that architecture schools propagate. The spread of this kind of architecture thus becomes a pedagogical problem:

> It is the philosophy that is preached as gospel in the majority of architecture schools. It is the philosophy of design.
> It brings sterility throughout the world instead of the possibility of the creative growth of the individual.
> It makes the metropolis into a mediocropolis.
> It is the architecture of termites, not of free, thinking, feeling people.
>
> Es ist die Philosophie, welche in einem Großteil der Architekturschulen als Evangelium gepredigt wird. Es ist die Philosophie des Design.
> Sie bringt Sterilität über die Welt statt Möglichkeit zur Entfaltung der Creativität [sic] der Einzelperson.
> Sie macht die Metropolis zur Mediocropolis.
> Sie ist eine Architektur der Termiten, nicht die freier, denkender, fühlender Menschen.
> (http://www.hollein.com/ger/Schriften/Texte/Zurueck-zur-Architektur).

20. In German, Hollein's 1963 essay reads: "Architektur ist elementar, sinnlich, primitiv, brutal, schrecklich, gewaltig, herrschend" (in Porsch, *Austrian Phenomenon I*, 21).

21. Ibid.

22. In "Back to Architecture," Hollein writes: "In actual fact many of the ideas of today's so-called modern architecture are not ideas born out of the spirit of the 20th century. Rather, they are ideas of the 19th century, the last phases of a machine romanticism." ("In Wahrheit sind viele der Ideen der heutigen, der sogenannten modernen Architektur gar keine Ideen geboren aus dem Geist des 20. Jahrhunderts. Sie sind vielmehr Ideen des 19. Jahrhunderts, letzte Ausläufe der Maschinenromantik," http://www.hollein.com/ger/Schriften/Texte/Zurueck-zur-Architektur).

23. The show includes Raimund Abraham's works. Abraham, an émigré to the United States, presented his important publication *Elementary Architecture* (*Elementare Architektur*) to the public in 1963. While his book draws on traditional rural architecture to argue for a simplified and timeless formal language, he is interested in entering into a dialogue with modernism. See Way Station 2.

24. Drexler's incisive description of the work of Hans Hollein, Walter Pichler, and Raimund Abraham is taken from one of the wall texts, "Architectural Fantasies: Drawings from the Museum Collection," written for the exhibition (rpt. in Porsch, *The Austrian Phenomenon I*, 41).

25. I quote the brief passage entitled "Architektur" in full: "It is born out of the strongest thoughts. For humans it will be coercion, they will either suffocate in it or they will live—live the way I mean it. Architecture is not the mantle for the primitive instincts of the masses. Architecture is the embodiment of the power and desires of the few. It is a brutal thing, which has not made use of art for a long time. It does not make allowance for stupidity and weakness. It never serves. It crushes those that cannot endure it. Architecture is the right [*Recht*] of those who do not believe in the law [*Recht*], but make it. Architecture is a weapon. Architecture uncompromisingly uses the strongest means at its disposal. Machines have taken hold of it and humans are only tolerated in its domain" ("Sie wird geboren aus den stärksten Gedanken. Für die Menschen wird sie Zwang sein, sie werden darin ersticken oder sie werden leben—leben, wie ich es meine. Architektur ist nicht die Hülle für die primitiven Instinkte der Massen. Architektur ist Verkörperung der Macht und Sehnsüchte weniger Menschen. Sie ist eine brutale Sache, die sich der Kunst schon lange nicht mehr bedient. Sie berücksichtigt die Dummheit und die Schwäche nicht. Sie dient niemals. Sie erdrückt die, die sie nicht ertragen. Architektur ist das Recht derer, die nicht an das Recht glauben, sondern es machen. Sie ist eine Waffe. Architektur bedient sich rückhaltslos der stärksten Mittel, die ihr jeweils zur Verfügung stehen. Maschinen haben sie ergriffen und die Menschen sind nur mehr geduldet in ihrem Bereich," rpt. in *The Austrian Phenomenon I*, 31).

26. See the reproduced pages from "Architektur," rpt. in *The Austrian Phenomenon I*, esp. 32–33.

27. See the reproductions of Hans Hollein's *Inflatable Room Furnishings* (*Aufblasbare Zimmereinrichtung*, 1965) and *Pneumatic Structures* (*Pneumatische Strukturen*, 1967), as well as Pichler's *Inflatable Chair* (*Aufblasbarer Stuhl*, 1966) and *Großer Raum* (1967), in *Bau* (1969), rpt. in *The Austrian Phenomenon I*, 75.

28. See the invaluable exhibition catalogue *Walter Pichler* from the Museum des 20. Jahrhunderts Wien and the Hamburger Kunsthalle (Salzburg: Residenz, 1971).

29. See Günther Dankl, "Raum und Expansion. Zum Aspekt des Konzeptionellen und Experimentellen bei Raimund Abraham, Ernst Caramelle, Bernhard Leitner, Max Peintner, Walter Pichler und Heinz Tesar," in his edited volume *Ex.Position—Avantgarde Tirol 1960/75* (Innsbruck: Tiroler Landesmuseum Ferdinandeum, 2004), 9–51, esp. 21.

30. Ibid., 16.

31. See Herbert Prader and Franz Fehringer, "Die nächste Generation: Konturen–Tendenzen," and Friedrich Achleitner, "Aufforderung," both in Porsch, *The Austrian Phenomenon I*, 855–58 and 848 resp.

32. Pichler, *Walter Pichler*, 17–19, 21.

33. Ibid., 25.

34. Ibid., 45–47, 48–49, 50–51.

35. Pichler's description of his unusual sculpture *Compact City with Climate Sheath* (*Kompakte Stadt mit Klimahülle,* 1964) with a white interior composed of rounded and stacked elements, encased in transparent plastic and resting on a concrete foundation, is unusual. Here he suggests an exchange between the various strata and a mediation between interior and exterior: "The living crust gets daylight. It is superimposed on the growing core" ("Die Wohnkruste erhält Tageslicht: Sie überlagert einen wachsenden Kern," in Pichler, *Walter Pichler*, 53–54).

36. In a slightly different context and with hindsight, Jürgen Hohmeyer speaks of Pichler's "scary science fiction architectures" of the 1960s ("schaurige Science-Fiction-Architekturen") in his article "Ein Haus für den Golem" in *Spiegel* (October 8, 1979): 250–52, http://www.spiegel.de/spiegel/print/d-39868637.html.

37. The daunting non-relation between in- and outside is further reflected upon in the *Prototypes* series Pichler designs only a few years later, from 1966–69. He picks up on the contemporary fascination with astronauts and the fear of nuclear catastrophe to create self-sufficient helmets and suits that work against man's extension into space through a reduction to the minimal necessities for life. *Small Space* (*Kleiner Raum,* 1967), which is composed of two stacked white spheres, is worn as a kind of helmet. It connects the wearer to the outside world through an interior microphone and a couple of ports for air and cooling. The globe encasing the human in *Intensive Box* (*Intensivbox,* 1960) offers a built-in television and diverse ports; it, too, shows how the self-sufficiency of the *Compact City* drawings can be carried over into a person's intimate space. In what is his most fascinating piece from the series, *TV-Helmet* (*Portable Living Room*)/*TV-Helm* (*Tragbares Wohnzimmer,* 1967), a phallic piece of molded plastic is placed over a person's head, and TV is piped into the helmet (*Walter Pichler*, 58–65). The shape hints at man's forward thrust and extension into surrounding areas, but the closed, smooth shape without eyeholes counteracts this impression. On these sculptures and their relation to the international Pop Art movement, see Georg Schöllhammer, "Die geschraubte Geste," in *Pichler: Prototypen/Prototypes*, ed. Sabine Breitwieser (Vienna: Generali, 1998), 35–58.

38. Richard Neutra, *Bauen und die Sinneswelt* (Dresden: Verlag der Kunst, 1977), 35.

39. See the essay "Blut für Mexiko," *Der Spiegel* (August 2, 1971): 105, http://www.spiegel.de/spiegel/print/d-43144766.html.

40. Apart from the MOMA, Pichler exhibits at the Documenta and Biennale.

41. See Walter Pichler, *111 Zeichnungen* (Salzburg: Residenz, 1973), 53, 173–75, 131.

42. Ibid., 57, 61, 59, 117, 119; and 121.

43. Ibid., 155, 160.

44. See the first fifty pages, where the novel charts this movement, esp. *V* 29–63.

45. Drexler, "Architectural Fantasies," in Porsch, *The Austrian Phenomenon I*, 41.

46. *Cn* 68; "Ich hatte aufeinmal den erfrischenden Gedanken, mich im letzten Moment aus meiner Gruft hinauszukatapultieren," *B* 90.

47. Bernhard's German text stresses the viewer's role in endowing what is before him with meaning. The "Betrachter" is unfortunately left out in the English translation, as is the need for various perspectives, "Gesichtspunkte," which give the viewer special insight into the relationship between edifice and (non) edification (*Ind* 123–24; *U* 80–81).

Way Station 2

1. I have chosen to preserve the original title, rather than use the 1995 translation, where the title is given as "Architectonics" (see B. Groihofer, ed. *(un)built* [Vienna: Springer, 1995; rpt. 2001, Salzburg: Pustet]). Terms similar to Hans Hollein's and Walter Pichler's recur numerous times in Raimund Abraham's *Elementare Architektur*: "elementar," "Wurzeln," "Ordnung," "am reinsten," "ursprünglichen" (Salzburg: Residenz, 1963), n.p. Also rpt. in *Reprint*: *Ein Lesebuch zu Architektur und Tirol*, ed. Arno Ritter (Innsbruck: Studienverlag, 2005), 153–57; and *The Austrian Phenomenon I*, 168, 746–47, where the publication date is given incorrectly as 1961. Walter Pichler and Ernst F. Graf do the layout for the book, which consists of Abraham's brief introduction and seventy-four pages of black-and-white illustrations. In an interview in 1986 with Dietmar Steiner and Christian Reder, Abraham discusses the book's distance from National Socialist discourse and its efforts to return to the roots of modernism (see "Raimund Abraham: Rund um den Nullpunkt," *Falter* 13 (1986), online at http://www.christianreder.net/pdf/p_86_13_falt.pdf).

2. Interestingly, Abraham opens his short introductory essay with an epigram from the nineteenth- and early twentieth-century architect Otto Wagner (1841–1918), suggesting the independence of architecture from nature and underlining the break with organic models: "Architecture has no model in nature, it is reliant on itself" ("Die Architektur hat kein Vorbild in der Natur, sie ist auf sich selbst gestellt," *Elementare*, n.p.). This seems to be an effort to guard against any quick condemnation of his undertaking as retrograde, when he stresses harmony between nature and architecture. In Abraham's argument, architecture and nature are much more interrelated than Wagner's words suggest. The epigram is not part of the reprint of Abraham's introduction in *The Austrian Phenomenon I*, 746–47.

3. This is, surprisingly, the same Abraham who develops visionary collages of a technoid future at the same time and, as his last completed work, builds a superlative, futuristic tower in New York, the Austrian Cultural Forum (2002). See his stunning drawings reproduced in Porsch, *The Austrian Phenomenon I*, 164–83. Thomas Bernhard intermingles a fictive place called Abraham with his real place names in *Gargoyles*. His description makes it sound like one of the landscapes in *Elementary Architectures*. It is an area covered with large orchards, old houses, and cider casks (*G* 43; *V* 45).

4. An aspect that deserves further study is the relationship between Abraham's conception and Konrad Wachsmann's teaching. Wachsmann, a colleague of Walter Gropius's and teacher in Salzburg during the summers, influenced Abraham's generation of architects. In his book *Aspects of Building* (*Aspekte des Bauens*), antedating *Elementary Architecture* by only two years, Wachsmann surveys the sites of classical European antiquity. A different conception of temporality informs his effort. In his introduction, he stresses the difficulties in understanding

the past. Its formal language can never be recuperated entirely in later epochs, for human beings can only really understand their own time, to which they have helped give shape. Any actualization or updating of earlier forms in contemporary understanding must necessarily be an abstraction and synthesis between past and present ("Im scheinbaren Wiedererkennen kann das Vergangene also nur in seiner Synthese als Abstraktion, als Deutung in den Gesichtskreis der Gegenwart rücken"). Any effort at imitation proceeds from this artificial standpoint ("künstlich gezogenen Kreis"), which must acknowledge the shaping hand of time ("des zeitgestaltenden Gedankens"). See Konrad Wachsmann, *Aspekte des Bauens* (Wiesbaden: Krausskopf, 1961), n.p. On the influence of Wachsmann on the architects Hollein, Achleitner, Kurrent, Spalt, etc., see Friedrich Achleitner, "Aufforderung zum Vertrauen," in Porsch, *Austrian Phenomenon I*, 846–54, esp. 848.

5. Abraham, *Elementare*, n.p. in Porsch, *Austrian Phenomenon I*, 746.

6. Abraham writes: "That means that each material can only be used according to its organic and technical possibilities. This is the basis for the demand for an exact familiarity with materials and their organic regularities as the precondition for any creative process at all. The natural feeling for material and structure, as it becomes palpable in the reduced constructions of primitive buildings, is necessary for all 'built' architecture, whether it arises from manual craft or owes its existence to perfected industrial fabrication" ("Das heißt, jedes Material kann nur in den Grenzen seiner organischen und technischen Möglichkeiten Verwendung finden. Darauf gründet die Forderung nach einer genauen Kenntnis der Werkstoffe und ihrer organischen Gesetzmäßigkeiten als der Voraussetzung jedes schöpferischen Prozesses überhaupt. Das natürliche Gefühl für Material und Gefüge, wie es in den reduzierten Konstruktionen primitiver Bauten spürbar wird, ist notwendig für alle 'gebaute' Architektur, ob sie nun handwerklicher Fertigung oder perfektionierter industrieller Fabrikation ihre Entstehung verdankt," Abraham, *Elementare*, n.p., in Porsch, *Austrian Phenomenon I*).

7. Roithamer's Cone in *Correction*, which is discussed in the conclusion, is motivated less by a desire for general edification of the kind we encounter in *Amras* or *Alte Meister* than as the personal achievement Mies van der Rohe criticizes at the end of this quotation.

8. Konrad Wachsmann, *Wendepunkt im Bauen* (Wiesbaden: Krausskopf Verlag, 1959), n.p. I have offered my own translation. See also *The Turning Point of Building: Structure and Design*, trans. Thomas E. Burton. (New York: Reinhold, 1961).

9. Wachsmann sees architecture as a subjugation of the malevolent forces of nature that uses the latest insights of technology—in the service of a new kind of harmony. His technologically friendly view stands in an uneasy relation of tension to Abraham's thoughts, even where the latter seems to quote him approvingly. I quote the passage from Wachsmann in full: "Building, which is, in the final analysis, a material battle against the destructive forces of nature, requires us to draw the consequences from science, the discoveries and developments of technology, in order to recognize the new laws of harmony between mass and space with all available means and methods. Completely different conditions revealed themselves in this way than those which determined the house built through handicraft; only resolute decisions, which were founded on the methodological and technological, were able to show the unique path in this new direction ("Das

Bauen, das letztlich ein materieller Kampf gegen die zerstörerischen Kräfte der Natur ist, verpflichtet, aus den Fortschritten der Wissenschaft, den Entdeckungen und den Erfindungen der Technik, die Konsequenzen zu ziehen, um durch alle erreichbaren Hilfsmittel und Methoden die neuen Gesetze der Harmonie zwischen Masse und Raum zu erkennen. Indem sich dadurch ganz andere Bedingungen zeigten als jene, die das handwerklich gebaute Haus bestimmten, konnten nur entschlossene Entscheidungen, die sich fest auf dem Methodischen und Technischen aufbauten, den einzigen Weg in die neue Richtung weisen" (Wachsmann, *Wendepunkt*, n.p.).

10. The quotations from Wachsmann, taken out of context, do not do justice to the breadth of his thinking. In his own book entitled *Aspects* (*Aspekte*, 1961), which Raimund Abraham's *Elementary Architecture* both complements and contradicts, Wachsmann reflects on some of the photos he made of Romanesque architecture in Italy (Wiesbaden: Krausskopf Verlag, n.p.). In this book, Wachsmann cautions against the desire to see formal continuities between different epochs; each epoch creates new forms in response to its own problems. The wish to see correspondences where there are completely different motives and causes should give pause. An insurmountable hurdle separates us from a past that we might resemble (the similarity of "das Gleiche"), but which does not allow itself to be intellectually assimilated or wholly incorporated (the equivalence of "dasselbe").

11. Much has been written on Bernhard's style; see, for example, Anne Betten, "'Das ist mir zu blöd, drei Seiten ein Satz': Anmerkungen zum Stil von Thomas Bernhards Prosa," in *Thomas Bernhard—Johannes Freumbichler—Hedwig Stavianicek*, ed. Manfred Mittermayer, *Rampe* (1999): 125–36; and Franz Eyckeler's chapter on "Sprache und Form" in *Reflexionspoesie: Sprachskepsis, Rhetorik und Poetik bei Thomas Bernhard* (Berlin: Schmidt, 1995), 72–131.

12. Hollein's brief prefatory text, entitled "Everything Is Architecture" ("Alles ist Architektur"), similarly works with these two elements: "Man is both—self-centered individual and part of a community. This determines his comportment" ("Der Mensch ist beides—selbstzentriertes Individuum und Teil der Gemeinschaft. Dies bestimmt sein Verhalten"), in Porsch, *Austrian Phenomenon I*, 1048–49.

13. See the novel's first page, from which these examples are taken (*A* 3; *Am* 111).

14. See, for instance, "Unterschied," "übergesund," "*Über*vorsicht," "Überdruck," "*Über*furcht", "untergrabende," "überblickbare," "unterhalb"; the word "unter" appears a number of times alone. Of course, not all of these are separable prefix words; "unter" is an intrinsic part of the words "Unterschied" and "unterhalb" (*Am* 114–16).

15. See the discussion of grammatical elements in Christian Norberg-Schulz, *Genius Loci: Towards a Phenomenology of Architecture* (New York: Rizzoli, 1979), 22.

16. On the elliptical perforations, see Juliane Vogel, "Vorüberlegungen zu Thomas Bernhards *Amras*," *Modern Austrian Literature* 42, no. 1 (2009): 41–44; see also Ena Jung, who links the ellipses to the representation of epilepsy in "Ellipses . . . Epilepsie," *Modern Austrian Literature* 42, no. 1 (2009): 87–98.

17. The "perforated" or "durchlöchert" existence of the brothers—their father's profligacy has ruined them—is visualized in this manner, with the thematic strain emerging on the formal level.

Chapter Two

1. The novella's opening underlines this dual aspect: "The tower, familiar to us from our childhood like no other building in all of Tyrol, was no dungeon to us" (*A* 3; "Der Turm war uns aus der Kindheit wie kein anderes Tiroler Gebäude vertraut, kein Kerker," *Am* 111).

2. Matthias Konzett speaks of *Amras* as being a "paradigmatic stock scenario" up to Bernhard's mid-career in his introduction "National Iconoclasm: Thomas Bernhard and the Austrian Avant-Garde," in *A Companion to the Works of Thomas Bernhard* (Rochester, N.Y.: Camden House, 2010), 1–22, esp. 8.

3. See Dietmar Steiner, "Österreichs Phänomen," in Porsch, *The Austrian Phenomenon I*, 907–8.

4. The etymological "shadows" cast their pall on the novel's predilection for darkness and other night states, contributing to a black romanticism that early reviewers were quick to note. See the essays in Anneliese Botond, ed., *Über Thomas Bernhard* (Frankfurt am Main: Suhrkamp, 1970).

5. *OM* 154; "lächerlicher Kleinstaat," "verstümmelte[r] Staat," *AM* 306.

6. The charming plan is reprinted in Alfred Auer, ed., *Meisterwerke der Sammlungen Schloss Ambras* (Vienna: Kunsthistorisches Museum/Skira, 2008), 19.

7. Here, he was perhaps sensitized to the interplay between space and viewer after a conversation with the famed architect Clemens Holzmeister (see notes to chapter 1). On Bernhard's participation in the Innsbruck Youth Culture Week and the function of the institution itself, see Christine Riccabona, "Begegnungen—Die Österreichischen Jugendkulturwochen in Innsbruck (1949–1969)," in *Ex.Position—Avantgarde Tirol 1960/75*, ed. Günther Dankl (Innsbruck: Tiroler Landesmuseum Ferdinandeum, 2004), 77–86, esp. 77–78; and her "Jugendkulturwochen," in *Ton Zeichen: Zeilen Sprünge: Die Österreichischen Jugendkulturwochen (1950–1969) in Innsbruck*, ed. Christina Riccabona, Erika Wimmer, and Milena Meller (Innsbruck: Studien Verlag, 2006), 47–53.

8. The lower halls were renovated and refurbished in 1974; see Alfred Auer, "Schloss Ambras und die Habsburger Porträtgalerie," *Vernissage* 8, no. 65 (July 2000): 6–11, esp. 8.

9. See the following passage: "My disquisitions on the chromonema, for example, on endomitosis, on isotopes and mitochondria, on the nucleolus, on pleiotropy, which had never failed to amaze my Walter, to give him pleasure, because to him, in his attitude, so dear to me, to the contemplation of a science that was arcane to him, Correns's and Mendel's formulas and theories had never been anything but poetry, crumbled on my very tongue . . . likewise, Walter's recitations of the verses of Baudelaire and Novalis or even the most ingenious attempt at an approach to the 'Sermon of the Dead Christ Delivered from the Vault of the Universe' only aroused panic in us, for they came to a pitiful end every time as soon as they had begun" (*A* 13; "Meine Erklärung des Chromonema zum Beispiel, der Endomitose, der Isotope und Mitochondrien, des Nucleolus, des Pleiotrops, die meinen Walter immer erstaunt, ihm Vergnügen bereitet hatte, denn ihm waren in seinem mir lieben Verhältnis zur Anschauung einer ihm 'spanischen' Wissenschaft Correns und Mendels Formeln und Theorien nur Poesie gewesen, zerbröckelten mir auf der Zunge . . . ebenso lösten Walters Rezitationen der Verse Baudelaires und Novalis' oder auch nur der naivste Versuch einer Annäherung an die 'Rede

des toten Christus vom Weltgebäude herab' in uns nur Entsetzen aus, denn sie endeten jedesmal kläglich schon in den Ansätzen," *Am* 124).

10. *A* 21; *Am* 133–35.

11. *A* 21; *Am* 135. Note the capitalization of "high" in the original German, which goes against standard usage.

12. We also find here an early permutation of the critic Reger's flights in *Old Masters*, which are conceived as a liberation from the strictures of prescribed learning as well as from the actual halls in which this learning, separated by disciplinary boundaries, takes place. However, the flights are not yet the sloppy reading habits of a wildly voracious, undiscerning reading public that Reger criticizes. Reger alludes to these flights in his use of the adjective "*hoch*gradig" to describe his talents as a page-turner (chapter 3).

13. *A* 16; *Am* 127. The English translation leaves out the capitalization of the section title in the original, which I have chosen to preserve here—it lends this section the necessary emphasis otherwise lacking.

14. Musil's novel *The Man without Qualities* is present in public discourse with the appearance of a new edition in 1952, ed. Adolf Frisé (parts had appeared in 1930, 1932, 1943, and 1952). I quote from this edition, since it is the one that would have been known to readers of the 1960s; the passages are the same as in the 1978 edition. Interestingly, Musil's magnum opus is not present in Bernhard's library, but many of his other works are (*Drei Frauen*, *Die Verwirrungen des Zöglings Törleß*, *Theater: Kritisches und Theoretisches*, *Nachlaß zu Lebzeiten*).

15. On the publication history of the journal and Bachmann's importance, see Patricia Preuss's "Leseprobe." *Undine: Ingeborg Bachmann Forum*, May 22, 2012, http://www.ingeborg-bachmann-forum.de/ibles-pp.htm.

16. Ingeborg Bachmann, "Ins Tausendjährige Reich," *Akzente* 1, no. 1 (February 1954): 27; *Werke*, vol. 4, ed. Christine Koschel et al. (Munich: Piper, 1978), 4–28.

17. In the interview "Three Days" ("Drei Tage"), Bernhard claims that Musil is one of the very great artists to whom he has succumbed entirely ("*restlos* verfallen")—and whom he has to subjugate ("niederdrücken," *Der Italiener* [Frankfurt am Main: Suhrkamp, 1989], 78–90, esp. 87).

18. Hans Höller was the first to remark on the fact that Musil's importance for *Amras* has been underestimated (*Bernhard*, 79).

19. Claude Haas has devoted a chapter to the similarities between Musil and Bernhard's incestuous dyads, relating it to Julia Kristeva's concept of abjection. See his *Arbeit am Abscheu: Zu Thomas Bernhards Prosa* (Munich: Fink, 2007), 213–36.

20. See, for e.g., Musil, *Mann*, 690, 700, 1024.

21. See, for e.g., Musil, *Mann*, 716–17; 702. In a different context, see the discussions of the tower in Alfred Pfabigan's chapter "Der Turm als Verlängerung der Familie und als Ort subversiver Reflexion," in *Thomas Bernhard: Ein österreichisches Weltexperiment* (Vienna: Zsolnay, 1999), 97–99; and Ulrich Kinzel's article on Bernhard and John Donne, "Gestaltung des Zerfalls: Thomas Bernhard und die Erfahrung John Donnes," in *Thomas Bernhard: Traditionen und Trabanten*, eds. Joachim Hoell and Kai Luehrs-Kaiser (Würzburg: Königshausen und Neumann, 1999), 119–128, esp. 126–27.

22. In another variation on *Amras*'s themes, written after the completion of the short novel and included in the volume of short texts entitled *Prosa* from 1967 (*Werke* 14, 9–95), Bernhard reverses the perspective. The uncle meets a young man, well versed in the arts and sciences, and discusses everything—"das Einundalles"—with him. In "Attaché in the French Embassy" ("Attaché an der französischen Botschaft"), the uncle's properties become the condition for the possibility of philosophical thought. The allusion to Musil's "sense of the possible" ("Möglichkeitssinn") is explicit. The uncle sees his own relation to his properties as the grounding ("*Grund*stücke") facilitating his philosophical speculations. This relation enables him to be a "practical man at the height of the twentieth century" ("Praktiker auf dem Höhepunkt des Zwanzigsten Jahrhunderts"): "My plots of land are my subject. I can imagine that a philosopher sees all his philosophies day and night, if he is an ideal philosopher. The art of it is that the philosopher always *sees through* all philosophies, while mine is, always, to *see through* all the plots of land. [. . .] Whatever it is, I always have to know it. The world is, as you know, a world of possibilities, as the philosophies are philosophies of possibilities. We are always thinking in terms of possibilities" (*P* 98, 97; "Meine Grundstücke sind meine Themen. Ich kann mir vorstellen, daß ein Philosoph Tag und Nacht alle seine Philosophien sieht, wenn er der ideale Philosoph ist. Die Kunst besteht darin, daß der Philosoph immer alle Philosophien *durchschaut*, wie die meinige darin besteht, immer alle Grundstücke zu *durchschauen*. [. . .] Immer muß ich wissen, was immer ist. Die Welt ist, wie Sie wissen, eine Möglichkeitswelt, meine Grundstücke sind Möglichkeitsgrundstücke, wie die Philosophien Möglichkeitsphilosophien sind. Wir denken alle immer in Möglichkeiten" (*Pr* 56–61, esp. 58). While it may seem bold to read the "durchschauen" in the uncle's statement—that his art is "immer alle Grundstücke zu *durchschauen*"—in the literal sense of "seeing through" rather than in the idiomatic sense of "being on to something," I'd like to argue that the art of possibility the "Grundstück" calls into being is precisely a synthesis of knowledge and private learning. On the "Durchblick" in Bernhard, see chapter 3.

23. See my article "Thomas Bernhard und die Tradition: 'Andere Zustände' in *Amras*," in *"Ist es eine Komödie? Ist es eine Tragödie?": Ein Symposium zum Werk von Thomas Bernhard*, eds. Attila Bombitz und Martin Huber (Vienna: Präsens, 2010), 161–76. See also Robert Leucht und Susanne Reichlin's piece, "'Ein Gleichgewicht ohne festen Widerhalt, für das wir noch keine rechte Beschreibung gefunden haben': Robert Musils 'anderer Zustand' als Ort der Wissensübertragung," in *Medien, Technik, Wissenschaft*, ed. Ulrich J. Beil et al. (Zurich: Chronos, 2011), 289–322.

24. The ceiling is reproduced in Auer, *Meisterwerke*, 64.

25. Anthony Vidler, *The Architectural Uncanny: Essays in the Modern Unhomely* (Cambridge, Mass.: MIT Press, 1992), esp. 3–14.

26. On the sense of "Unheimlichkeit" in Bernhard, compare Claude Haas's analysis of *Extinction* (*Arbeit*, 132–40).

27. This alternation should not be imagined as fixed positions that are "achieved"—in line with their threshold space and their middle position in the tower, these are fluid gender identities through which the brothers transition.

28. On the influence of Novalis's "Zauberworte" or "magical words" on Bernhard's composite nouns, see Ingrid Petrasch, *Die Konstitution von Wirklichkeit in*

Thomas Bernhard: Sinnbildlichkeit und groteske Überzeichnung (Frankfurt am Main: P. Lang, 1986), 90–94.

29. *A* 3; "zwei Roßdecken," *Am* 111.

30. *A* 9; "zwei Geschwistermädchen, ein Brüderpaar, zwei Professoren," *Am* 118–19.

31. *A* 24; "verdoppelt," *Am* 138.

32. *A* 28; "jeweils zwei übereinander," *Am* 144.

33. *A* 43; "Es gibt aber keine erste und keine letzte Gestalt des Bruders . . . keinen Bruder . . . Walter *ist.* [. . .] der Tod unterbricht ja nicht," *Am* 161.

34. Robert Musil, *The Man without Qualities*, vol. 3, trans. Eithne Wilkins and Ernst Kaiser (London: Pan Books, 1979), 89; *Der Mann ohne Eigenschaften* (Reinbek bei Hamburg: Rowohlt, 1978), 752.

35. Musil, *Man* 3: 99–100; *Mann*, 767.

36. The translation here reads "excessively healthy," "overcaution," "excessive strain," and excessive fear" and approximates the repetitive element through the intonation of the adjective "excessive" (*A* 5–7; *Am* 115–16).

37. *A* 8–23; *Am* 116–35. While the English translations sometimes preserve the original repetition of "hoch," or "higher" (e.g., "higher education," 21), this is not always the case, e.g., "sibling torpor" (4), "institutional martyrdom" (21–22).

38. On the whole, the prose works evince a kind of similarity, as Alfred Pfabigan has written in *Thomas Bernhard: Ein österreichisches Weltexperiment* (Vienna: Zsolnay, 1999), 39.

39. Later Bernhard novels, written as one unbroken paragraph (*Playing Watten* [*Watten*, 1969], *Lime Works* [*Kalkwerk*, 1970], *Walking* [*Gehen*, 1971], *Concrete* [*Beton*], *Wittgenstein's Nephew* [*Wittgensteins Neffe*], 1982), mimic the tower on a purely typographic level.

40. On a website from the University of Vienna, a diagrammatic treatment of the term "structuration" or "structuredness" ("Strukturiertheit") moves through the various phases of defining the problem, selecting and calibrating the method, training the observer, observing, recording, and sharing the recorded observations (and bears no resemblance to Anthony Giddens's sociological concept of structuration). One synonym that has been given for this kind of "structuration" is "standardization," but I find this a bit misleading, since it implies a homogeneity among teaching situations and teachers that is neither intended nor possible. See http://www.didactics.eu/index.php?id=826.

41. See also Anthony Vidler, *The Architectural Uncanny: Essays in the Modern Unhomely* (Cambridge, Mass.: MIT Press, 1992), 167–68.

42. This element in Bernhard needs to be distinguished from the fears about surveillance that were heavily thematized in art and public discourse during the 1960s and 1970s, with the worries about homegrown terrorism and the overweening power of the surveillant state in the Federal Republic of Germany.

43. On the Ambraser cabinet of curiosities, see Way Station 3.

44. See Gabriele Beßler, *Wunderkammern: Weltmodelle von der Renaissance bis zur Kunst der Gegenwart* (Berlin: Dietrich Reimer Verlag, 2009), 20–21.

45. Hans Hollein, "Alles ist Architektur," http://www.hollein.com/eng/Writings/Texte/Alles-ist-Architektur.

46. See the protagonist Reger's accolades for Novalis in *Old Masters*: "I have loved Novalis from the start, he said, when he had closed the book with the

Novalis maxims [. . .] and I still love him today" (*OM* 131; "Novalis habe ich von Anfang an geliebt, sagte er, nachdem er das Buch mit den Novalis-Sätzen wieder zugeklappt hatte [. . .] und ich liebe ihn noch heute," *AM* 262).

47. Bernhard rewrites Novalis so that the original is often altered. A Novalis epigram from *Physikalische und medizinische Bermerkungen*, for instance, opens the edition by Walter Rehm: "Das Wesen der Krankheit ist so dunkel als das Wesen des Lebens." Bernhard's misquotation and correction of the Novalis aphorism in the typescript closest to the final version of Amras is telling: Bernhard crosses out "of death" ("Todes") in "Das Wesen der Krankheit ist so dunkel als das Wesen des Todes," replacing it with the correct word "Lebens." He is here foreshadowing the cut that he undertakes to Novalis's *Brouillon*, curtailing the fragmentary encyclopedia's transcendent thrust in favor of a purely secular, this-worldly text (see Schmidt-Dengler and Huber's afterword to *Amras*, 347–56).

48. Novalis, *Notes*, sect. 526, 93; "Alles *Höhere* gehört zusammen—alles *Niedre*," *Brouillon*, sect. 526, 356.

49. See translator David Wood's introduction to the English translation of Novalis's *Notes to a Romantic Encyclopedia* (ix–xxix). Also see Joseph Vogl's discussion of Novalis and his response to the new objects of study and fields of inquiry in *Kalkül und Leidenschaft: Poetik des ökonomischen Menschen*, 2nd ed. (Zurich: Diaphanes, 2004), esp. 258–64.

50. Novalis, *Notes*, sect. 76, 12; *Brouillon*, sect. 76, 253.

51. Novalis, *Notes*, sect. 526, 93; "Wenn mein Unternehmen zu groß in der Ausführung werden sollte—so geb ich nur die Methodik des Verfahrens—und Beyspiele—den *allgemeinsten Theil* und Bruchstücke aus den Besondern Theilen," *Brouillon*, sect. 526, 356).

52. Novalis, "*Alle W[issenschaft] ist Eine*," *Brouillon*, sect. 526, 356.

53. Novalis writes: "[M]it der Vervollständigung und Erhöhung des Schemas klärt sich der Versuch auf, wird mannichfacher und höher grädig. Alle Beobachtung ist um so mehr *Beobachtung*, je specificirender oder classificirender—und zwar je *richtiger* classificirend sie ist. Auch die richtige Ordnung in der Vermannichfachung gehört zum höhern Grade" (*Brouillon*, sect. 528, 357).

54. In a section entitled "Physik" in the Novalis paperback, Bernhard marks a few aphorisms with thick roller-ball pen. We here see Bernhard's fascination with space. One such highlighted aphorism reads: "Wenn ein Körper im ganzen in ein Verhältnis tritt, so treten seine Teile in ein ähnliches Verhältnis, wie der ganze Körper." Another marked passage (also with the notation "Marx" next to it) reads: "Trieb und Raum haben viel Ähnlichkeit—Jeder Körper ist ein ausgefüllter Trieb." Two unmarked passages on the same page state: "Zeit ist innrer Raum—Raum ist äußere Zeit" and "Der Raum als Niederschlag aus der Zeit" (Rehm, *Novalis* [Frankfurt am Main: Fischer, 1956], 189, 192–93).

55. See Rehm's introduction, *Novalis*, 7–13.

56. Bruce Donehower, *The Birth of Novalis* (Albany: SUNY Press, 2007), 7.

57. Rehm, introduction, *Novalis*, 11.

58. The erotic connotations are also present in the German: "In diesem Sinn und auf dieses Ziel hin müssen auch die Aufsätze und Fragmente des Novalis gelesen werden: als ein Vor-Spiel der Dichtung" (Rehm, introduction, *Novalis*, 13).

59. Compare the reading Bernhard Judex offers, in his note to "Böden und Mauern," *Amras: Text und Kommentar* (Frankfurt am Main: Suhrkamp, 2006),

133. For him, *Amras* shows the impossibility of recuperating the romantic writer's closeness to nature.

60. See Typescript 15/2 of *Amras* in the Bernhard-Archive, p. 63, where these reflections immediately precede K.'s narration of Walter's jump to his death.

61. See, for instance, *A* 32–33, *A* 58–59; *Am* 161, 174.

62. *A* 56; "Gleichgewichtsstörungen, Kopfschmerz und Ohnmacht [. . .] beim Umblättern einer Bücherseite," *Am* 175–76. As such it is no coincidence that the narrator's brother suffers from "Fallsucht," or "falling" sickness. Compare Armin Schäfer, for whom the opening of entryways and exits in the encounter with the written word produces a loss of stability ("Existenzmöglichkeiten: Versuch über die Auflösung des sensomotorischen Schemas in Thomas Bernhards *Amras*," *Modern Austrian Literature* 42, no. 1 [2009]: 45–61).

63. *A* 56–57; *Am* 175–76. The method Reger envisions (chapter 3)—entering a page like a landscape, traversing it with care and penetrating it—is present here as well, with the parents "reading" the Tyrolean landscape ("tirolische Erdoberfläche") like a penal code ("Strafgesetzbuch"), which condemns them, their progeny, and their descendants to lifelong imprisonment ("eingeschlossen," *Am* 175–76).

64. In Bernhard the tower also functions as a kind of utopian space that ends a forbidden incest with nature and replaces it with a Musil-inspired one. The physical proximity to incest stands in a clear relationship to the aesthetic experience of physical beauty. The first-person narrator at first denies this proximity, only to affirm it indirectly later on (*Am* 24). The repeated description of the brothers' bodily contiguity ("body to body" ["Körper an Körper"], *A* 22; *Am* 27) is a precondition for the dissolution of boundaries in the "Other Condition" and the "doubled face of nature," which Musil describes and Bernhard puts into practice. Ena Jung links the homoerotic and incestuous aspects to this collapse of individuality in her careful reading of *Amras*'s typography: "The collapse of individuality is explicit in their signature at the end of their first two letters, written to explain their situation: 'K.M.W.M.' [. . .] The two sets of initials are pressed together, representing literally the way their two bodies were found in bed upon the suicide attempt [. . .] 'K.M.W.M' as the typographic representation of the incestuous and homoerotic embrace of the two brothers" (Jung, "Ellipses . . . Epilepsie," *Modern Austrian Literature* 42, no. 1 [2009]: 87–98, esp. 94–95).

65. See Juliane Vogel's compelling foreword to the special issue of *Modern Austrian Literature* devoted to *Amras* ("Vorüberlegungen zu Thomas Bernhards *Amras*," *Modern Austrian Literature* 42, no. 1 [2009]: 41–44).

66. Novalis, *Notes*, sect. 113, 18; *Brouillon*, sect. 113, 261.

Way Station 3

1. On the Wunderkammer see, e.g., Elisabeth Scheicher, *Die Kunst- und Wunderkammer der Habsburger* (Vienna: Molden, 1979); *Sammeln als Institution: Von der fürstlichen Wunderkammer zum Mäzenatentum des Staates*, ed. Barbara Marx and Karl-Siegbert Rehberg (Munich: Deutscher Kunstverlag, 2006); Thomas Richter, *Wunderkammer: Kunst, Natur und Wissenschaft in Renaissance und Barock* (Zürich: Chronos, 2005); Gabriele Beßler, *Wunderkammern: Weltmodelle von der Renaissance bis zur Kunst der Gegenwart* (Berlin: Dietrich Reimer Verlag, 2009); Horst Bredekamp, *The Lure of Antiquity and the Cult of the Machine: The Kunstkammer and the Evolution of Nature, Art, and*

Technology, trans. Allison Brown (Princeton, N.J.: Markus Wiener, 1995). Bredekamp's book was originally published in German as *Antikensehnsucht und Maschinenglauben: Die Geschichte der Kunstkammer und die Zukunft der Kunstgeschichte* (Munich: Wagenbach, 1993); all citations are from this edition.

2. Julia Teresa Friehs, "Die Kunstkammer auf Schloss Ambras," http://www.habsburger.net/de/kapitel/die-kunstkammer-auf-schloss-ambras.

3. See Friederike Klauner's brief introduction to *Die Kunstkammer*, ed. Elisabeth Scheicher et al. (Vienna: Kunsthistorisches Museum, 1977), 7–8.

4. Beßler, *Wunderkammern*, 15.

5. For a precise description and inventory, see the section "Antiquarium," in Scheicher, *Kunstkammer*, 157–94. The niches, while present in earlier documentation, in their current form probably date to 1730. Interestingly, the restoration in 1974 eliminates "all too baroque" ("allzu Barockes") in favor of the "character" of the sixteenth century, suggesting that the principles of selection I mention are in operation (158–59). This selectiveness goes against Klauner's assertion in the introduction that the 1970s favored a more inclusive taste and showed openness toward the "fantastic gimmickry" ("phantastischen Spielereien") of mannerism, which estrange man and nature (8).

6. Beßler, *Wunderkammern*, 6.

7. See his acceptance speech when he receives the Literary Prize of Bremen in 1965 (*MPr*, 117–20, esp. 120).

8. As Elisabeth Scheicher et al. write: "Seinem Wesen nach ist das Antiquarium ein Studiolo, daß heißt ein Raum, in den sich der Sammler zum Zweck seiner wissenschaftlichen Beschäftigung zurückzog, was im Fall von Ambras durch die räumliche Verbindung mit der Bibliothek zum Ausdruck kommt" (*Kunstkammer*, 157).

9. Samuel Quiccheberg, *The First Treatise on Museums: Samuel Quiccheberg's Inscriptiones 1565*, trans. and ed. Mark A. Meadow and Bruce Robertson (Los Angeles: Getty Research Institute, 2013).

10. See Bruce Robertson, preface, vi–xi, and Mark A. Meadows, introduction, *The First Treatise*, 1–41; Auer, *Meisterwerke*, 18; and Thomas Brakensiek, "Samuel Quicchelberg: Gründungsvater oder Einzeltäter? Zur Intention der *Inscriptiones vel Tituli Theatri amplissimi* (1565) und ihrer Rezeption im Sammlungswesen Europas zwischen 1550 und 1820," http://www.metaphorik.de/14/Brakensiek. See also Margot Rauch, "Monster und Mirakel: Wunderbares in der Kunstkammer von Schloss Ambras," exhibition brochure, Castle Ambras (Innsbruck: Heimatwerbung, 2003), n.p.

11. Quiccheberg, *The First Treatise*, 61.

12. Brakensiek discusses Francis Yates's magisterial *The Art of Memory* ("Samuel Quiccheberg," 241); Bredekamp, *The Lure of Antiquity*, 53.

13. See Quiccheberg, *The First Treatise*, 72; and Meadows, introduction to *The First Treatise*, 2.

Chapter Three

1. In their commentary to the volume of *Old Masters* in the collected edition, Wendelin Schmidt-Dengler and Martin Huber speak of Bernhard's final written work as "Schlußstein im Gewölbe des Romanwerks von Thomas Bernhard" (*AM* 240).

2. Ferdinand II's cabinet of curiosities contained many surviving items from other collections belonging to Emperors Frederick III, Maximilian I, and Ferdinand I. It later enters the Kunstkammer, or Collection of Sculpture and Decorative Arts, of the Art History Museum in Vienna. In the early nineteenth century, the collection was moved from Tyrol to the Lower Belvedere in Vienna to safeguard it from Napoleonic troops. A reorganization in 1875 under Franz Joseph I led to its partial inclusion in the Kunsthistorisches Museum (see Cäcilia Bischoff, *The Kunsthistorisches Museum in Vienna* [Munich: Prestel, 2007], 74).

3. The translation from Horst Bredekamp's *The Lure of Antiquity and the Cult of the Machine: The Kunstkammer and the Evolution of Nature, Art and Technology*, trans. Allison Brown (Princeton, N.J: Markus Wiener, 1995) is my own. The published translation is more abbreviated: "The *Kunstkammer* became a metaphor for the human brain gradually reacquiring Edenic wisdom" (40–41). See Horst Bredekamp's original: "Die Kunstkammer wird zu einem Analogon des Gehirnes der Menschheit, das die gelöschte Weisheit des Paradieses allmählich zurückgewinnt." This analogical function is trumpeted in an early treatise about the "Kunst- und Naturalien-Kammern" from 1674, in which the cabinets are seen as restoring the erased mental tablet of humanity, "Taffel seines Gehirn . . . darinaufgezeichnete Dinge . . . außgelescht" (*Antikensehnsucht und Maschinenglauben: Die Geschichte der Kunstkammer und die Zukunft der Kunstgeschichte* [Berlin: Klaus Wagenbach, 1993], 43).

4. *A* 25; "verbotenen Äpfelgärten," *Am* 139.

5. See Brian O'Doherty's seminal essay "Inside the White Cube: Notes on the Gallery Space" in *Artforum*, in which he polemically takes the museum to task for its enshrinement of a certain view of modernist art. The rise of the museal space—which endows meaning and confers status—is linked to the "elementary architecture" of the white cube: "An image comes to mind of a white, ideal space that, more than any single picture, may be the archetypal image of 20th-century art. And it clarifies itself through a process of historical inevitability usually attached to the art it contains." O'Doherty breaks down this "pure" space further, arguing that the fundamental plane is the wall—it endows works with meaning and narrative coherence within a larger history of art. The problem is that the hollow space of the museum gallery with its white walls does not emplace artworks in a meaningful manner. He writes: "We enter the era where works of art conceive the wall as a no-man's land on which to project their concept of the territorial imperative. And we are not far from the kind of border warfare that often Balkanizes museum group shows. There is a peculiar uneasiness in watching artworks attempting to establish territory but not place in the context of the placeless modern gallery" (n.p.), http://www.societyofcontrol.com/whitecube/insidewc.htm.

6. See Anne-Marie Bonnet and Gabriele Kopp-Schmidt, *Kunst ohne Geschichte? Ansichten zu Kunst und Kunstgeschichte heute* (Munich: C.H. Beck, 1995), 7–12.

7. Jacopo Robusti, *Portrait of a White-Bearded Man*, 92.4 × 59.5 cm, Kunsthistorisches Museum, Vienna. The painting is one of Tintoretto's late works; see Paola Rossi, *Jacopo Tintoretto* (Milan: Electa, 1994), 140–41.

8. *OM* 17; "ein hochgradig talentierter Umblätterer," *AM* 26.

9. Speed is always the problem, as in the case of the Prince Saurau in *Gargoyles*, whose thinking is highly problematic: "To me my thought is: Velocities

that I cannot see" (*G* 185; "Mir ist mein Denken: Geschwindigkeiten, die ich nicht sehen kann," *V* 186).

10. Hence comes the privilege bestowed on movement *per pedes* in Bernhard's oeuvre.

11. Carl Schorske convincingly argues that the Ringstrasse inverts baroque values: the dynamic horizontality of the street does not magnify the buildings' splendor, but leads to the street's independence. "They [the Ringstrasse designers] organized all the elements in relation to a central broad avenue or corso, without architectonic containment and without visible destination." The street leads an "independent life, unsubordinated to any other spatial entity" (32). Schorske interestingly does not devote any time to the museum buildings themselves, focusing elsewhere on the importance of Semper—the theater builder for Richard Wagner—for the Viennese cityscape. See his chapter on "The Ringstrasse and the Birth of Urban Modernism" in *Fin-de-Siècle Vienna: Politics and Culture* (New York: Knopf, 1979), 24–115.

12. As Reger states: "I have not read a book at home for years, here in the Bordone Room I have read hundreds of books, but that is not to say that I read all those books in the Bordone Room *through to the end*, I have never in my life read a single book *through to the end*, my way of reading a book is that of a highly talented page turner, that is of a person who would rather turn the pages than read, who therefore turns dozens, or at times hundreds, of pages before reading a single one" (*OM* 17; "Zu Hause lese ich schon seit Jahren kein Buch mehr, hier im Bordone-Saal habe ich schon Hunderte Bücher gelesen, aber das heißt nicht, daß ich alle diese Bücher im Bordone-Saal *aus*gelesen hätte, ich habe niemals in meinem Leben ein einziges Buch *aus*gelesen, meine Art zu lesen ist die eines hochgradig talentierten Umblätterers, also eines Mannes, der lieber umblättert, als liest, der also Dutzende von Seiten umblättert, bevor er eine einzige liest," *AM* 26–27).

13. The lighting system itself is quite complex. Bischoff describes the Picture Gallery on the top floor of the museum in detail: "light from above streams into the great halls that face the courtyard, while the side rooms surrounding them receive the necessary light through window openings on the outside wall. In line with the state of technological development at the time it was built, the entire building was designed and used as a daylight museum" (*Kunsthistorisches Museum*, 18).

14. See esp. *OM* 9; *AM* 16.

15. See Hans Belting's revision of his text, *Das Ende der Kunstgeschichte?* (Munich: Deutscher Kunstverlag, 1983) twelve years later (*Das Ende der Kunstgeschichte: Eine Revision nach zehn Jahren* [Munich: C.H. Beck, 1995]), in which he claims that the museum has taken over the job of consecrating art "products" or "wares" and furthering the art market's goals. See also Martin Warnke, "Theorie und Praxis in der Endzeit," in Bonnet and Kopp-Schmidt, *Kunst*, 113–16.

16. Sorg succinctly distinguishes Reger's two approaches, without delving into depth. One is the "Lust an der Destruktion des Falschen, Mediokren und allgemein Überschätzten," the other the "melancholische Akzeptierung der Imperfektion jedes Kunstwerks." The former leads, according to Sorg, to indiscriminate criticism ("Mäkelei"), the latter to the hierarchization of life and art, with the subordination of art to life (Sorg, *Thomas Bernhard* [Munich: C.H. Beck, 1992], 116–17).

17. Elaine Scarry, *On Beauty and Being Just* (London: Duckworth, 2001), esp. 65–67, 80–82.

18. Scarry actually speaks of "lateral disregard," by which she means that beauty is often disparaged for its ability to make us neglect other, less beautiful things, i.e., "the problem that whatever benefits accrue to an object through its being the focus of our attention are not being equally enjoyed by nearby objects in the same class" (*On Beauty and Being Just*, 65–66).

19. Dilettantism's etymological relation to "delectare" is an indication of the formerly positive meaning of the word. It becomes a common term in Italy between the sixteenth and eighteenth century and refers to the nobility interested in art. In England, the extra-institutional role of the aristocracy in matters pertaining to art leads to the fusion of the tradition of gentleman, scholar, and dilettante. The Society of Dilettanti in London cultivates Italian art history and classical archaeology. On the development of dilettantism as a concept and its prevalence in fin-de-siècle Vienna (which strongly influences Bernhard's non-synchronous characters), see Cathrine Theodorsen, "Zur Rolle des Dilettantismus im Prozess der Ausdifferenzierung einer österreichischen Literatur aus der deutschen Literatur," *Nordlit* 9 (2001): 45–61.

20. The sentiment of love, underpinning the experience of beauty, is at the center of Scarry's treatise.

21. On the role of Anglophilia as a mark of distinction, see my article "Dialectic at a Standstill: The Discourse of Victimhood in Thomas Bernhard's *Heldenplatz*," *German Quarterly* 75, no. 4 (2003): 409–22, esp. 413–14.

22. See, for instance, *OM* 34, 38; *AM* 47, 51.

23. "Durchschauen," the word used in *Gargoyles* in connection with such moments, carries overtones of unmasking something nefarious. "Durchblick," on the other hand, is more positive, with resonances of savvy and mental sharpness. Gregor Hens has argued that the "Durchblick" subordinates the spatial coordinates of the novel to its temporal ones and is related to the mannerist distortion of space in *Alte Meister* (*Thomas Bernhards Trilogie der Künste: Der Untergeher, Holzfällen, Alte Meister* [Columbia, S.C.: Camden House, 1999], 152).

24. Friderike Klauner, *Die Gemäldegalerie des Kunsthistorischen Museums in Wien: Vier Jahrhunderte europäischer Malerei* (Salzburg: Residenz, 1978), 5–8, esp. 8.

25. See his statement: "In London I had lived, in Vienna I have never truly lived, in London my head felt well (*OM* 97; "In London hatte ich gelebt, in Wien habe ich nie wirklich gelebt, in London hat sich mein Kopf wohlgefühlt," *AM* 121). Changes in the various corrected page proofs of *Alte Meister* make clear that Bernhard sought to mask the Jewishness of the main character—it remains, in this way, a more subtle criticism of the Austrian Republic and its population's anti-Semitism. For example, Reger's wife is, in an earlier version 8/3a, a Jewess (in the final corrected version she is no longer an "intelligent, wealthy Jewess," but an "elegant, wealthy cosmopolitan," see *AM* 123). Reger's own Jewishness is only mentioned peripherally ("There was also a massive Jewish contribution," *OM* 46; "es hat auch einen kräftigen jüdischen Einschlag gegeben," *AM* 61). A similar statement in Version 8/3a reads: "thankfully, I had a dash of Jewishness" ("zum Glück hatte ich auch einen Schuß Judentum"). On the topic see Wendelin Schmidt-Dengler and Martin Huber's afterword to vol. 8 (197–247; esp.

219–20). Mention is also made of Frau Reger's burial in a white shroud (*AM* 170), and Reger's easy familiarity with the Hungarian Jews in the Hotel Ambassador (*AM* 108–9).

26. Scarry, *On Beauty and Being Just*, 82–86.

27. This is Stanley Corngold's description of Kant's spectator in his *Complex Pleasures: Forms of Feeling in German Literature* (Stanford, Calif.: Stanford University Press, 1998). Corngold's words are applicable here, but go beyond my scope: "Kant's example shows us, at the origin of the thesis of self-reflexivity of fiction, how self-reflection might and indeed must contain a bearing on social reality. It evokes in every reader of the beautiful fiction the existence of fellow consciousnesses entirely sane, a whole society of consciousness, all the time preserving in aesthetic awareness a dimension of irreducible solitude" (46–47).

28. Scarry, *On Beauty and Being Just*, 89.

29. The English reads "misuse," rather than "violate" or "abuse," compare *OM* 144; *AM* 178.

30. See Way Station 1.

31. Michel Chaouli, *The Laboratory of Poetry: Chemistry and Poetics in the Work of Friedrich Schlegel* (Baltimore, Md.: Johns Hopkins University Press, 2002), 49–50.

32. We could see Scarry's treatise as an attempt to restore the intersubjective aspect to the experience of beauty.

33. See, for instance, *OM* 41–46, *AM* 55–60.

34. Reger does not comment explicitly on the German philosopher's thoughts in "Building Dwelling Thinking" ("Bauen Wohnen Denken").

35. Giorgio Agamben, *The Man without Content*, trans. Georgia Albert (Stanford, Calif.: Stanford University Press, 1999), 13.

36. The translation here is my own. See Jean de la Bruyêre, *Les Caractères de Théophraste traduits du grec avec Les Caractères ou les Moeurs de ce siècle*, ed. Marc Escola (Paris: Editions Champion, 1999): "Le plaisir de la critique nous ôte celui d'être vivement touchés de très belles choses," 20[I], 164.

37. See Scarry, *On Beauty and Being Just*, 73, where she describes the figure in *Phaedrus* who beholds the beautiful boy and sprouts wings in public. His interior dislocation is matched by his exterior transformation.

38. Agamben charts the same process for the artist, who feels more and more exposed to hostile forces in the artistic process, unable to achieve the *promesse de bonheur* of creation. Unmoored from a social milieu that vigorously intervenes in the creative process and from the materials with which he works, he finds no content outside of him in a world where all certainties have disappeared. Thrown back upon the creative formal principle, the artist—having evolved from artisan to inspired genius—is faced with "absolute abstract inessence" (Agamben, *The Man without Content*, 54).

39. This figure can be related to the artistic judge or "Kunstrichter" of Jürgen Habermas (see Matthias Konzett, *The Rhetoric of National Dissent in Thomas Bernhard, Peter Handke, and Elfriede Jelinek* [Rochester, N.Y.: Camden House, 2000], 25–56).

40. Scarry, *On Beauty and Being Just*, 74; Agamben, *The Man without Content*, 7–15.

41. On Bernhard's indebtedness to romanticism, see Sylvia Kaufmann, *The Importance of Romantic Aesthetics for the Interpretation of Thomas Bernhard's "Auslöschung. Ein Zerfall" and "Alte Meister: Eine Komödie"* (Stuttgart: Hans-Dieter Heinz, 1998), esp. 107–14.

42. *AM* 28, 187. I prefer this translation to Ewald Oser's "massive mistake" in *Old Masters* (19), since it preserves the formality of Reger's German phrase. It also retains the flavor of tragedy inherent in the classical Greek conception of flaws, with their intimations of future peril and destruction.

43. As Bischoff writes: "There are few works from early stylistic phases, works striving solely for inner fulfillment, no thirteenth- or fourteenth-century material, scarcely anything of the Italian quattrocento, no 'struggling, brooding types,' few sketches. [. . .] Eccentricity was not favoured. The qualities that aroused admiration were seemingly effortless mastery and incontestable elegance. Habsburg taste was orthodox without actually lapsing into bigotry" (*Kunsthistorisches Museum*, 130).

44. Compare *OM* 20; *AM* 29.

45. Compare Bianca Theisen on fragmentation in Bernhard, *Silenced Facts: Media Montages in Contemporary Austrian Literature* (Amsterdam: Rodopi, 2003), esp. 31–55.

46. Sorg speaks of the "humane Substanz der Kunst" that manifests itself when art absorbs empirical reality and transposes it, with all its limitations, into the medium of aesthetic contemplation (Sorg, *Thomas Bernhard*, 118).

47. On the interplay of fragment and totality, see the preface to Klauner's book, on which Bernhard drew for his novel: "Freilich," she writes, "ein Kunstwerk ist nie in seiner Totalität, sondern nur annäherungsweise zu erkennen und aufzufassen, und die Gegenwart wird sich von alter Kunst außer der Erkenntnis ihrer jeweiligen Qualität nur das nehmen, wozu aus der gegebenen Situation heraus ohnehin Neigung und Verwandtschaft besteht" (Klauner, *Gemäldegalerie*, 7).

48. Semper conceived "his huge square in such a way as to challenge the sovereignty of Förster's circulating space. The forum would be an axis bisecting the Ringstrasse. Great arches were to link the two museums in the foreground to two extensions of the imperial Hofburg in the background. The axis would thus break the cincture of pavement with which the Ringstrasse had replaced the cincture of stone fortifications around the inner city. It would bind old and new: the court and the popular centers of high culture, the residence of ancient royalty and the institutes of bourgeois science and art, the inner city and the outer city" (Schorske, *Fin-de-Siècle Vienna*, 101).

49. See Cäcilia Bischoff's description of the stylistic hodgepodge of building styles: "[E]ach of the four façades of the rectangular building is dedicated to a different period in the history of art. The figures on the façade facing the Babenbergerstrasse represent antiquity; those on the Lastenstrasse are from the Middle Ages; the side facing Maria-Theresien Platz celebrates the Renaissance; and finally that on the Burgring illustrates modern times." In its basic structure, the museum alludes to Leo von Klenze's Alte Pinakothek in Munich, with a nod to the baroque Palazzo Reale in Caserta (*Kunsthistorisches Museum*, 14–18).

50. Martin Jay uses this phrase to describe the opinions on mimesis of Roland Barthes, Paul de Man, and Gilles Deleuze; see his "Mimesis and Mimetology: Adorno and Lacoue-Labarthe," in *Cultural Semantics: Keywords of Our Time*

(Amherst: University of Massachusetts Press, 1998), 120–37, esp. 120–21. Also see Corngold on Paul de Man (*Complex Pleasures*, 20, 45–46).

51. Scarry describes the effect of the beautiful with these terms; the nonsentient comes to life or seems life-like (*On Beauty and Being Just*, 68).

52. This is stressed in Klauner's description, in the art historical survey in Bernhard's possession (*Gemäldegalerie*, 200). While Tom Nichols warns that recent scholarship on Tintoretto focuses too exclusively on the painter's alienation, he also cautions against an anodyne view of the artist as fully integrated in his artistic surroundings (Nichols, *Tintoretto: Tradition and Identity* [London: Reaktion Books, 1999], 97–99).

53. Hens, *Thomas Bernhards Trilogie*, 148.

54. In the book *The Kunsthistorische Museum Vienna*, which contains highlights from the collection, Tintoretto's *The Flagellation of Christ* (c. 1585/90), *Lorenzo Soranzo* (1553), *Sebastiano Venier* (c. 1571), and *Susanna and the Elders* (c. 1555/56) are depicted. See Manfred Leithe-Jasper, Rudolf Distelberger, and Wolfgang Prohaska's *The Kunsthistorische Museum Vienna*, trans. Elsie Callander and Ilse Seldon (London: Philip Wilson, 1984), 148–49. Prohaska's edition from 1997 likewise depicts *Lorenzo Soranzo* (28), *Susanna and the Elders* (29), and the *Flagellation* (32); see his *Kunsthistorisches Museum, Vienna: The Paintings* (London: Scala Books, 1997). An older catalogue, edited by Gustav Glück and entitled *Die Gemäldegalerie des Kunsthistorischen Museums in Wien* (Vienna: Kunstverlag Anton Schroll, 1925), includes *Old Man and a Boy* in addition to the *Veniers* portrait and the *Susanna* painting (45–47). The 1950 catalogue *Vienna Treasures* (New York: Art Foundation, 1950, 39–41), which accompanied a traveling exhibition to the United States, does as well. This exhibition itself did, however, include Tintoretto's *White-Bearded Man* (6). A short catalog, *Art Treasures from the Vienna Collection* (Washington, D.C.: National Gallery of Art, 1949–52), also does not include *The White-Bearded Man*.

55. See the critical edition and Schmidt-Dengler and Huber's afterword to *Alte Meister* (2008, 197–247), where they reproduce the page from Klauner's book that Bernhard had underlined and circled. In the marked passage, Klauner singles out the pseudo-expressionism of the image, which renders "das allgemeine Bild einer Gruppe, eines Standes in dramatisch übersteigerte Form [. . .] , ohne dabei die jeweilige Porträtähnlichkeit einem übergeordneten Gedanken zu opfern. [. . .] Tintorettos Bildnisse kennzeichnen den Ausbruch aus der Ausgewogenheit des Menschenbildes der Renaissance und den Beginn einer Betrachtungsweise, die betont einseitig das schöne Bild auflösen will und erschreckende Finsternis einbrechen läßt, die nur wie in einem Gewitter durch Blitze erhellt wird und nicht so sehr das ästhetische Bewußtsein befriedigt als Gefühlsbewegungen auslöst" (*Gemäldegalerie*, 193).

56. In a highly interesting article on the role of the modern museum from 1984, Klauner raises many of the issues that Reger does: what is the role of the museum as it has evolved since the Enlightenment period? How does the museum vouchsafe the appropriate aesthetic presentation of the artwork, above and beyond the documentary quality the artwork may evince? How does the intermediary—the museum director or curator—manage to do justice to the artwork and the viewer, fulfilling his role as an agent of *Bildung*? See her "Stationäre Präsentation im Museum aus der Sicht des Objekts, der Besucher und der Verantwortlichen,"

in *Bewahren und Ausstellen, die Forderung des kulturellen Erbes in Museen*, ed. Hermann Auer (Munich: Saur, 1984), 57–61, esp. 57.

57. Hens, *Thomas Bernhards Trilogie*, 153.

58. Scarry, *On Beauty and Being Just*, 89.

59. See Ingeborg Hoesterey, "Visual Art as Narrative Structure: Thomas Bernhard's *Alte Meister*," *Modern Austrian Literature* 21, no. 3-4 (1988): 117–22, esp. 120.

60. *OM* 150; *AM* 186. Note the similarity in the German ("mit Haut und Haaren") in this assertion—it links it to Reger's description of reading, quoted at the outset.

61. In his *Theatrum Pictorium*, a catalogued inventory created a few years after the gallery pictures, the painter seems to be providing more of a guide for the visitor strolling through the gallery than an important index to each work's singular importance. In his commentary, he stresses the arrangement of the objects rather than the names of the artists (Agamben, *The Man without Content*, 28–29). See also Gudrun Swoboda, *Die Wege der Bilder: Eine Geschichte der kaiserlichen Gemäldesammlungen von 1600 bis 1800* (Vienna: Kunsthistorisches Museum, 2008), 40–87.

62. Agamben, *The Man without Content*, 28–39.

63. Teniers was commissioned not only to give an inventory of the collection, but also its arrangement.

64. Agamben, *The Man without Content*, 28–39, esp. 31.

65. To be sure, what has been reduced in the modern gallery is the element of "bad" taste that may be embarrassing about a cabinet of curiosities. The side-by-side arrangement of "high" and "low" art or even non-art (e.g., the unicorn's horn next to the delicate inlaid altar) does not yet embarrass the viewer in the sixteenth century.

66. This type of painting was widespread from the early seventeenth century onward. Margret Klinge argues that Teniers was less interested in the genre's allegorical or fictive representation of galleries than in representing existent pictures. For him, these gallery pictures attest to the eminence of painting as an art form (Klinge, *David Teniers the Younger: Paintings—Drawings*, trans. David R. McLintock [Ghent: Snoeck-Ducaju & Zoon, 1991], 220–21). See also Peter C. Sutton, *The Age of Rubens* (Boston: Museum of Fine Arts, 1993), 576, 581; Matías Díaz Padrón and Mercedes Royo-Villanova, *David Teniers, Jan Brueghel y Los Gabinetes de Pinturas* (Madrid: Museo del Prado, 1992), 36; Prohaska, *Kunsthistorisches Museum*, 79.

67. *The Archduke Leopold Wilhelm in His Gallery in Brussels*, 123 × 163 cm, and *Archduke Leopold Wilhelm in His Picture Gallery*, 70 × 86 cm, are both in the Kunsthistorisches Museum. Other very similar representations are in the Petworth House in Sussex, England, the Bayerische Staatsgemäldesammlung, Munich, the Prado in Madrid, and the Brussels Museum. There are approximately ten views of the gallery in all (Klinge, *David Teniers the Younger*, 220–21, 228–29). Tintoretto's *White-Bearded Man* appears in Tenier's gallery paintings in Munich, Vienna, Madrid, and the Petworth House.

68. He does so in a manner reminiscent of John Ruskin, *The Lamp of Beauty*, ed. Joan Evans (London: Phaidon, 1959).

69. Scarry, *On Beauty and Being Just*, 76.

70. Reger unleashes his vitriol on art historians, mimicking Plato's banishment of the artist from the ideal space of the Republic: "The art historians' trade is the vilest trade there is, and a twaddling art historian, but then there are only twaddling art historians, deserves to be chased out with a whip, chased out of the world of art, Reger said, all art historians deserve to be chased out of the world of art, because art historians are the real wreckers of art and we should not allow art to be wrecked by the art historians who are really art wreckers" (*OM* 15; "Das Geschäft der Kunsthistoriker ist das übelste Geschäft, das es gibt, und ein schwätzender Kunsthistoriker, und es gibt ja nur schwätzende Kunsthistoriker, gehört mit der Peitsche verjagt, aus der Kunstwelt hinausgejagt, sagte Reger, hinausgejagt aus der Kunstwelt gehörten alle Kunsthistoriker, denn die Kunsthistoriker sind die eigentlichen Kunstvernichter und wir sollten uns die Kunst nicht von den Kunsthistorikern als Kunstvernichter vernichten lassen," *AM* 23).

71. *OM* 22; *AM* 31–32.

72. The English translation gives the "Kunstkenner" as an "art connoisseur" (*OM* 76), obviously implying a difference from the dilettante and setting him off from the "Kunstvernichter," or "art wreckers." A "Kunstfachmann" is aptly translated as an "art expert" (*OM* 76; *AM* 97).

73. Reger says of him: "The people who use *Aqua brava* all have good taste" (*OM* 73; "Die Leute, die *Aqua brava* verwenden, haben alle einen guten Geschmack," *AM* 92).

74. Uwe Betz discusses the problematic aspects of the man from Wales and his pecuniary interest in art (*Polyphone Räume und karnevalisiertes Erbe: Analysen des Werks Thomas Bernhards auf der Basis Bachtinscher Theoreme* [Würzburg: Ergon, 1997], 80–82).

75. Klinge, *David Teniers the Younger*, 278–79.

76. On the practice of making copies of the images within the Habsburg collection, see Swoboda's fascinating *Die Wege der Bilder*, esp. 18–19.

77. *OM* 79; *AM* 99–100. Count Seilern's collection is now in the Courtauld Institute of Art in London.

78. As scholars such as Allan Bloom, Francisco Gonzales, and James Arieti have argued, the injunction against mimesis is slightly misleading and should not be taken at face value. See Allan Bloom, introduction, *The Republic of Plato* (New York: Basic Books, 1991), 307–436; Francisco J. Gonzales, *Dialectic and Dialogue: Plato's Practice of Philosophical Inquiry* (Evanston, Ill.: Northwestern University Press, 1998), 129, 138–43; and James Arieti, *Interpreting Plato: The Dialogues as Drama* (Savage, Md.: Rowman and Littlefield, 1991), 242.

79. Furthermore, the movement between the beautiful object and similar things of the same class would be arrested by the existence of two equivalents. For Scarry, singular beauty acts as a democratic force, advancing our concern for related, albeit less beautiful objects. It requires a certain hierarchical difference, which the existence of identical doubles would make impossible.

80. The Welshman's final apodictic judgment returns us to the genius-centered ideology from which Reger distanced himself. The gentleman explains the existence of an identical image not by returning to the fake nature of either canvas, but by appealing to the absolute superiority of Tintoretto as an artist: "Only a great artist like Tintoretto, the Englishman said, Reger said, could have succeeded in painting a second picture not *as a totally similar but as a totally identical one*"

(*OM* 79; "Nur einem so großen Künstler wie Tintoretto mag es, so der Engländer, so Reger, tatsächlich gelungen sein, ein zweites Gemälde nicht *als ein vollkommen gleiches, sondern als vollkommen dasselbe zu malen,*" *AM* 100).

81. See Rüdiger Görner, "The Broken Window Handle: Thomas Bernhard's Notion of *Weltbezug*," in *A Companion to the Works of Thomas Bernhard*, ed. Matthias Konzett (Rochester, N.Y.: Camden House, 2010), 89–104.

82. See, for example, *OM* 5; *AM* 10.

83. Thomas Cousineau offers a critical reading of Reger in his book *Three Part Inventions: The Novels of Thomas Bernhard*, in which he stresses the "proprietary control" Reger seeks to exert on his wife and masterworks (Newark: University of Delaware Press, 2008), esp. 134.

84. This is Luce Irigaray's phrase to describe patriarchal social orders dependent on the circulation of women among men. See her chapter "Women on the Market" in *This Sex Which Is Not One*, trans. Catherine Porter (Ithaca, N.Y.: Cornell University Press, 1985), 170–91.

85. One could argue that Reger's wife—who has passed away by the time the novel begins—must necessarily be dead to make this model of *Bildung* succeed. There is simply no room for her in this scheme, not even as a parrot of her husband's ideas. Ria Endres allusively discusses misogynist elements in Bernhard's writing in *Am Ende angekommen: Dargestellt am wahnhaften Dunkel der Männerporträts des Thomas Bernhard* (Frankfurt am Main: Fischer, 1980), 98–101.

86. Peter Humfrey, *Painting in Renaissance Venice* (New Haven, Conn.: Yale University Press, 1995), 186–94; Nichols, *Tintoretto*, 29–48; Klauner, *Gemäldegalerie*, 191.

87. The published English translation is somewhat misleading, reading "imaginary father" (*OM* 10; *AM* 18).

88. *OM* 95; *AM* 109–10.

Way Station 4

1. Nicolas Mahler, *Alte Meister* (Berlin: Suhrkamp, 2011), 29; 87–89, 92–93.

2. Ibid., 45, 50, 51, 59.

3. Ibid., 130. The image closes the bracket opened on p. 37, where the point symbolizes the "Fluchtpunkt" (both "vanishing point" and the point to which he flees) of Reger's thoughts on the Old Masters.

4. Compare p. 114, where Reger is seated in front of Tintoretto with a dotted outline surrounding him and p. 115, where the outline has disappeared. Coming together with Reger's pronouncement that Irrsigler was the only person he found acceptable after his wife's death ("der einzige mögliche Mensch"), this frame suggests that Reger has regrounded himself through his pedagogical mission—with his former student and the Tintoretto painting.

5. Ibid., 142–51, 157.

6. Ibid., 40–41, 102–3.

7. Mahler does not use the word "Mißbrauch," which Reger uses, in the graphic novel, but fittingly stresses Reger's use of the word "karikieren," meaning "to caricature" (*Alte*, 72–74).

8. I do not use the term here in the manner in which Stephen Best and Sharon Marcus do in their important introduction "Surface Reading," where they argue in favor of new reading strategies that do not rely on symptomatic readings

empowering the interpreter. Instead, they argue for an interest in the "evident, perceptible, apprehensible [. . .] ; what is neither hidden nor hiding; what, in the geometrical sense has length and breadth but no thickness, and therefore covers no depth. A surface is what insists on being looked *at* rather than what we must train ourselves to see *through*" (9). Their 2009 essay responds to a legitimacy crisis in the humanities, where methods of interpretation no longer equal political activism. Reger is clearly interested in exploring the surface to "see through" as well as "look at" it. See Stephen Best and Sharon Marcus, "Surface Reading: An Introduction," *Representations* 108 (Fall 2009): 1–21.

9. See the preceding chapter and Scarry, *On Beauty and Being Just*, esp. 3.

10. Today, web-based gallery visits give us an inkling of the kind of gliding, tactile vision Reger's method requires. They realize the potential that has always been inherent in the gallery space itself, from its earliest instantiation in the cabinet of curiosities onward. These Internet excursions achieve the gallery's interconnectivity, transcending any confinement and mediating between outer and inner, haptic and optic. I recommend the gallery tours on the website of German photographer Thomas Struth, whose "Museum Photographs" look at people engaged in the act of looking in temples of high culture—including in the Kunsthistorisches Museum (1989). On his website, we see the careful layout of Struth's shows in the very museums he photographed for the series. We "move" through virtual space by manipulating an arrow on the floor plan while looking at Struth's museum pictures among other works from his career. The view of specific images is often from an adjoining room as the cursor takes us through virtual space. See Thomas Struth's website: http://thomasstruth25.com/all/html/800_museum.htm.

Conclusion

1. See Jelinek's obituary for Bernhard, "Der Einzige und wir, sein Eigentum," where she paraphrases Max Stirner's title to his magnum opus, *Profil* 20 (February 20, 1989): 72–73. Bernhard wins the Franz-Theodor Csokor Prize, the Grillparzer and Adolf Grimme Prizes only two years after receiving what is one of the most prestigious awards in the German-speaking world, the Georg Büchner Prize in 1970. His travails, the affronts he suffers, and the outrages he perpetrates are wonderfully described in *My Prizes* (*Meine Preise*, 2009). In Bernhard's brilliant recollections about receiving the Csokor Prize, he describes two "scenes of instruction," where the Austrian novelist George Saiko functions as a teacher to the younger writer. Once, on the occasion of Saiko's visit to Salzburg, Bernhard leads him around the city and is forced to listen to a four-hour lecture on a theory of the novel. On another visit in Vienna, Saiko teaches him that the best time to try on shoes is at 4 p.m. Bernhard discusses his recalcitrance to Saiko as an overbearing pedagogue, laconically remarking that he remembered the second lesson much better than the first (*MP* 91–99; *MPr* 93–101).

2. The Kobernaußerwald is already mentioned in *Gargoyles*.

3. *C* 270; "Über Altensam und alles, das mit Altensam zusammenhängt, mit besonderer Berücksichtigung des Kegels," *K* 317.

4. We read: "I had suddenly grabbed the knapsack and turned it over and dumped its contents on the sofa" (*C* 132; "ich hatte den Rucksack plötzlich gepackt und umgestülpt und den Inhalt auf den Diwan geleert," *K* 160).

5. See *C* 141, 213; *K* 170, 253.

6. In an artfully extended variation on this childhood home as a jail, Roithamer's "childhood prison" becomes *the* penal institution per se: "Possibly I was kept in prison, in my parents' dungeon, Altensam, to atone for their crime [. . .] my parents were also my prosecutors, they had conceived and born me directly into that dungeon. [. . .] We can dream of escape but we can never escape because, once escaped from our parental dungeon, we'd perish in no time. [. . .] We've taken up the struggle against the dungeon, against the institution of this dungeon" (*C* 172; "Möglicherweise büßte ich für das Verbrechen meiner Eltern im Gefängnis, im Kerker meiner Eltern, in Altensam [. . .] meine Eltern waren ja gleichzeitig meine Ankläger gewesen, sie hatten mich sofort in den Kerker *hineingezeugt und hineingeboren* gehabt. [. . .] Wir können an Flucht denken, aber wir können nicht fliehen, weil wir, aus diesem Elternkerker geflohen, zugrunde gingen in der kürzesten Zeit [. . .] wir haben den Kampf gegen der Kerker und gegen die Institution dieses Kerkers [. . .] aufgenommen," *K* 206).

7. The name "Altensam" contains both the allusion to old age ("alt"), Roithamer's reproach against his parents, and isolation ("einsam"), Roithamer's reflections on the relationship between sequestration and emotional and intellectual loneliness. With the money from the sale of Altensam, Roithamer plans to help former prison inmates: "Use the money to do everything possible for those people, so Roithammer [. . .] build homes, buildings for them, taking into account my experiences with the Cone project, so Roithamer, always near the centers, population centers, avoid anything contributing to isolation, disregarding the fact that *everything is isolation*" (*C* 149; "Mit dem Geld alles tun für diese Leute, was möglich ist, so Roithamer, Heimstätten, Gebäude bauen, unter Berücksichtigung meiner Erfahrungen mit dem Kegelbau, so Roithamer, immer nahe an den Zentren, Menschenansammlungen, alles vermeiden, was Isolation fördert, abgesehen davon, daß *alles Isolation ist*," *K* 179).

8. *C* 170, 178–79; "Erkerzimmer," *K* 202, 210–14.

9. The description is indeed that of a Pichlerian inner core that is doubly closed off, with fake openings: "So she'd lock me up in the turret room which never was unlocked all summer long except to lock me up in it, it was opened for no other purpose, nor were the windows in the turret room ever opened, the window bolts had been immobilized by rust for decades, so the windows couldn't have been opened, that's where she'd lock me up where the air, the hot, sunbaked air, had long since been suffocated and thousands, hundreds of thousands of dead flies lay about on the floor and on all the furniture, heaps of dead flies, in this turret room with its terrible smell, with those windows covered from the top to the bottom with fly shit by all those flies in all those years of their hectic death throes, this room left in an indescribable state of filth" (*C* 176; "Daß sie mich also in das Erkerzimmer eingesperrt hat, in welchem, weil dieses Erkerzimmer den ganzen Sommer über niemals aufgesperrt worden ist, außer, ich bin in das Erkerzimmer hineingesperrt worden, zu keinem anderen Anlaß ist es geöffnet worden, und die Fenster des Erkerzimmers sind niemals aufgemacht worden, die Fensterriegel sind schon jarhzehntelang eingerostet gewesen und es wäre gar nicht mehr möglich gewesen, die Fenster des Erkerzimmers aufzumachen, daß sie mich dahinein gesperrt hat, wo die Luft, die heiße Sonnenluft, längst erstickt gewesen war und Tausende und Hunderttausende Fliegenkadaver auf dem Boden und auf allen

Möbelstücken herumgelegen sind, ganze Haufen von abgestorbenen Fliegen, in dieses Erkerzimmer mit seinem fürchterlichen Geruch, durch dessen Fenster, die von den Fliegen von oben bis unten in jahrelanger Verzweiflungshektik verdreckt und in einem unbeschreiblichen Verschmutzungszustand sich befunden haben," *K* 210–11).

10. The reflection on taste in *Old Masters* (chapter 3) is here present in kernel form: "Offended against so-called good taste, against which I've always offended. [. . .] Once we fail to offend against so-called good taste by doing something tasteful, we can say good-bye to our character, our reason, our self" (*C* 152; "Gegen den sogenannten Guten Geschmack verstoßen, gegen den ich immer verstoßen habe. [. . .] Verstoßen wir einmal nicht gegen den sogenannten Guten Geschmack, weil wir etwas sogenanntes Geschmackvolles tun, haben wir den Charakter verloren, unseren Verstand, unser Wesen aufgegeben," *K* 182).

11. *C* 180–81; *K* 215–16.

12. *C* 178; "exzentrischer," *K* 213.

13. *C* 175; "Wir [. . .] müssen [. . .] den Versuch machen, diese Welt nach unseren Vorstellungen zu verändern, zuerst im Hintergrund, unscheinbar, dann aber mit aller Gewalt und ganz deutlich, so daß wir nach einiger Zeit sagen können, *wir leben in unserer Welt, nicht in der uns vorgegebenen*, [. . .] von unseren Eltern uns vorgegebenen," *K* 209.

14. See the description of the attic room's perfect size and location for furthering Roithamer's thoughts about another building: "At the very instant I entered Hoeller's garret for the first time together with Hoeller who wanted to show me his garret because he thought it might be a suitable place for me to think especially about building the Cone. [. . .] I'd known at that earliest instant that Hoeller's garret could enable me, as no other retreat had enabled me, to get on with my thinking" (*C* 168–69; "Schon im ersten Augenblick, wie ich die höllersche Dachkammer zum erstenmal gemeinsam mit dem Höller betreten habe, weil er, wie er, Höller, mir die höllersche Dachkammer zeigen wollte aus seiner Ansicht heraus, daß mir die höllersche Dachkammer vielleicht ein geeigneter Ort für meine Denkzwecke vor allem im Hinblick auf den Kegelbau sein könne, [. . .] schon in diesem ersten Augenblick hatte ich gewußt, daß die höllersche Dachkammer mir ermöglicht, was mir kein anderer Denkplatz bis dahin mehr ermöglicht hat," *K* 201).

15. See the English translation "thinking on a scene," *C* 167 (*K* 199).

16. See Jean-Marie Pérouse de Montclos, *Etienne-Louis Boullée 1728–1799: Theoretician of Revolutionary Architecture*, trans. James Emmons (New York: Georges Braziller, 1974), esp. 41.

17. In an interesting discussion of Boullée, Margarete Kohlenbach alerts readers to the desire for absolute order and perfection underpinning both Roithamer's and Boullée's architectural designs. See her *Das Ende der Vollkommenheit: Zum Verständnis von Thomas Bernhards "Korrektur"* (Tübingen: G. Narr, 1986), esp. 103–9. The "image de l'ordre," which Boullée envisions, functions because the architecture he designs is immediately comprehensible ("saisible au premier aspect," qtd. in Kohlenbach 108); this direct view of architecture goes against the multifaceted experience of buildings in the Bernhard novels under discussion.

18. Pérouse de Montclos, *Theoretician*, 35–39. While I refer above to Jean-Marie Pérouse de Montclos's 1974 translated work on Boullée, I would like to

also mention his greatly expanded French edition (*Etienne-Louis Boullée* [Paris: Flammarion, 1994]). See in particular his chapter on "L'Architecture funéraire," which relates Boullée's monuments to what Richard Etlin describes as the changing practices of dealing with the dead in *The Architecture of Death: The Transformation of the Cemetery in Eighteenth-Century Paris* (Cambridge, Mass.: MIT Press, 1984), 150–65. Bernhard Sorg has noted the parallel between the Cone and pyramids in *Thomas Bernhard* (Munich: Beck, 1977), 180.

19. See Anthony Vidler's chapter on "Dark Space," in *The Architectural Uncanny: Essays in the Modern Unhomely* (Cambridge, Mass.: MIT Press, 1992), 167–77, esp. 169–73; compare Hermann Helms-Derfert, *Die Last der Geschichte: Interpretationen zur Prosa von Thomas Bernhard* (Cologne: Böhlau, 1997), 109.

20. Qtd. in Vidler, *Architectural Uncanny*, 170; Pérouse de Montclos, *Theoretician* 36.

21. In this context it is worth mentioning Neutra's German publications *Mensch und Wohnen* (Stuttgart: Koch, 1956), *Welt und Wohnung* (Stuttgart: Koch, 1962), and *Naturnahes Bauen* (Stuttgart: Koch, 1970), with its near simultaneous publication in English as *Building with Nature* (New York: Universe, 1971). His English book, *Survival through Design*, entered its fourth edition in 1964, bespeaking Neutra's intellectual currency during the decade in which Bernhard articulates the architectonic ideas that pervade his work (New York: Oxford University Press, 1954).

22. Neutra, *Auftrag*, 325, also qtd. in Helms-Derfert, *Die Last der Geschichte*, 111. In *Mission for Tomorrow*, Neutra argues that an individual's porous nature allows him to receive outside input and to act on these impressions. Note his description of the person as structure: the individual "possesses pretty permeable membranes and many openings; through them, he swallows impressions in order to become active. He could not exist in a vacuum or separated from the outside world" ("besitzt ziemlich durchlässige Membranen und eine Menge Öffnungen; durch sie schluckt es Eindrücke auf, um wirksam zu werden. In einem Vakuum oder von der Außenwelt geschieden, könnte es nicht bestehen," *Auftrag*, 16).

23. *C* 160; *K* 191–92. See also Helms-Derfert, *Die Last der Geschichte*, 110–13.

24. In the same volume, Neutra discusses simplicity in design as a result of increasing specialization and as a neuronal necessity. Because "organic associations" of designers and workmen no longer exist and the "methods of collaboration and transmission" have changed, designs have to be simpler. Modern reduction and simplification arises as a result of the division of labor: "the canon of transmission of our architectural ideas is largely planimetric presentation; that is, the drawing of floor plans, elevations, and sectional layouts of a house or any spatial concept on a flat piece of paper. This imposes unavoidable and grave limitations on the concept itself. It will have to be simple enough to be understood by those expected to execute the plan. Many spatial concepts cannot be represented intelligibly by these particular means" (*Survival*, 298–99).

25. When it comes to imagining a city, Neutra argues, the design cannot only be geometric: "The Euclidean contestant entering the arena with his static paraphernalia of T-square, triangle, and compass will look from the start a bit hopeless and forlorn. Biological balance is not easily housed in our gridiron towns even

when they are garnished with a few special geometrical gems; a lack of human dimension in daily behavior has been forced upon us" (*Survival*, 340).

26. The director of the Architecture Department at MOMA, Arthur Drexler, who devotes monographs to Richard Neutra, Mies van der Rohe, and writes a text on the Austrian visionary architects (Chapter 1), is nearly apologetic about discussing Neutra. In his view, Neutra is a regional rather than an international architect whose large-scale works do not hold up to sustained scrutiny. See Drexler and Thomas Hines, *The Architecture of Richard Neutra: From International Style to California Modern* (New York: Museum of Modern Art, 1982).

27. I refer here to Peter Blake's study *The Master Builders: Le Corbusier, Mies van der Rohe, Frank Lloyd Wright* (New York: Knopf, 1960), translated into German as *Drei Meisterarchitekten*, trans. Hermann Stiehl (Munich: Piper, 1962). Similarly, A. James Speyer's catalog *Ludwig Mies van der Rohe* is translated into German in 1968; his foreword is reproduced in English, while the rest of the text is translated. Arthur Drexler published *Ludwig Mies van der Rohe* in London in 1960.

28. The similarity among the rooms, inside and outside, is underlined in the following description: "that the individual chambers in the Cone are not to be specifically designated, it must be possible to live in a building in which the individual chambers are undesignated, though it is only natural for the chamber constructed as a meditation chamber to be designated as a meditation chamber. The chambers are all whitewashed. No windows but look-outs that are neither to be opened nor shut, natural airing of the inner spaces always without having to open or shut the look-outs. Solar energy for heating. Stone, bricks, glass, iron, nothing else. The Cone is whitewashed outside as well as inside. The Cone's height is the same as the height of the forest so that it's impossible to see the Cone unless one is standing directly in front of it" (*C* 163/64; "daß die einzelnen Räume im Kegel nicht zu bezeichnen sind, es muß möglich sein, in einem Gebäude zu leben, in dem die einzelnen Räume ohne Bezeichnung sind, aber es ist naturgemäß, daß der Raum, welcher als Meditationsraum konstruiert ist, als Meditationsraum bezeichnet wird. Die Räume sind sämtliche weiß gekalkt. Die Ausblicke sind keine Fenster, es sind Ausblicke, die nicht zu öffnen und also auch nicht zu schließen sind, die Lüftung ist, ohne daß die Ausblicke geöffnet oder geschlossen werden müssen, immer naturgemäß. Sonnenenergie als Heizung. Steine, Ziegel, Glas, Eisen, sonst nichts. Wie innen, ist der Kegel außen weiß gekalkt. Die Höhe des Kegels ist die Höhe des Waldes, so daß es unmöglich ist, den Kegel zu sehen, außer man steht unmittelbar davor," *K* 195).

29. Furthermore, Mies van der Rohe is willing to go against established opinion. In the introductory essay to the catalogue from 1968, Speyer stresses Mies van der Rohe's role as an innovative pedagogue at the Illinois Institute of Technology, overturning the curriculum and working closely with his students. Significantly, van der Rohe himself argues in the same catalogue that his role as a teacher forced him to think more clearly as an architect: "Teaching forced me to clearly formulate my ideas about architecture" ("Die Lehre zwang mich, meine Gedanken über Architektur klar zu formulieren," Speyer, *Mies van der Rohe*, n.p.).

30. The ambivalent character of Altensam is brought to the fore at the beginning of the second section, and the imbrications of walls and man stressed: "What was Altensam, where I come from [. . .] ? A composite of masonry and men where

action was taken without prior thought" (*C* 143; "Was ist Altensam, aus dem ich bin [. . .] ? Ein Gebilde aus Mauern und Menschen, in welchem ohne zu denken gehandelt worden ist," *K* 172).

31. *C* 158; "Zuerst, der Kegel hat Ausblicke nach allen Richtungen, dann der Kegel hat nur nach Süden Ausblicke und nach Norden, dann, nur nach Westen und nach Osten, schließlich nur nach Norden," *K* 189.

32. In Bernhard's letter to Siegfried Unseld from July 1970, he begs to have Bloch's publications: "Alles von Ernst Bloch!" The sixteen volumes are sent to him (Bernhard, *Briefwechsel*, 185–86).

33. Ernst Bloch, *The Principle of Hope*, vol. 2, trans. Neville Plaice, Stephen Plaice, and Paul Knight (Cambridge, Mass.: MIT Press, 1986), 743; *Das Prinzip Hoffnung*, vol. 2 (Frankfurt am Main: Suhrkamp, 1973), 869.

34. See Bloch's section "New Houses and Real Clarity," in *Principle*, 733–37; "Neue Häuser und wirkliche Klarheit," in *Prinzip*, 858–63. See also Hilde Heynen, *Architecture and Modernity: A Critique* (Cambridge, Mass.: MIT Press, 1999), esp. 124–26.

35. These words are Robert Venturi's, describing modernist puritanism. See his "Gentle Manifesto" in *Complexity and Contradiction in Architecture* (New York: Museum of Modern Art, 2002), esp. 16.

36. See Gerhard Brunner, "Sturm ums Haus Wittgenstein," *Stuttgarter Zeitung*, August 9, 1971, rpt. in Bernhard Leitner, *Wittgenstein-Haus: Ein Pressespiegel Juni/Juli/August 1971* (Vienna: Secession, 1989), 49: "Baukörper [. . .] von unerhörter Strenge," "fanatische[s] Ordnungsstreben," and "spartanische Kargheit."

37. See also Gerhard Brunner, "Denkmalpflege mit der Spitzhacke," *Die Welt*, June 15, 1971, rpt. in Leitner, *Pressespiegel*, 37; "fanatische Besessenheit" and "logische Strenge."

38. See Hilde Spiel, "Demolierer am Werk," *Frankfurter Allgemeine Zeitung*, June 14, 1971, rpt. in Leitner, *Pressespiegel*, 31. Spiel enjoins Bernhard to write about the philosopher. He declines with a philosophical reply, but returns to the Wittgensteins in his writings (such as *Wittgenstein's Nephew/Wittgensteins Neffe*, 1982, and *Ritter Dene Voss*, 1986). See Martin Klebes, *Wittgenstein's Novels* (New York: Routledge, 2006), esp. 49–86.

39. See also Günther Feuerstein's article "Die Spitzhacke ist keine Antwort," from the Austrian daily *Kurier*, June 23, 1972. He, too, argues for the "ascetic sparseness" of the building, whose "authorship" cannot be denied: "Fascinating is not only the strict and stringent structure (main body) with the slim windows, the terraces, the connection to the garden, but also the wraithlike, ascetic frugality of the details, whose authorship not even the preservation commission can deny. [. . .] A house, in which 'each millimeter was important,' where measure, object, order and precision were built and thought reality" ("Faszinierend ist nicht nur der strenge, straffe Baukörper mit den schlanken Fenstern, den Terrassen, der Verbindung zum Garten, sondern auch die durchgeistigte asketische Kargheit der Details, deren Autorschaft nicht einmal das Denkmalamt leugnen kann. [. . .] Ein Haus, in dem es 'auf den Millimeter ankam', in dem Maß, Objekt, Ordnung, Präzision gebaute und gedachte Wirklichkeit sind," rpt. in Leitner, *Pressespiegel*, 27). See also Brunner's article "Denkmalpflege mit der Spitzhacke," which is similarly negative about the role of the preservation commission in denigrating Wittgenstein's masterpiece (rpt. in Leitner, *Pressespiegel*, 37).

40. Leitner quotes Dr. Pötschner's words printed in *Die Presse* on April 10, 1970: "Any arbitrary meaning can be given to such a strange structure; crazy ideas and *cupiditas rerum novarum* may create quite charming effects but not genuine form, and any architect could be degraded to a mere assistant if he were to give in to the thousand wishes and ideas of his client and adjust his work of art accordingly" ("Einem so eigenartigen Gebilde kann jeder beliebige 'Sinn' unterlegt werden, Spleen und cupiditas rerum novarum können zwar reizvolle Effekte, aber noch keine echte Form schaffen und jeder Architekt könnte zum bloßen Erfüllungsgehilfen degradiert werden, brächte man die 1000 Wünsche und Einfälle der Bauherrschaft vom künstlerischen Ganzen in Abzug," rpt. in Leitner, *Pressespiegel*, 42). See also Reinhard Ablinger, "'Hobbyhaus' eines Philosophen erregt Wiener Gemüter," from the *Oberösterreichische Nachrichten* from Bernhard's region, which speaks of Wittgenstein's "hobby house" and the work of an "amateur" (Aug. 12, 1971; rpt. in Leitner, *Pressespiegel*, 65).

41. Nana Last, *Wittgenstein's House: Language, Space, and Architecture* (New York: Fordham, 2008), 2.

42. The writer Ingeborg Bachmann had, as in the case of Robert Musil, sought to draw attention to Wittgenstein, his lack of public prominence, and the reified image of him as ascetic in a short essay entitled "Ludwig Wittgenstein—Zu einem Kapitel der jüngsten Philosophiegeschichte," *Gedichte, Erzählungen, Hörspiel, Essays* (Munich: Piper, 1981), 284–95. In her description of Wittgenstein's early philosophy (the *Investigations* had just been published in England), she emphasizes the mystical aspect toward which Wittgenstein's logical assertions repeatedly gesture, making him into Musil's kindred spirit. Her essay was first published in *Frankfurter Hefte* in July 1953, a few months before the appearance of "Ins tausendjährige Reich," her essay on Musil in *Akzente* (Feb. 1954) mentioned in chapter 2.

43. See Last, *Wittgenstein's House*, 115, 177.

44. As Bernhard Leitner argues, this ratio is not geometrically or technically perfect (the floor plan is actually a rectangle), but the aesthetic effect of a square is created through the interplay of elements. See his book *Das Wittgenstein Haus* (Ostfildern-Ruit: Hatje Cantz, 2000), 66; translated into English as *The Wittgenstein House* (New York: Princeton Architectural Press, 2000), 66.

45. See the images in Leitner with the original floor plans (*House*, 64–65; *Haus*, 64–65).

46. See Last's account in her chapter entitled "The Practice of Architecture," in *Wittgenstein's House*, 95–124.

47. Leitner, *House*, 70; *Haus*, 70.

48. Leitner, *House* 66; *Haus*, 66.

49. Leitner, *House*, 64; *Haus*, 64.

50. Leitner, *House*, 76–78; *Haus*, 76–78.

51. The idea of being a kind of self-taught architect such as Wittgenstein (who early on designed his own bedstead and even the door handles in his sister's home) must have held its appeal for Bernhard, who furnishes his homes with lamps and tables of his own design. These can be seen in the apartment of the Thomas-Bernhard-Society in Vienna's First District, not far from the Bernhardian triangle with which I began this book. On Wittgenstein's work as a teacher, see

the book in Bernhard's library: Konrad Wünsche, *Der Volksschullehrer Ludwig Wittgenstein* (Frankfurt am Main: Suhrkamp, 1985).

52. Martin Heidegger, "Building, Dwelling, Thinking," *Basic Writings: From Being and Time (1927) to "The Task of Thinking" (1964)*, ed. David Farrell Krell (San Francisco, CA: HarperSanFrancisco, 1993), 343–64; "Bauen Wohnen Denken," *Vorträge und Aufsätze* (Frankfurt am Main: Vittorio Klostermann, 2000), 146–64. Of course the last word of *Correction* is "Lichtung" or "clearing," a link to Heidegger's reflection on the opening of Being. I do not pursue this connection here, since it would take me too far afield. Bernhard links the clearing to death, since Roithamer commits suicide in a clearing midway between Altensam on the mountain and the town of Stocket below. See the editors' remarks to *Korrektur* in vol. 4 (354–57). Among the earliest reflections on the relation to Heidegger, they note Peter Kampits's essay "Tod und Reflexion: Philosophische Bemerkungen zum Werk Thomas Bernhards," in *Thomas Bernhard. Literarisches Kolloquium Linz 1984*, ed. Alfred Pittertschatscher (Linz: Adalbert-Stifter-Institute, 1985), 18–28; and Gudrun B. Mauch's excellent chapter, "Thomas Bernhards Roman 'Korrektur': Zum autobiographisch fundierten Pessimismus Thomas Bernhards," in *Studien zur österreichischen Erzählliteratur der Gegenwart*, ed. Herbert Zeman (Amsterdam: Rodopi, 1982), 87–106. See her discussion of Heidegger as well as the novel's focus on the middle, esp. 88–93, 96–97.

53. See Gregory B. Smith, *Martin Heidegger: Paths Taken, Paths Opened* (Lanham, Md.: Rowman and Littlefield, 2007), esp. 175–202. See also Karsten Harries, who examines the homelessness underpinning Heidegger's essay in "Unterwegs zur Heimat," *Wolkenkuckucksheim* 3, no. 2 (June 1998), http://www.cloud-cuckoo.net/openarchive/wolke/deu/Themen/982/Harries/harries_t.html.

54. See David R. Cerbone, "Dwelling on Rough Ground: Heidegger, Wittgenstein, Architecture," in *Wittgenstein and Heidegger*, eds. David Egan, Stephen Reynolds, Aaron Wendland (New York: Routledge, 2013), 245–60.

55. Heidegger describes an old farm in the Black Forest, built in the shadow of a mountain, protected from the elements and beholden to God; here, all ages find a proper dwelling ("Building," 361–62; "Bauen," 162).

WORKS CITED

Primary Works by Thomas Bernhard

German

Werkausgabe. Edited by Wendelin Schmidt-Dengler, Martin Huber, and Hans Höller. Frankfurt am Main: Suhrkamp, 2003–2012.

Alte Meister: Komödie. Vol. 8 (2008).

Amras. In *Erzählungen I*. Vol. 11 (2004).

Auslöschung: Ein Zerfall. Vol. 9 (2009).

Autobiographie (*Die Ursache*; *Der Keller; Der Atem; Die Kälte; Ein Kind*). Vol. 10 (2004).

Der Italiener. In *Erzählungen I*. Vol. 11 (2004).

Der Untergeher. Vol. 6 (2003).

"Ebene." In *111 Zeichnungen,* by Walter Pichler. Salzburg: Residenz, 1973. Reprinted in *Erzählungen, Kurzprosa*. Vol. 14 (2003).

Ereignisse. In *Erzählungen, Kurzprosa*. Vol. 14 (2003).

Frost. Vol. 1 (2003).

Heldenplatz. In *Dramen VI*. Vol. 20 (2012).

Holzfällen: Eine Erregung. Vol. 7 (2007).

In der Höhe: Rettungsversuch. Unsinn. In *Erzählungen I*. Vol. 11 (2004).

Ja. In *Erzählungen III*. Vol. 13 (2008).

Kalkwerk. Vol. 3 (2004).

Korrektur. Vol. 4 (2005).

"Meine eigene Einsamkeit." *Die Presse* [December 24, 1965]. Reprinted in *Thomas Bernhards Häuser*, edited by Wieland Schmied and Erika Schmied. Salzburg: Residenz, 1995, 5–6.

Meine Preise. (2009).

Prosa. Vol. 14 (2003).

Verstörung. Vol. 2 (2003).

Wittgensteins Neffe. In *Erzählungen III*. Vol. 13 (2008).

———, with Siegfried Unseld. *Der Briefwechsel*. Edited by Raimund Fellinger, Martin Huber, and Julia Ketterer. Frankfurt am Main: Suhrkamp Verlag, 2009.

English

Amras. Translated by Peter Jansen. In *Three Novellas*, edited by Kenneth J. Northcott. Chicago: University of Chicago Press, 2003.

Concrete. Translated by David McLintock. New York: Vintage, 1984; 2010.

Correction. Translated by Sophie Wilkins. New York: Random House, 1983.

Extinction. Translated by David McLintock. New York: Alfred A. Knopf, 1995.

Frost. Translated by Michael Hofmann. New York: Vintage, 2006.

Gathering Evidence. A Memoir (*A Child, An Indication of the Cause, The Cellar: An Escape, Breath: A Decision, In the Cold*). Translated by David McLintock. New York: Alfred A. Knopf, 1985.
Gargoyles. Translated by Richard Winston and Clara Winston. Chicago: University of Chicago Press, 1986.
My Prizes: An Accounting. Translated by Carol Janeway. New York: Alfred A. Knopf, 2010.
Old Masters: A Comedy. Translated by Ewald Osers. Chicago: The University of Chicago Press, 1992.
On the Mountain: Rescue Attempt, Nonsense. Translated by Russell Stockman. Marlboro, Vt.: Marlboro, 1991.
Prose. Translated by Martin Chalmers. London: Seagull, 2010.
Wittgenstein's Nephew: A Friendship. Translated by David McLintock. Chicago: University of Chicago Press, 1989.

Critical Literature

Abraham, Raimund J. *Elementare Architektur*. Salzburg: Residenz, 1963.
Achleitner, Friedrich. "Der 'Aufbau' und die Aufbrüche." In *Architektur im 20. Jahrhundert*. Reprinted in Porsch, *The Austrian Phenomenon I*, esp. 833–35.
———. "Aufforderung zum Vertrauen." Reprinted in Porsch, *Austrian Phenomenon*, 846–54.
———. *Österreichische Architektur im 20. Jahrhundert*. Salzburg: Residenz, 1980.
———. *Quadratroman*. Salzburg: Residenz, 1972.
———. "Schlusslicht im Schulbau. Neues Bauen kritisch betrachtet: Tiroler Schulen." In Ritter, *Reprint*, 164.
Adorno, Theodor W. *Dissonanzen: Musik in der verwalteten Welt*. In *Gesammelte Schriften*, vol. 14, 7–167. Frankfurt am Main: Suhrkamp, 1990.
———. "Education for Maturity and Responsibility." Translated by Robert French, Jem Thomas, and Dorothee Weymann. In *History and the Human Sciences* 12, no. 3 (1999): 21–34.
———. "Erziehung nach Auschwitz." In *Gesammelte Werke*, vol. 10.2, 674–90. Frankfurt am Main: Suhrkamp, 1977.
———. "Erziehung zur Mündigkeit." In *Vorträge und Gespräche mit Hellmut Becker 1959–1969*, edited by Gerd Kadelbach, 133–47. Frankfurt am Main: Suhrkamp, 1970.
Agamben, Giorgio. *The Man without Content*. Translated by Georgia Albert. Stanford, Calif.: Stanford University Press, 1999.
Anderson, Mark M. "Fragments of a Deluge: The Theater of Bernhard's Prose." In Konzett, *Companion*, 119–35.
Arendt, Hannah. *The Human Condition*. Chicago: University of Chicago Press, 1958.
Arieti, James. *Interpreting Plato: The Dialogues as Drama*. Savage, Md.: Rowman and Littlefield, 1991.
Auer, Alfred, ed. *Meisterwerke der Sammlungen Schloss Ambras*. Vienna: Kunsthistorisches Museum/Skira, 2008.
———. "Schloss Ambras und die Habsburger Porträtgalerie." *Vernissage* 8, no. 65 (July 2000): 6–11.

Bachelard, Gaston. *La Poétique de l'éspace*. Paris: Presses Universitaires de France, 1958.

———. *The Poetics of Space*. Translated by Maria Jolas. Boston: Beacon, 1994.

Bachmann, Ingeborg. "Ins Tausendjährige Reich." In *Werke*, vol. 4, edited by Christine Koschel et al. Munich: Piper, 1978, 4–28; *Akzente* 1, no. 1 (February 1954): 27.

———. "Ludwig Wittgenstein—Zu einem Kapitel der jüngsten Philosophiegeschichte." In *Gedichte, Erzählungen, Hörspiel, Essays*, 284–95. Munich: Piper, 1981.

Belting, Hans. *Das Ende der Kunstgeschichte?* Munich: Deutscher Kunstverlag, 1983.

———. *Das Ende der Kunstgeschichte: Eine Revision nach zehn Jahren*. Munich: C.H. Beck, 1995.

———. *Florenz und Bagdad: Eine westöstliche Geschichte des Blicks*. Munich: C.H. Beck, 2008.

Bentmann, Reinhard, and Michael Müller. *Die Villa als Herrschaftsarchitektur*. Frankfurt am Main: Syndikat, 1970.

Bentz, Oliver. *Thomas Bernhard: Dichtung als Skandal*. Würzburg: Königshausen & Neumann, 2000.

Bernstein, Susan. *Housing Problems: Writing and Architecture in Goethe, Walpole, Freud, and Heidegger*. Stanford, Calif.: Stanford University Press, 2008.

Betten, Anne. "'Das ist mir zu blöd, drei Seiten ein Satz': Anmerkungen zum Stil von Thomas Bernhards Prosa." In "Thomas Bernhard—Johannes Freumbichler—Hedwig Stavianicek," edited by Manfred Mittermayer, *Rampe* (1999): 125–36.

Betz, Uwe. *Polyphone Räume und karnevalisiertes Erbe: Analysen des Werks Thomas Bernhards auf der Basis Bachtinscher Theoreme*. Würzburg: Ergon, 1997.

Bischoff, Cäcilia. "Architectural History of the Kunsthistorisches Museum." Introduction to *The Kunsthistorisches Museum in Vienna*, 13–19. Munich: Prestel, 2007.

Blake, Peter. *Drei Meisterarchitekten*. Translated by Hermann Stiehl. Munich: Piper, 1962.

———. *The Master Builders: Le Corbusier, Mies van der Rohe, Frank Lloyd Wright*. New York: Knopf, 1960.

Bloch, Ernst. *Das Prinzip Hoffnung*. Vol. 2. Frankfurt am Main: Suhrkamp, 1973.

———. *Pädagogica*. Frankfurt am Main: Suhrkamp, 1971.

———. *The Principle of Hope*. Vol. 2. Translated by Neville Plaice, Stephen Plaice, and Paul Knight. Cambridge, Mass.: MIT Press, 1986.

Bloom, Allan. Translation and introduction to *The Republic of Plato*, 307–436. New York: Basic Books, 1991.

Bode, Peter, and Gustav Peichl. *Architektur aus Österreich seit 1960*. Salzburg: Residenz, 1980.

Böhme, Gernot. *Architektur und Atmosphäre*. Munich: Fink, 2006.

Bonnet, Anne-Marie, and Gabriele Kopp-Schmidt. *Kunst ohne Geschichte? Ansichten zu Kunst und Kunstgeschichte heute*. Munich: C.H. Beck, 1995.

Borsche, Tilman. *Wilhelm von Humboldt*. Munich: C.H. Beck, 1990.

Botond, Anneliese, ed. *Über Thomas Bernhard*. Frankfurt am Main: Suhrkamp, 1970.

Boys-Remonds, Manuela du. *Strategien kompensatorischer Erziehung: Das Beispiel der USA*. Frankfurt am Main: Suhrkamp, 1971.

Brakensiek, Thomas. "Samuel Quicchelberg: Gründungsvater oder Einzeltäter? Zur Intention der *Inscriptiones vel Tituli Theatri amplissimi* (1565) und ihrer Rezeption im Sammlungswesen Europas zwischen 1550 und 1820." http://www.metaphorik.de/14/Brakensiek.

Bredekamp, Horst. *Antikensehnsucht und Maschinenglauben: Die Geschichte der Kunstkammer und die Zukunft der Kunstgeschichte*. Berlin: Klaus Wagenbach, 1993.

———. *The Lure of Antiquity and the Cult of the Machine: The Kunstkammer and the Evolution of Nature, Art and Technology*. Translated by Allison Brown. Princeton, N.J.: Markus Wiener, 1995.

Brodsky, Claudia. *In the Place of Language: Literature and the Architecture of the Referent*. New York: Fordham University Press, 2009.

Bruyère, Jean de La. *Les Caractères de Théophraste traduits du grec avec Les Caractères ou les Moeurs de ce siècle*. Edited by Marc Escola. Paris: Editions Champion, 1999.

Buckley, Craig. "From Absolute to Everything: Taking Possession in 'Alles ist Architektur.'" *Grey Room* 28 (2007): 108–22.

Bürger, Peter. *Theorie der Avantgarde*. Frankfurt am Main: Suhrkamp, 1974.

Carstensen, Thorsten. "Keine Spuren hinterlassen: Bauen, Wohnen und Erben bei Thomas Bernhard." *Gegenwartsliteratur: Ein germanistisches Jahrbuch* 13 (2014): 111–35.

Cassirer, Ernst. *Philosophie der symbolischen Formen: Mythisches Denken*. Vol. 2. Darmstadt: Wissenschaftliche Buchgesellschaft, 1977.

———. *Philosophy of Symbolic Forms: Mythical Thought*. Vol. 2. Translated by Ralph Manheim. New Haven, Conn.: Yale University Press, 1955.

Cerbone, David R. "Dwelling on Rough Ground: Heidegger, Wittgenstein, Architecture." In *Wittgenstein and Heidegger*, edited by David Egan, Stephen Reynolds, and Aaron Wendland, 245–60. New York: Routledge, 2013.

Certeau, Michel de. *L'Invention du quotidien*. Paris: Union générale d'éditions, 1980.

———. *The Practice of Everyday Life*. Translated by Steven Rendall. Berkeley: University of California Press, 1984.

Chaouli, Michel. *The Laboratory of Poetry: Chemistry and Poetics in the Work of Friedrich Schlegel*. Baltimore, Md.: Johns Hopkins University Press, 2002.

Cook, Peter. *Experimental Architecture*. New York: Universe Books, 1970.

Corngold, Stanley. *Complex Pleasures: Forms of Feeling in German Literature*. Stanford, Calif.: Stanford University Press, 1998.

Cousineau, Thomas. *Three-Part Inventions: The Novels of Thomas Bernhard*. Newark: University of Delaware Press, 2008.

Csáky, Moritz, ed. *Kommunikation—Gedächtnis—Raum: Kulturwissenschaften nach dem "Spatial Turn."* Bielefeld: Transcript, 2009.

Dankl, Günther, ed. "Raum und Expansion: Zum Aspekt des Konzeptionellen und Experimentellen bei Raimund Abraham, Ernst Caramelle, Bernhard Leitner,

Max Peintner, Walter Pichler und Heinz Tesar." In *Ex.Position—Avantgarde Tirol 1960/75*. Innsbruck: Tiroler Landesmuseum Ferdinandeum, 2004.

Day, Christopher. *Places of the Soul: Architecture and Design as a Healing Art*. London: Harper Collins, 1993.

———. *Spirit and Place: Healing Our Environment*. London: Architectural, 2002.

Dimendberg, Ed. *Diller Scofidio + Renfro: Architecture after Images*. Chicago: University of Chicago Press, 2013.

———. *Film Noir and the Spaces of Modernity*. Cambridge, Mass.: Harvard University Press, 2004.

———. "The Limits to Emplacement." *Rethinking History* 11, no. 4 (December 2007): 513–16.

Dittmar, Jens, ed. *Thomas Bernhard: Werkgeschichte*. Frankfurt am Main: Suhrkamp, 1981.

Donehower, Bruce. *The Birth of Novalis*. Albany: SUNY Press, 2007.

Donnenberg, Josef. *Thomas Bernhard und Österreich: Studien zu Werk und Wirkung 1970–1989*. Stuttgart: Hans-Dieter Heinz, 1997.

Döring, Wolfgang. *Perspektiven einer Architektur*. Frankfurt am Main: Suhrkamp, 1973.

Dowden, Stephen D. *Understanding Thomas Bernhard*. Columbia, S.C.: University of South Carolina Press, 1991.

Downing, Eric. *After Images: Photography, Archaeology, and Psychoanalysis and the Tradition of Bildung*. Detroit: Wayne State University Press, 2006.

Drexler, Arthur. "Architectural Fantasies: Drawings from the Museum Collection." In Porsch, *Austrian Phenomenon I*, 41.

———. *Ludwig Mies van der Rohe*. New York: G. Braziller, 1960.

Drexler, Arthur, and Thomas Hines. *The Architecture of Richard Neutra: From International Style to California Modern*. New York: Museum of Modern Art, 1982.

Dünne, Jörg, and Stephan Günzel, eds. *Raumtheorie: Grundlagentexte aus Philosophie und Kulturwissenschaften*. Frankfurt am Main: Suhrkamp, 2006.

Endres, Ria. *Am Ende angekommen: Dargestellt am wahnhaften Dunkel der Männerporträts des Thomas Bernhard*. Frankfurt am Main: Fischer, 1980.

Etlin, Richard. *The Architecture of Death: The Transformation of the Cemetery in Eighteenth-Century Paris*. Cambridge, Mass.: MIT Press, 1984.

Eyckeler, Franz. *Reflexionspoesie: Sprachskepsis, Rhetorik und Poetik bei Thomas Bernhard*. Berlin: Schmidt, 1995.

Feuerstein, Günther. "Thesen zu einer inzidenten Architektur." Reprinted in Porsch, *The Austrian Phenomenon I*, 59. Also "Thesen zur 'inzidenten' Architektur." Reprinted in Porsch, *The Austrian Phenomenon I*, 275.

———. "Visionäre Architektur im Österreich der sechziger und siebziger Jahre." Reprinted in Porsch, *The Austrian Phenomenon I*, 866–69.

Feyerabend, Paul. *Erkenntnis für freie Menschen*. Frankfurt am Main: Suhrkamp, 1979.

Fliedl, Konstanze, Marina Rauchenbauer, and Joanna Wolf. *Handbuch der Kunstzitate: Malerei, Skulptur, Fotografie in der deutschsprachigen Literatur der Moderne*. Berlin: De Gruyter, 2011.

Foucault, Michel. "Des espaces autres." *Architecture, Mouvement, Continuité* 5 (October 1984): 46–49.

———. "Of Other Spaces." Translated by Jay Miskowiec. *Diacritics* 16, no. 1 (Spring 1986): 22–27.

Glück, Gustav. *Die Gemäldegalerie des Kunsthistorischen Museums in Wien.* Vienna: Kunstverlag Anton Schroll, 1925.

Gonzalez, Francisco J. *Dialectic and Dialogue: Plato's Practice of Philosophical Inquiry.* Evanston, Ill.: Northwestern University Press, 1998.

Görner, Rüdiger. "The Broken Window Handle: Thomas Bernhard's Notion of *Weltbezug.*" In Konzett, *Companion*, 89–104.

Gutschmidt, Holger. "Von der 'Idee einer Universität' zur 'Zukunft unserer Bildungsanstalten'—Bildungsbegriff und Universitätsgedanke in der deutschen Philosophie von Schiller bis Nietzsche." In Stolzenberg, *Bildung als Kunst*, 149–67.

Haas, Claude. *Arbeit am Abscheu: Zu Thomas Bernhards Prosa.* Munich: Fink, 2007.

Hallet, Wolfgang, ed. *Raum und Bewegung in der Literatur: Die Literaturwissenschaften und der Spatial Turn.* Bielefeld: Transcript, 2009.

Handke, Peter. *Ich bin ein Bewohner des Elfenbeinturms.* Frankfurt am Main: Suhrkamp, 1972.

Harries, Karsten. "Unterwegs zur Heimat." *Wolkenkuckucksheim* 3, no. 2 (June 1998). http://www.cloud-cuckoo.net/openarchive/wolke/deu/Themen/982/Harries/harries_t.html.

Hays, K. Michael, ed. *Architecture Theory since 1968.* Cambridge, Mass.: MIT Press, 1998.

Heidegger, Martin. "Bauen Wohnen Denken." In *Vorträge und Aufsätze*, 146–64. Frankfurt am Main: Vittorio Klostermann, 2000.

———. "Building, Dwelling, Thinking." In *Basic Writings: From Being and Time (1927) to "The Task of Thinking" (1964)*, edited by David Farrell Krell, 343–64. San Francisco: HarperSanFrancisco, 1993.

Helms-Derfert, Hermann. *Die Last der Geschichte: Interpretationen zur Prosa von Thomas Bernhard.* Cologne: Böhlau, 1997.

Hennetmair, Karl Ignaz. *Ein Jahr mit Thomas Bernhard: Das notariell versiegelte Tagebuch 1972.* Salzburg: Residenz, 2000.

Hens, Gregor. *Thomas Bernhards Trilogie der Künste: Der Untergeher, Holzfällen, Alte Meister.* Columbia, S.C.: Camden House, 1999.

Heydorn, Heinz-Joachim. *Zu einer Neufassung des Bildungsbegriffs.* Frankfurt am Main: Suhrkamp, 1972.

Heynen, Hilde. *Architecture and Modernity: A Critique.* Cambridge, Mass.: MIT Press, 1999.

Hoell, Joachim. *Der literarische Realitätenvermittler: Die Liegenschaften in Thomas Bernhards Roman Auslöschung.* Berlin: VanBremen, 1995.

Hoell, Joachim, and Kai Luehrs-Kaiser, eds. *Thomas Bernhard: Traditionen und Trabanten.* Würzburg: Königshausen und Neumann, 1999.

Hoesterey, Ingeborg. "Visual Art as Narrative Structure: Thomas Bernhard's *Alte Meister.*" *Modern Austrian Literature* 21, no. 3–4 (1988): 117–22.

Hollein, Hans, and Walter Pichler. *Architektur.* Vienna: Galerie nächst St. Stephan, 1963. Reprinted in Porsch, *Austrian Phenomenon I*, 15–37.

Höller, Hans. *Der unbekannte Thomas Bernhard*. Mattighofen: Korrektur Verlag, 2014.

———. *Kritik einer literarischen Form: Versuch über Thomas Bernhard*. Stuttgart: Heinz, 1979.

———. *Thomas Bernhard*. Reinbek bei Hamburg: Rowohlt, 1993.

Höller, Hans, and Irene Heidelberger-Leonard, eds. *Antiautobiografie: Zu Thomas Bernhards Auslöschung*. Frankfurt am Main: Suhrkamp, 1995.

Honneger, Gitta. *Thomas Bernhard: The Making of an Austrian*. New Haven, Conn.: Yale University Press, 2001.

Honold, Alexander, and Markus Joch, eds. *Thomas Bernhard—Die Zurichtung des Menschen*. Würzburg: Königshausen und Neumann, 1999.

Huber, Martin. *Thomas Bernhard und seine Lebensmenschen: Der Nachlass*. Frankfurt am Main: Suhrkamp, 2002.

Humboldt, Wilhelm von. *Gesammelte Schriften*. Berlin: B. Behr, 1903.

Humfrey, Peter. *Painting in Renaissance Venice*. New Haven, Conn.: Yale University Press, 1995.

Hundertwasser, Friedrich. "Verschimmelungsmanifest gegen den Rationalismus in der Architektur." In *Schöne Wege: Gedanken über Kunst und Leben*, 216. Munich: Langen Müller, 2004. Reprinted in Porsch, *The Austrian Phenomenon I*, 780–82.

Irigaray, Luce. *This Sex Which Is Not One*. Translated by Catherine Porter. Ithaca, N.Y.: Cornell University Press, 1985.

Jansen, Georg. *Prinzip und Prozess Auslöschung: Intertextuelle Destruktion und Konstitution des Romans bei Thomas Bernhard*. Würzburg: Königshausen und Neumann, 2005.

Jarzombek, Mark. "Corridor Spaces." *Critical Inquiry* 36 (2010): 728–70.

Jay, Martin. *Cultural Semantics: Keywords of Our Time*. Amherst, Mass.: University of Massachusetts Press, 1998.

Judex, Bernhard. *Thomas Bernhard: Epoche, Werk, Wirkung*. Munich: C.H. Beck, 2010.

Jung, Ena. "Ellipses . . . epilepsie." *Modern Austrian Literature* 42, no. 1 (2009): 87–98.

Jurgensen, Manfred. *Thomas Bernhard: Der Kegel im Wald, oder die Geometrie der Verneinung*. Bern: P. Lang, 1981.

Kampits, Peter. "Tod und Reflexion: Philosophische Bemerkungen zum Werk Thomas Bernhards." In *Thomas Bernhard: Literarisches Kolloquium Linz 1984*, edited by Alfred Pittertschatscher, 18–28. Linz: Adalbert-Stifter-Institute, 1985.

Kaufmann, Sylvia. *The Importance of Romantic Aesthetics for the Interpretation of Thomas Bernhard's "Auslöschung. Ein Zerfall" and "Alte Meister. Eine Komödie."* Stuttgart: Hans-Dieter Heinz, 1998.

Kinzel, Ulrich. "Gestaltung des Zerfalls: Thomas Bernhard und die Erfahrung John Donnes." In Hoell, *Thomas Bernhard*, 119–28.

Klauner, Friderike. *Die Gemäldegalerie des Kunsthistorischen Museums in Wien: Vier Jahrhunderte europäischer Malerei*. Salzburg: Residenz, 1978.

———. "Stationäre Präsentation im Museum aus der Sicht des Objekts, der Besucher und der Verantwortlichen." In *Bewahren und Ausstellen, die Forderung des kulturellen Erbes in Museen*, edited by Hermann Auer, 57–61. Munich: Saur, 1984.

Klebes, Martin. *Wittgenstein's Novels*. New York: Routledge, 2006.
Klenner, Jens. "Ektopia: Skizze einer topographischen Anatomie in Thomas Bernhards Amras." *Modern Austrian Literature* 1 (2009): 63–84.
Klinge, Margret. *David Teniers the Younger: Paintings—Drawings*. Translated by David R. McLintock. Ghent: Snoeck-Ducaju & Zoon, 1991.
Kohlenbach, Margarete. *Das Ende der Vollkommenheit: Zum Verständnis von Thomas Bernhards "Korrektur."* Tübingen: G. Narr, 1986.
Konzett, Matthias, ed. "National Iconoclasm: Thomas Bernhard and the Austrian Avant-Garde." In *A Companion to the Works of Thomas Bernhard*, 1–22. Rochester, N.Y.: Camden House, 2010.
———. *The Rhetoric of National Dissent in Thomas Bernhard, Peter Handke, and Elfriede Jelinek*. Rochester, N.Y.: Camden House, 2000.
Lackner, Josef. "Die acht naiven Giganten." In Ritter, *Reprint*, 152–53.
Last, Nana. *Wittgenstein's House: Language, Space, and Architecture*. New York: Fordham University Press, 2008.
Lefebvre, Henri. *La Production de l'espace*. Paris: Éditions Anthropos, 1974.
———. *The Production of Space*. Translated by Donald Nicholson-Smith. Cambridge, Mass.: Blackwell, 1991.
Lehnert, Gertrud, ed. *Raum und Gefühl: Der Spatial Turn und die neue Emotionsforschung*. Bielefeld: Transcript, 2011.
Leithe-Jasper, Manfred, Rudolf Distelberger, and Wolfgang Prohaska. *The Kunsthistorische Museum Vienna*. Translated by Elsie Callander and Ilse Seldon. London: Philip Wilson, 1984.
Leitner, Bernhard. *Das Wittgenstein Haus*. Ostfildern-Ruit: Hatje Cantz, 2000.
———. *Wittgenstein Haus: Ein Pressespiegel Juni/Juli/August 1971*. Vienna: Secession, 1989.
———. *The Wittgenstein House*. New York: Princeton Architectural, 2000.
Lempert, Wolfgang. *Leistungsprinzip und Emanzipation*. Frankfurt am Main: Suhrkamp, 1971.
Leucht, Robert Leucht, and Susanne Reichlin. "'Ein Gleichgewicht ohne festen Widerhalt, für das wir noch keine rechte Beschreibung gefunden haben': Robert Musils 'anderer Zustand' als Ort der Wissensübertragung." In *Medien, Technik, Wissenschaft*, edited by Ulrich J. Beil et al., 289–322. Zurich: Chronos, 2011.
Long, J. J. *The Novels of Thomas Bernhard: Form and Its Function*. Rochester, N.Y.: Camden House, 2001.
Lughofer, Johann Georg. *Thomas Bernhard: Gesellschaftliche und politische Bedeutung der Literatur*. Vienna: Böhlau, 2012.
Mahler, Nicholas. *Alte Meister: Eine Komödie*. Frankfurt am Main: Suhrkamp, 2011.
Mauch, Gudrun B. "Thomas Bernhards Roman 'Korrektur': Zum autobiographisch fundierten Pessimismus Thomas Bernhards." In *Studien zur österreichischen Erzählliteratur der Gegenwart*, edited by Herbert Zeman, 87–106. Amsterdam: Rodopi, 1982.
McQuaid, Matilda, ed. *Envisioning Architecture: Drawings from the Museum of Modern Art*. New York: Museum of Modern Art, 2002.
Miller, Alice. *Am Anfang war Erziehung*. Frankfurt am Main: Suhrkamp, 1980.
Mittermayer, Manfred. *Thomas Bernhard*. Stuttgart: Metzler, 1995.

———. *Thomas Bernhard*. Frankfurt am Main: Suhrkamp, 2006.

———, ed. *Thomas Bernhard, Johannes Freumbichler, Hedwig Stavianicek: Bilder, Dokumente, Essays*. Linz: R. Trauner, 1999.

Musil, Robert. *Der Mann ohne Eigenschaften*. Vol. 1. Reinbek bei Hamburg: Rowohlt, 1978.

———. *The Man without Qualities*. Vol. 3. Translated by Eithne Wilkins and Ernst Kaiser. New York: Capricorn, 1965.

Naqvi, Fatima. "Dialectic at a Standstill: The Discourse of Victimhood in Thomas Bernhard's *Heldenplatz*." *German Quarterly* 75, no. 4 (2003): 409–22.

———. "Of Dilettantes and Men of Taste: Thomas Bernhard's Pedagogical Project in *Alte Meister* (1985)." *Monatshefte* 96, no. 2 (2004): 252–72.

———. "Thomas Bernhard und die Tradition: 'Andere Zustände' in *Amras*." In *"Ist es eine Komödie? Ist es eine Tragödie?": Ein Symposium zum Werk von Thomas Bernhard*, edited by Attila Bombitz und Martin Huber, 161–76. Vienna: Präsens, 2010.

———. *Trügerische Vertrautheit: Filme von Michael Haneke*. Vienna: Synema, 2010.

———. "Von Türhütern, Meistern und Untergängern: Dilettantismus in Thomas Bernhards *Der Untergeher*." In *Österreichische Literatur ohne Grenzen. Gedenkschrift für Wendelin Schmidt-Dengler*, edited by Attila Bombitz et al., 317–34. Vienna: Präsens, 2009.

Nesbitt, Kate. *Theorizing a New Agenda for Architecture: An Anthology of Architectural Theory 1965–1995*. Princeton, N.J.: Princeton Architectural, 1996.

Neutra, Richard. *Auftrag für morgen*. Hamburg: Claasen, 1962.

———. *Bauen und die Sinneswelt*. Dresden: Verlag der Kunst, 1977.

———. *Building with Nature*. New York: Universe Books, 1971.

———. *Naturnahes Bauen*. Stuttgart: Alexander Koch, 1970.

———. *Survival through Design*. New York: Oxford University Press, 1954.

Nichols, Tom. *Tintoretto: Tradition and Identity*. London: Reaktion Books, 1999.

Nienhaus, Birgit. *Architekturen und andere Räume: Raumdarstellung in der Prosa Thomas Bernhards*. Marburg: Tectum Verlag, 2010.

Nietzsche, Friedrich. *Die Zukunft unserer Bildungsanstalten*. In *Sämtliche Werke: Kritische Studienausgabe*, vol. 1, 641–752. Munich: Deutscher Taschenbuch Verlag, 1988.

———. *On the Future of Our Educational Institutions*. Translated by J. M. Kennedy. Edinburgh: T. N. Foulis, 1910. http://www.gutenberg.org/files/28146/28146-h/28146-h.htm.

Norberg-Schulz, Christian. *Architecture: Presence, Language, Place*. Milan: Skira, 2000.

———. *Genius loci: Towards a Phenomenology of Architecture*. New York: Rizzoli, 1979.

Novalis. *Das Allgemeine Brouillon (Materialien zur Enzyklopädistik 1798/99)*. In *Schriften*, vol. 3 (*Das philosophische Werk II*), 207–478, ed. Richard Samuel, Hans-Joachim Mähl, and Gerhard Schulz. Stuttgart: W. Kohlhammer, 1960.

———. *Notes for a Romantic Encyclopaedia: Das Allgemeine Brouillon*. Translated by David W. Wood. Albany: SUNY Press, 2011.

O'Doherty, Brian. *Inside the White Cube: The Ideology of the Gallery Space*. San Francisco: Lapis, 1986.

———. "Inside the White Cube: Notes on the Gallery Space." http://www.societyofcontrol.com/whitecube/insidewc.htm.

Padrón, Matías Díaz, and Mercedes Royo-Villanova. *David Teniers, Jan Brueghel y Los Gabinetes de Pinturas*. Madrid: Museo del Prado, 1992.

Pérouse de Montclos, Jean-Marie, *Etienne-Louis Boullée*. Paris: Flammarion, 1994.

———. *Etienne-Louis Boullée 1728–1799: Theoretician of Revolutionary Architecture*. Translated by James Emmons. New York: Georges Braziller, 1974.

Petrasch, Ingrid. *Die Konstitution von Wirklichkeit in der Prosa Thomas Bernhards: Sinnbildlichkeit und groteske Übersetzung*. Frankfurt am Main: Lang, 1987.

Pfabigan, Alfred. *Thomas Bernhard: Ein österreichisches Weltexperiment*. Vienna: Zsolnay, 1999.

Pichler, Walter. "Architektur." In Porsch, *The Austrian Phenomenon I*, 31.

———. *Pichler: Prototypen/Prototypes 1966–69*. Edited by Sabine Breitwieser. Vienna: Generali, 1998.

———. *Skulpturen Gebäude Projekte*. Salzburg: Residenz Verlag, 1983.

———. *Walter Pichler: Austria*. Catalogue for the Biennale. Salzburg: Residenz, 1982.

———. *Walter Pichler: Museum des 20. Jahrhunderts Wien and the Hamburger Kunsthalle*. Salzburg: Residenz, 1971.

———. *Walter Pichler: 111 Zeichnungen*. Salzburg: Residenz, 1973.

Porsch, Johannes, ed. *The Austrian Phenomenon: Architektur Avantgarde Österreich 1956–1973*. Basel: Birkhäuser, 2009.

Prader, Herbert, and Franz Fehringer. "Die nächste Generation, Konturen—Tendenzen." In Porsch, *Austrian Phenomenon I*, 855–58.

Prohaska, Wolfgang. *Kunsthistorisches Museum, Vienna: The Paintings*. Vol. 2. London: Scala Books, 1997.

Purdy, Daniel. *On the Ruins of Babel: Architectural Metaphor in German Thought*. Ithaca, N.Y: Cornell University Press, 2011.

Quiccheberg, Samuel. *The First Treatise on Museums: Samuel Quiccheberg's Inscriptiones 1565*. Translated and edited by Mark A. Meadow and Bruce Robertson. Los Angeles: Getty Research Institute, 2013.

Rauch, Margot, "Monster und Mirakel: Wunderbares in der Kunstkammer von Schloss Ambras." Exhibition brochure, Castle Ambras. Innsbruck: Heimatwerbung, 2003.

Rauch, Margot, et al. *Fernsucht: Die Suche nach der Fremde vom 16. bis 19. Jahrhundert*. Vienna: Kunsthistorisches Museum, 2009.

Readings, Bill. *The University in Ruins*. Cambridge, Mass.: Harvard University Press, 1996.

Rehm, Walter, ed. and intro. *Novalis*. Frankfurt am Main: Fischer, 1956.

Rhodes, John David, and Elena Garfinkel, eds. *Taking Place: Location and the Moving Image*. Minneapolis: University of Minnesota Press, 2011.

Riccabona, Christine. "Begegnungen—Die Österreichischen Jugendkulturwochen in Innsbruck (1949–1969)." In Dankl, *Ex.Position*, 77–86.

Riccabona, Christine, Erika Wimmer, and Milena Meller. *Ton Zeichen: Zeilen Sprünge. Die Österreichischen Jugendkulturwochen (1950–1969) in Innsbruck*. Innsbruck: Studien Verlag, 2006.

Ritter, Arno, ed. *Reprint: Ein lesebuch zu architektur und tirol*. Innsbruck: Studienverlag, 2005.

Rossi, Paola. *Jacopo Tintoretto*. Milan: Electa, 1994.

Ruskin, John. *The Lamp of Beauty*. Edited by Joan Evans. London: Phaidon, 1959.

Rutschky, Katharina, ed. *Schwarze Pädagogik: Quellen zur Naturgeschichte der bürgerlichen Erziehung*. Berlin: Ullstein, 1977.

Scarry, Elaine. *On Beauty and Being Just*. Princeton, N.J.: Princeton University Press, 1999.

Schäfer, Armin. "Existenzmöglichkeiten: Versuch über die Auflösung des sensomotorischen Schemas in Thomas Bernhards *Amras*." *Modern Austrian Literature* 42, no. 1 (2009): 45–61.

Scheicher, Elisabeth. *Die Kunst- und Wunderkammer der Habsburger*. Vienna: Molden, 1979.

Schmidt-Dengler, Wendelin. *Der Übertreibungskünstler: Studien zu Thomas Bernhard*. Vienna: Sonderzahl, 1989.

Schmied, Wieland, and Erika Schmied. *Thomas Bernhards Häuser*. Salzburg: Residenz, 1995.

———. *Thomas Bernhards Österreich: Schauplätze seiner Romane*. Salzburg: Residenz, 2000.

Schöllhammer, Georg. "Die geschraubte Geste/The Stilted Gesture." In Pichler, *Prototypen/Prototypes*, 35–58.

Schorske, Carl. *Fin-de-siècle Vienna: Politics and Culture*. New York: Vintage, 1981.

Schütte, Uwe. *Thomas Bernhard*. Cologne: Böhlau, 2010.

Schweidler, Walter. "Friedrich Nietzsche: Über die Zukunft unserer Bildungsanstalten." In *Hauptwerke der Pädagogik*, edited by Winfried Böhm, Birgitta Fuchs, and Sabine Seichter, 317–19. Paderborn: Schöningh, 2009.

Sebald, W. G. *Die Beschreibung des Unglücks: Zur österreichischen Literatur von Stifter bis Handke*. Frankfurt am Main: Fischer, 2003.

Sekler, Eduard. *Josef Hoffmann: Das architektonische Werk*. Salzburg: Residenz, 1982.

Simons, Oliver. *Raumgeschichten: Topographien der Moderne in Philosophie, Wissenschaft und Literatur*. Munich: Fink, 2007.

Smith, Gregory B. *Martin Heidegger: Paths Taken, Paths Opened*. Lanham, Md.: Rowman and Littlefield, 2007.

Sorg, Bernhard. *Thomas Bernhard*. Munich: C.H. Beck, 1992.

Speyer, A. James, and Frederick Koeper. *Ludwig Mies van der Rohe: Ausstellung anläßlich der Berliner Bauwochen 1968*. Berlin: Art Institute of Chicago and Akademie der Künste Berlin, 1968.

———. *Ludwig Mies van der Rohe*. Chicago: Art Institute of Chicago, 1968.

Stolzenberg, Jürgen, and Lars-Thade Ulrichs. *Bildung als Kunst: Fichte, Schiller, Humboldt, Nietzsche*. New York: De Gruyter, 2010.

Stütz, Gisela. *Berufspädagogik unter ideologiekritischem Aspekt*. Frankfurt am Main: Suhrkamp, 1970.

Sutton, Peter C. *The Age of Rubens*. Boston: Museum of Fine Arts, 1993.

Swoboda, Gudrun. *Die Wege der Bilder: Eine Geschichte der kaiserlichen Gemäldesammlungen von 1600 bis 1800*. Vienna: Kunsthistorisches Museum, 2008.

Theisen, Bianca. *Silenced Facts: Media Montages in Contemporary Austrian Literature*. Amsterdam: Rodopi, 2003.

Theodorsen, Cathrine. "Zur Rolle des Dilettantismus im Prozess der Ausdifferenzierung einer österreichischen Literatur aus der deutschen Literatur." *Nordlit* 9 (2001): 45–61.

Venturi, Robert. *Complexity and Contradiction in Architecture*. New York: Museum of Modern Art, 2002.

Vidler, Anthony. *The Architectural Uncanny: Essays in the Modern Unhomely*. Cambridge, Mass.: MIT Press, 1992.

Vogel, Juliane. "Vorüberlegungen zu Thomas Bernhards *Amras*." *Modern Austrian Literature* 42, no. 1 (2009): 41–44.

Vogl, Joseph. *Kalkül und Leidenschaft: Poetik des ökonomischen Menschen*. Zurich: Diaphanes, 2004.

Wachsmann, Konrad. *Aspekte des Bauens*. Wiesbaden: Krausskopf, 1961.

———. *Wendepunkt im Bauen*. Wiesbaden: Krausskopf, 1959.

Warnke, Martin. "Theorie und Praxis in der Endzeit." In Bonnet and Kopp-Schmidt, *Kunst*, 113–16.

Welzig, Maria, and Gerhard Steixner, eds. *Die Architektur und ich: Eine Bilanz der österreichischen Architektur seit 1945*. Vienna: Böhlau, 2004.

Wünsche, Konrad. *Der Volksschullehrer Ludwig Wittgenstein*. Frankfurt am Main: Suhrkamp, 1985.

INDEX

Page numbers in **boldface** refer to illustrations.